Sephardim

Sephardim

THE JEWS FROM SPAIN

Paloma Díaz-Mas

Translated by George K. Zucker

THE UNIVERSITY OF CHICAGO PRESS
Chicago & London

PALOMA DÍAZ-MAS is professor of
Sephardic studies at the Universidad del Pais Vasco
and author of
numerous articles on Spanish Jewry.

THE UNIVERSITY OF CHICAGO PRESS, CHICAGO 60637
THE UNIVERSITY OF CHICAGO PRESS, LTD., LONDON
© 1992 by The University of Chicago
All rights reserved. Published 1992
Printed in the United States of America
01 00 99 98 97 96 95 94 93 92   5 4 3 2 1
ISBN (cloth): 0-226-14483-6

Originally published as *Los Sefardíes: Historia, Lengua y Cultura,*
© Riopiedras Ediciones, Barcelona, 1986.

Library of Congress Cataloging-in-Publication Data

Díaz Mas, Paloma.
   [Sefardíes. English]
   Sephardim : the Jews from Spain / Paloma Díaz-Mas ; translated by
George K. Zucker.
      p. cm.
   Translation of: Los sefardíes.
   Includes bibliographical references and index.
   1. Sephardim—History.   2. Ladino philology.   I. Title.
DS134.D52413   1992
909'.04924—dc20   92-15523
                                                                  CIP

CONTENTS

TRANSLATOR'S FOREWORD

When I first saw *Los sefardíes: Historia, lengua y cultura* in early 1987, I found the book exciting. It was the only text I had ever seen that collected basic historical, linguistic, and cultural material on the Sephardim—precisely the kind of book needed to provide introductory material to readers interested in Sephardic studies, either personally or academically. In their review of the book, the editors of *Aki Yerushalayim* state: "asta agora son relativamente pokos los livros ke tratan de estos temas i ke pueden ser fasilmente konsultados" ["up to now there have been relatively few books that treat these themes and that can be easily consulted"]. They go on to report: "Este livro . . . prezenta . . . un panorama jeneral de todos los aspektos de la erensia kulturala sefaradi, tokando a kada uno de eyos de una manera serioza, klara i bien dokumentada" ["This book . . . presents . . . a general panorama of all aspects of the Sephardic cultural heritage, treating each one of them seriously, clearly and in well documented form"] (*Aki Yerushalayim* 9, no. 32–33 [Jan.–June 1987]: 44).

This edition, however, is not identical to the original, because Professor Díaz-Mas updated relevant sections of the text, as well as the bibliography, specifically for this translation. For example, when she wrote the book, diplomatic relations between Spain and Israel had not yet been established; she made changes in the text (chapter 5) to reflect those relations.

Professor Díaz-Mas has wonderful control of her native Spanish. She was able to maintain a pleasant, conversational tone in the original while packing useful data into every sentence. Because I subscribe to the belief that any translation that reads like a translation is a bad one, the translation of the text is not verbatim, although I have made every effort to retain the content, including the nuances, of the original. The same is true of the translations of the Judeo-Spanish quotes that appear in the text.

The original text was written for Spanish readers, and many cultural references required no explanation. Since American readers are not likely to have this cultural background at their fingertips, I have added several notes to the English translation to explain those Spanish cultural references. The designation [AN] at the beginning of a note indicates that it is the author's note and appeared in the original Spanish text. My translator's notes are unmarked.

Again, because the target audience of the original work consisted of Spaniards, the Recommended Reading sections at the end of each chapter contained sources mostly in Spanish. Here they have been expanded to include more works in English when possible. The additional titles are reflected in the Translator's Additional Bibliography, which is separate from the author's updated bibliography. The additional bibliography is an efficient way to let the reader know of the existence of texts that were not used in writing this book, either because they were unavailable to the author or because they were published after she updated the bibliography for this translation.

While quotes in other languages have simply been translated into English, those in Judeo-Spanish have been left in the original to let the Sephardim speak in their own voice. Those quotes were taken from sources written in the Roman alphabet and the original spelling has been preserved; English translations are provided. I was unable to locate two sources, however, so the quotes from the Ferrara Bible and from the play *Los Maranos* have not been checked.

Historically, Judeo-Spanish was written using the Hebrew alphabet, as is explained in chapter 3 (this is known as *aljamia, aljamiado,* or *aljamiada* writing). It was not until recently that the language was commonly written in other alphabets. Consequently, there are ongoing problems of how to represent those words in the Roman alphabet.

The Hebrew alphabet consists of consonants only; vowels, when they are used, are represented by dots or dashes above, below, or beside the letters. Yet the vowels are often semantically significant both in Spanish and Judeo-Spanish: for example, *mes* [month], *más* [more]; *lo* (masculine direct object pronoun), *la* (feminine direct object pronoun), *le* (indirect object pronoun). The *aljamiado* writing system partially solved this problem by using some consonants for those vowel sounds. More problematic are the Hebrew letters *yod* (representing both *e* and *i*) and *vav* (which may stand for either *o* or *u*).

Consonants, too, can cause difficulties. There are consonantal sounds in Judeo-Spanish that did not exist in Spanish at the time the Jews were expelled from Spain (when phonetic development of Judeo-Spanish stopped following the same course as it had in Spain), as well as sounds that do not exist in Hebrew. The question of how to represent the sounds *ch* and the Old Spanish sibilant *j* or *g* before a front vowel was solved by incorporating a *rafĕ*, a tick above the Hebrew letter, with *gimel* and *zayin*. But now the reader must rely on the scribe to include the *rafĕ* where it belongs and not to write it otherwise, an assumption that does not always hold true. In a language written by native speakers for native speakers, words would be recognized with or without the *rafĕ*.

There are also cases where a single sound can be represented by more than one Hebrew consonant. The most troublesome of those cases deals with the *s,* which can be written with either the *samekh* or the *sin*. *Sin* is used more frequently, both within words and in word-final position as the sign of plurality in nouns and adjectives, and to indicate second-person singular in verbs. But that does not necessarily mean that the *samekh* represents a different *s* sound; it may simply be an alternation of phonetic equals.

An additional problem posed by the *sin* is that the same letter, with a dot on the opposite upper corner, is the *shin,* pronounced /sh/. That sound, which does not exist in modern Spanish, was part of the late fifteenth-century Spanish phonetic inventory and is still present in Judeo-Spanish. (It appeared as the letter *x* in Old Spanish.)

These problems involved in reading a document written in *aljamiado* are also reflected in attempts to transcribe such documents into the Roman alphabet. Unfortunately, these are not the only problems of transcription. There are dialectal differences in Judeo-Spanish as well. Do we, upon finding *aleph yod zayin* with *rafĕ vav,* write *ijo* or *iju*? Since *vav* represents both of those final vowels, both are legitimate, contemporary pronunciations of the Judeo-Spanish word for "son" or "child"; the difference is regional. A further question is whether or not to include the silent initial *h* that appears in the Spanish word *hijo*.

The transcription system of the original text, preserved in the translation, was developed at the Instituto Arias Montano in Madrid (currently a part of the Instituto de Filología, still within the Consejo Superior de Investigaciones Científicas). It represents the sounds of the Judeo-Spanish words but keeps the spelling as close as possible to standard Spanish. The quotes, however, are by authors with a variety of linguistic backgrounds, so that there will be some discrepancies with the transcription system described in the introduction. Those differences reflect the various origins of the authors of the quotes and their educational backgrounds: for example, the sound represented in English by *sh* is spelled *ch* in French and in Turkish appears as ş.

Modern Spanish does not use that sound at all; it is generally represented here by š. The problems raised by the lack of a single transcription system for Judeo-Spanish will quickly become apparent to readers of *Sephardim*.

Spelling of Hebrew words (for example, *huppa, Shabbat*) follows Ashkenazic rather than Sephardic practice, because the Ashkenazic forms of those words are the ones most familiar to American readers.

This compendium should allow an increasing number of institutions to offer introductory courses in Sephardic studies, because instructors will no longer have to spend months seeking and copying appropriate text materials from a wide variety of books and journals so that their students may have necessary basic references at their disposal.

This translation would have taken years longer to complete had it not been for a Professional Development Leave awarded to me by the University of Northern Iowa and the Iowa Board of Regents. My thanks to the University of Northern Iowa's Graduate College, the College of Humanities and Fine Arts, my home department of modern languages, and the Maurice Amado Foundation. Their support and generosity allowed me to complete this translation. Thanks, too, to my colleagues who bore with good humor my "preposition runs" down the hall, as well as to Ed Wagner and his entire Interlibrary Loan staff, who performed wonders in getting me all of the texts needed to prepare this translation. Special thanks go to Jennie Ver Steeg and Dan Power, who generously offered to read the translation to be certain that the result was good, clear English, and to Isaac Jack Lévy, who checked the accuracy of translations from Judeo-Spanish. I am solely to blame for the faults that remain in the translation.

When Antonio Nebrija's *Gramática castellana* first appeared in 1492, it was a notable advance—the first grammar of a spoken language published in Western Europe. After that grammar had been available for a while, however, it became obvious that additional material would be desirable, and several subsequent grammars were written in Spain during the sixteenth century. It is my hope that *Sephardim,* in like manner, will inspire future research and publication in the field of Sephardic studies. This book certainly provides a thorough background for anyone interested in "los diversos askpektos de la kultura djudeo-espanyola: la lengua, las romansas, los kuentos i mas" ["the various aspects of Judeo-Spanish culture: the language, the ballads, the stories and more"] (Ibid.).

GEORGE K. ZUCKER
University of Northern Iowa

INTRODUCTION

In 1492 the Catholic monarchs[1] decreed the expulsion of the Spanish Jews, most of whom left Spain and settled in various parts of Europe, North Africa, and the then-powerful Turkish Empire. Those who had been expelled called themselves Sephardim, and many of their descendants retained the Spanish language and a culture with Hispanic roots for nearly five hundred years.

At the beginning of this century, Senator Ángel Pulido moved public opinion with his campaign of information and publicity about the people he called "Spaniards without a homeland." Since that time, much has been written in Spain about the Sephardim, but not everything that has been said and written—by Spaniards or others—reflects the truth. Spanish authors have not always examined the Sephardim with scientific documentation nor have they all approached the subject free of prejudice. The treatment of the Sephardim in general is marked by an abundance of misinformation and ignorance of the situation of Jews of Spanish origin, along with biased interpretations of their culture. Consequently, commonplace beliefs about the Sephardim have been propagated, ideas that are heard time and again and that serve as obstacles to true knowledge about this aspect of Hispanic culture, the culture sustained by Spanish Jews in exile.

Where and how the interested layperson can acquire information is a problem, as the most reliable and best documented works to date present two major obstacles to nonspecialists. First, they cover very narrowly specific aspects of Sephardic studies, but they do not give a general overview of Sephardic history and culture. Second, these works are usually located in academic sources (in journals, for example) not easily accessible to the general

1. Ferdinand II of Aragon and Isabella I of Castile.

public. Unfortunately, widely distributed publications tend (with notable exceptions) to include the biases and offending opinions mentioned above.

The paper "Los sefardíes como tópico" ["The Sephardim as a topic"] presented by Iacob M. Hassán at the Congreso sobre la España olvidada: Los judíos [Conference on the forgotten Spain: The Jews] (organized in Zamora by the Ramos del Castro Foundation, June 18–20, 1981) and a subsequent conversation with its author gave me the idea of writing a book. My aim, in addition to refuting some of the most often-repeated beliefs, would be to give the general reader worthwhile, truthful, and well-documented information about the Sephardim, their history, their language, their culture, and their relations with Spain, along with some basic bibliography for those who were interested in studying any of these topics further. The result is this book, which has been divided into six chapters.

The first chapter provides the reader with much of the background data necessary for in-depth understanding of the Sephardim. It presents an outline of the history of the Jews in Spain prior to their expulsion; clarifies some necessary terms, such as Sephardic, Ashkenazi, and others; and gives a brief outline of the fundamental principles and practices of Judaism, both Sephardic and Ashkenazi.

Chapter 2 examines the history of the Sephardim in the countries where they settled after the expulsion (the Turkish Empire, North Africa, the Low Countries, Italy, and so on), and in the countries where they traveled after the Second Diaspora, which began in the nineteenth century (the United States, South America, Israel, and Western Europe).

Many believe that the language of the Sephardim—Judeo-Spanish, which some also call Ladino—is fifteenth-century Spanish that miraculously has been fossilized or mummified over the course of five centuries. This is not the case, however. Chapter 3 discusses Sephardic language in its various forms, its conservatism and innovation, its Hispanic base and the influence of other languages on it, the evolution of the dialect, and its various speech registers.

Another commonly held belief is that Sephardic literature is limited to traditional orally transmitted genres, mainly ballads. In response, chapter 4 provides a synthesis of the major literary genres in Judeo-Spanish, some of which are certainly deeply rooted in the Spanish tradition (ballads, songs, stories, proverbs), although they also have been influenced by other literatures such as Turkish, Greek, and Arabic. There are other specifically Jewish genres (rabbinic commentary), one genre (the *coplas*) in which Jewish and Spanish traditions are fused, and other more recent genres that imitate Western literatures (novel, theater, journalism, autograph poetry).

Chapter 5 presents an analysis of an area in which misinformation, bias, sentimentalism, and patriotism abound—the relationship between the Sephardim and Spain. I attempt here to present an objective view of how relations between the two groups have developed since the expulsion and to track, especially from the mid-nineteenth century to the present, Spain's attitude toward the Sephardim and the Sephardic attitudes toward their country of origin.

Chapter 6, is an overview of the Sephardic situation today. It tells where the Sephardic communities are, how they have evolved since World War II, to what degree they retain their own cultural identity, and the probable future for Sephardic ethnic identity. The chapter gives special attention to the Jewish communities in Spain. It also discusses the state of Sephardic studies in Spain and throughout the world.

The purpose of the book is not only to inform but also to provide a background for those who wish to pursue these topics further. Consequently, each chapter ends with a brief Recommended Reading section including works relevant to that chapter. I have attempted to give timely and accurate lists, to include works that are easily found in bookstores or (more frequently) in libraries, and that are in languages many people can read (English, Spanish, and French). Works in less commonly known languages (for example, Hebrew) have not been included, although there are many such works. Though essential and valuable to the study of the Sephardim, they are not accessible to the general public. Nevertheless, given the scarcity of works on some topics, it has not always been possible to include easily found and recent titles on all topics.

Finally, the book ends with a bibliography that includes the works cited in notes and in the Recommended Reading sections of each chapter. The bibliography also gives the full citations for the abbreviated titles used in the text. There are also indexes: one defines terms used, one gives names, and one contains the titles and first lines of works mentioned.*

Some observation must be made about the transcription system used for Hebrew and Judeo-Spanish words. The text follows the system advocated by Iacob M. Hassán in "Transcripción normalizada de textos judeoespañoles" ["Transcription system for Judeo-Spanish texts"] *Estudios Sefardíes* 1 (1978): 147–50. The advantage of this sytem is that it will be easily accessible to Spanish-speaking readers while still representing all the phonetic peculiarities

---

*The original Spanish text contained three indexes; they have been combined into a single index here.

of Judeo-Spanish. The symbols used, and their phonetic equivalents, are as follows:

ḅ, b-, v: voiced bilabial occlusive [b], like English *b*.

ć, ś, ź: voiced dentoalveolar fricative [z], like the *s* in *rose*.

ĝ, ĵ, ẑ: voiced prepalatal affricate [y], like English *j*.

ĵ, ŝ, ý: voiced prepalatal fricative, like French *j*.

ǰ, š: unvoiced prepalatal fricative, like English *sh* or French *ch*.

ŝ: voiceless dentoalveolar affricate, like the German or Italian *z*.

ḥ: unvoiced pharyngeal fricative, like English *h* or Spanish *j*.

': voiced pharyngeal fricative *ʿayin*, without equivalent in Western languages.

A dot below *b, d,* or *v*, or above *g* indicates that the sound is occlusive in places where it would not be occlusive in Spanish.

A dot between *l.l* indicates that the group should be read as a double *l*, and not as the Spanish *ll* (as in English mi*lli*on).

The following sounds are not indicated because they are general characteristics that always occur in Judeo-Spanish: pronunciation of *c* before *e* or *i*, or of *z*, as [s]; pronunciation of Spanish *ll* as *y;* pronunciation of labiodental fricative [v] or bilabial fricative [b] in all cases except where marked as v.

Except for indications to the contrary, original spelling has been retained in quotes, generally reflecting Sephardic spelling, such as the use of *ch* for /sh/.

I cannot end this introduction without expressing my gratitude to the individuals and institutions that have helped me. First, to Spain's Ministry of Culture, whose Grant for Literary Creation allowed me to write this book. Also to the Instituto Arias Montano (now part of the Instituto de Filología) in the CSIC, where I was educated for six years and in whose vast Sephardic Studies Library I was able to find most of the bibliographic material I needed. To the former director of that institute, José Luis Lacave, for his information on the history of the Jews in the Middle Ages. To my constant teacher, Iacob M. Hassán, for his continuous aid and advice. To Samuel Toledano, of the Israelite Community of Madrid, who provided me with valuable data about the Jewish communities in contemporary Spain. To Bárbara Fernández, who willingly accepted the thankless task of typing my original copy. And to María Dolores Mas and María Fernanda and Miguel Díaz Mas, for their continual and selfless support.

I hope that the reader will find this book useful. If it is also enjoyable to read, so much the better.

ONE

HISTORICAL BACKGROUND

HISTORICAL BACKGROUND IS needed to discuss meaningfully anything that is truly Sephardic.

JEWS IN THE IBERIAN PENINSULA
In Ancient, Visigothic, and Muslim Spain

It is generally known that Jews lived in the Iberian Peninsula in the remote past.[1] Diverse legends fix the date that the first Jews settled there in the period of Nebuchadnezzar (sixth century B.C.E.).[2] At this time the refugees or captives resulting from the destruction of the first temple in Jerusalem spent their exile or captivity in the peninsula. More daring traditions date the arrival of the first Jews as far back as the era of Solomon (tenth century B.C.E.), suggesting that they reached the Mediterranean shores along with Phoenician traders.

But these hypotheses have no historical value. They are merely legends that originated in Al-Andalus (Muslim Spain) in the tenth century, at a time when

---

1. [AN] Because there is considerable confusion of terminology, it is best to establish the meaning of some terms: *Jew* (which originally meant "from the tribe of Judah") is the most general term. Nearly synonymous, *Hebrew* is generally used for the Jewish people of biblical times; used adjectivally, it alludes to the Hebrew language. Thus, *Hebrew literature* is not necessarily written by Jews but is written in the Hebrew language. Similarly, if a literature or culture is called *Hispano-Hebraic* or *Hebreo-Spanish,* that term refers to a culture developed in Hebrew by Spanish Jews. The term *Israelite* (derived from *Israel,* the name given to the patriarch Jacob by an angel) is synonymous with *Jewish,* but it should not be confused with *Israeli,* which applies only to a citizen of modern Israel (Jewish or not). Some people nevertheless use the terms *Hebrew* and *Israelite* as euphemisms for *Jew,* a word that seems pejorative to them. Other expressions, such as *people of God* and *chosen people,* imply strictly religious concepts. The terms *Sephardic* and *Ashkenazi* are explained later in the text.

2. B.C.E., Before the Common Era, is equivalent to the Christian B.C.; Christian A.D. is denoted as C.E., the Common Era.

Spanish Jews were enjoying a period of splendor. Such legends were an attempt to explain the extraordinary Jewish success by attributing splendid and venerable origins to their communities. In subsequent centuries, these legends were spread, amplified, and embellished, and the Christian population came to accept them as well.

Reliable historical data, nevertheless, is so scarce that hardly any conclusions can be drawn. It can legitimately be assumed that from earliest times Jews settled in the commercial ports of the Mediterranean coast and that other Jews came as refugees in the first century c.e., following the destruction of the second temple in Jerusalem. But the oldest documentary evidence comes from the late Roman period: a gravestone found in Adra (dated from the third century but now lost) marked the burial of a girl (surely a slave) with the Judaic name of Salomonula. Another gravestone, from Tortosa, and an inscription on the synagogue of Elche are both from the fourth century. There is also the famous trilingual stone from Tarragona (now in the Sephardic Museum in Toledo), on which inscriptions in Hebrew, Latin, and Greek are combined with Judaic symbols. The date of the stone remains questionable, with estimates ranging from the first through the sixth century.

In any case, the Jewish population in the peninsula was considerable, and the Jews were well integrated with the Christians in the fourth century, at the time of the Council of Elvira. That Council not only prohibited mixed marriages but also other practices that must have been common at the time and that clearly indicate the coexistence of the two religions. For example, it barred Jews and Christians from celebrating feasts together, and forbade Jews from blessing Christian fields and harvests.

More serious difficulties began in the Visigothic period, specifically in the seventh century, when the crown changed the state religion from Aryanism to Catholicism. Subsequent Councils in Toledo promulgated anti-Jewish measures that would inspire the Christian kingdoms to legislate against their Jewish subjects seven or eight centuries later (during the outbreak of activity against the Jews in the fourteenth and fifteenth centuries). At first the prohibitions focused on Jews holding Christian serfs (by itself quite severe in a rural society, where serf-holding insured that the land would be worked). The celebration of mixed marriages also was forbidden, and Jews were not allowed to hold public office. The measures gradually became harsher. King Sisebut (612–21) even proclaimed a law ordering Jews either to convert to Christianity or to leave the kingdom. This is probably the first occurrence of the *converso* [convert] problem in the Iberian Peninsula. It is no wonder that, when the Moorish invasion occurred in 711, the oppressed Jews gladly joined the new settlers, who not only tolerated the Jewish religion, customs, and folkways but occasionally even entrusted to the Jews the defense of recently conquered areas (Granada, Cordova, Seville, Toledo).

In the Caliphate of Cordova, the Jewish element became more and more important, reaching its peak in the tenth century, a period in which Hebrew science and letters flourished (with figures such as the grammarian Menaḥem ben Saruc and the poet Dunáš ben Labrat), and the children of Israel achieved political eminence through Ḥasday ben Šaprut, secretary to Abderraman III. When the Caliphate disintegrated in the eleventh century as the result of civil wars, many influential Jews remained in the small Moorish kingdoms. A good example is Šemuel Hanaggid, whose power was virtually unlimited in the kingdom of Granada. On his death, he was succeeded by his son Yosef, whose abuse of power resulted in an uprising in 1066, the first slaughter of Jews in peninsular history. In that revolt, Yosef, his family, and his closest collaborators perished. However, this was not an anti-Jewish uprising by the Moors in Granada but rather a reaction against a specific family. Shortly afterward, influential Jews were again in the court in Granada.

The situation changed radically at the end of the eleventh century with the arrival of the Almoravides and the Almohades,[3] whose religious fundamentalism resulted in a massive exodus of Jews to the Christian realms.

From the Eleventh Century to the Expulsion

But what did they find there? How did Jewish life develop in Christian Spain?

In the north of the peninsula, small Jewish communities were in existence before the tenth century; there is evidence of Jewish colonies in Galicia and Leon from that time. In tenth-century Catalonia, Jews seem to have been largely, but not exclusively, involved in agriculture; a century later there was a sizable urban community in Barcelona, made up mainly of tailors, cobblers, silversmiths, and goldsmiths. In the twelfth century, Catalan legal documents were generally written in Hebrew when they dealt with matters between Jews, and in both Hebrew and Latin when they had to do with affairs involving both Jews and Christians. In that same era, the Counts of Barcelona considered the Jews as their property, and consequently subject to special legal status that was more protective than discriminatory.

A similar situation existed in Castile from the tenth century: first the counts, then the kings, established the rights of Jews by means of privi-

3. Two Arabic Muslim dynasties that invaded and occupied the Moorish territory of the Iberian Peninsula. The Almoravides held power in that territory from 1055 to 1147. They were conquered by the Almohades, who held control from 1147 to 1269.

leges accorded the Jewish colonies. Especially significant was the policy of Alfonso VI (eleventh century), who offered Jews coming from the Moorish kingdoms the opportunity to settle in Castile. To some of them he entrusted the organization of fiscal matters, and he authorized their appointment in the court. This was the case of Yosef ibn Ferrusel (known as "Cidiello"), to whom Yehuda ha-Levi refers in his famous poem:

Desd' cand' meu Cidiello venyd	Since my Cidiello arrived
Tan bona albixara!	what good news!
Com' rayo de sol exid	As a ray of sunshine he arose
en Wad al-haŷara.	in Guadalajara.

The Aragonese king Alfonso I the Battler also favored the Jews. During his reign in the twelfth century, Jewish colonies were established in Aragon and Navarre, and the status of the Jews was respected in the areas reconquered from the Moors, such as Zaragoza.

Also in the twelfth century, Castile saw the basis of the interreligious cultural flowering that was to blossom in the following century. The Archbishop of Toledo, Raimundo de Salvetat, founded the famous Translators' School in which Christian and Jewish intellectuals collaborated, and through which the European Christian world received not only the works of Eastern knowledge but also much of classical antiquity, which had been conserved only in Arabic versions. In its first stage, the mission of the school was the translation of Arabic into Latin, going through a rough draft in Romance. Alfonso X's great innovation (in the thirteenth century) was to lavish great attention on the Romance translations. Thus, the Spanish Jews not only contributed to the cultural and scientific enrichment of Castile—and, through Castile, of the rest of Christian Europe—but they also actively collaborated on the consolidation of the Castilian language as a vehicle for artistic and technical expression.

At the same time as this coexistence and exchange flourished among the intellectual classes, some legislation began to show characteristics not at all favorable to the Jews. Other legislation, however, reflected the monarchy's traditional protection of this group. The *Siete Partidas*[4] insist, for example, that the Jews "descend from those who crucified Our Lord Jesus Christ" and require them to live apart from Christians and wear a distinctive sign on their clothing. Yet at the same time the Christians were obliged to respect the

---

4. A compilation of laws and customs of Castile, written under the direction of Alfonso X "the Wise" (1252–84), reflecting the Spanish society of the time.

synagogue, because it was a "house in which the name of God is praised." The *Fuero Real*[5] and legislative sessions that took place during the thirteenth century gave with one hand and took away with the other. Jews and Christians were prohibited from marrying each other or even living under the same roof, but Jewish landowners were permitted to employ Christian laborers; forced baptism was forbidden, but conversion to Judaism drew the death penalty.

Aversion to the Jews was becoming more pronounced in Castile as well as in Aragon and Catalonia. In the latter, a veritable campaign to force Jews to abjure their faith arose, a campaign in which the Dominican friars were very active. The campaign culminated in the Dispute of Barcelona in 1263, in which the Christian participants included the convert Pablo Cristiano and Raimundo Martín, a disciple of Raimundo Peñafort. For the Jews, the famous Moses ben Nahman (Nahmanides, known as Rambam among the Jews and to the Christians as Bonastruc de Porta) participated. The dispute, presided over by King Jaime I, eased the way for the growing wave of anti-Judaism that was to explode across the whole peninsula toward the end of the following century.

In fact, hostility toward the Jews continued to grow in the Christian kingdoms from the end of the thirteenth century. Among the contributing factors were financial scandals involving some of Alfonso X's Jewish courtiers; the spread of accusations, originating in central Europe, of ritual crimes and profanation of Eucharistic wafers; and the concentration of Jews in unpopular professions related to moneylending and tax collecting.

The situation deteriorated still further with the Castilian battles of the Trastamaras and the consequent social tensions.[6] Finally, in 1391, an extensive wave of killings and popular assaults against the Jewish communities broke out. Beginning in Seville as a result of the preachings of the Archdeacon of Ecija, the assaults extended throughout the peninsula and resulted in the destruction of entire communities, some of which (like the community in Barcelona, which had been so prosperous) disappeared forever.

Many Jews died as a result of the violence of 1391, and Jewish communities suffered substantial economic losses, mass flights, and—of great importance to the future history of Spain—a large number of forced conversions.

5. Law code Alfonso X ordered compiled in 1254.
6. The Trastamara dynasty in Castile begins with Enrique II in 1369. This period is characterized by the ascendancy of the nobility, and Castilian involvement in conflicts in Western Europe, such as the Hundred Years' War in France.

After the disaster, the monarchs themselves tried to reconstruct the Jewish areas and repair the damages. Juan I of Aragon entrusted this difficult task to Hasday Crescas, but Spanish Jewry had suffered a mortal blow.

Moreover, the forced conversions were the origin of the extremely serious problem of converts who practiced Judaism in secret and who, years later, would be persecuted by the Inquisition. This institution, born in twelfth-century France to combat the Albigensian heresy, had come to Aragon in 1232, subsequently extending to Navarre. Its mission was not to persecute the Jews but rather to watch over the purity of the Christian faith. Consequently, Inquisitorial trials were not directed against practicing Jews but against those converts who were suspected of not having abandoned their Jewish practices completely. No Inquisition was established in Castile until the late fifteenth century, when the Catholic monarchs[7] instituted the so-called "National" or "New" Inquisition.

The fifteenth century was a time of contrasts for the Jewish communities in Spain, who were still feeling the effects of the great material and spiritual damage of the massacres of 1391. On the one hand, events very prejudicial to Hispanic Jewry occurred during that century. Inquisition trials of converts continued. The two-year-long Dispute of Tortosa (1412–14), provoked by the convert Jerónimo de Santa Fe, took place, resulting in the baptism of several eminent rabbis, to the great discouragement of their coreligionists. Slander and vitriolic anti-Semitic texts were spread with increasing impetus, often by converts. At the same time, however, Hispanic Jewry achieved moments of splendor. In 1432, representatives of the Castilian Jewish communities met in Valladolid and composed the famous *Taqqanot* [Laws], an important legal text that was to govern those communities henceforth. And there were nobles who did not hesitate to favor Jews, as was the case of the Master of the Order of Calatrava,[8] who entrusted to Rabbi Moshe Arragel de Guadalajara an annotated translation of the Bible, known today as the Alba Bible.

After the civil war that brought Isabella to Castile's throne, she and her husband, Ferdinand, followed the same policy as their predecessors, regarding the Jews as "royal property" under their protection. Why the same

7. Ferdinand II of Aragon and Isabella I of Castile who, having married in 1469, united their realms ten years later. Their reign included the establishment of the Inquisition (1480), the conquest of Granada (last of the Moorish territory in the Iberian Peninsula), the expulsion of the Jews, and the discovery of the New World (all in 1492), and the annexation of Navarre to their territory (1512).

8. The Order of Calatrava was a military-religious knightly order founded in 1158 for the purpose of defending the city of Calatrava from the Moors.

monarchs, years later, decreed their expulsion has been a matter of great contention. The expulsion edict itself was justified by the claim that Jewish presence in Spain brought temptation for converts to continue Jewish practices, for which reason the Inquisition had urged the monarchs to take such a measure. Some historians explain the expulsion as Spain's desire to enrich its supposedly indebted treasury by expropriating the exiles' property. Others interpret it as a royal concession to popular pressure. And there are those who attribute it to irrational religious fanaticism. It is likely that more than one of these motives played a part in the final decision. In any case, on March 31, 1492, Ferdinand and Isabella signed the decree that gave the Jews four months to leave Spain.

The exact number of Jews who left is unknown, as is how many Spanish Jews underwent conversion to Catholicism rather than be forced to leave what they considered their homeland. Recent estimates put the number at some one hundred thousand exiles, distributed among the countries open to them: Portugal (from which they would soon have to flee again), Italy, the Low Countries, southern France, North Africa, and, above all, the eastern Mediterranean, where the then-powerful Ottoman Empire welcomed them gladly.

The exiles called themselves Sephardim, meaning people from *Sepharad,* the Hebrew name for their native Spain.

Why *Sepharad?* Definition of the Term *Sephardi*

What is the origin of the Hebrew place name the Spanish Jews use for their mother country?

The name *Sepharad* appears in the prophecy of Obadiah (Obad. 20) as one of the places where the Jews exiled from Jerusalem lived. The biblical allusion is probably to Sardis, a city in Asia Minor. But Jewish tradition, especially since the eighth century C.E., tended to identify Sepharad with the western edge of the known world—the Iberian Peninsula. Thus, during the entire Middle Ages, and especially during the Golden Age of Hispano-Hebraic culture, Spanish Jews called themselves Sephardim,[9] a name they subsequently used (and not without a certain pride in their glorious peninsular past) in the diaspora following their expulsion from Spain.

The term *Sephardi* is often used in contrast to *Ashkenazi,* which refers to another major ethnocultural branch of Judaism—the Franco-German-Slavic branch. As in the case of Sepharad, Ashkenaz is also a biblical place name (it

---

9. *Sephardim* is the Hebrew plural of *Sephardi;* the adjective is either *Sephardi* or *Sephardic.*

appears in Gen. 10:3, Chron. 1:6, and Jer. 51:27), which originally seems
to have meant a country in the upper Euphrates valley bordering Armenia,
but which medieval rabbinic literature identified with the earliest Jewish settlements in central Europe—first Germany and northern France, then Poland
and Lithuania. A cultural tradition grew from this nucleus, one with its own
folkways and customs, rich folklore, religious and literary currents, a strong
philosophy, and its own liturgy. Linguistically, the Ashkenazi branch of Judaism is characterized by its particular pronunciation of Hebrew in religious
texts and by the use of Yiddish—a derivative of High German influenced by
Slavic, other European languages, and, naturally, Hebrew—in daily life. Successive migrations have placed the Ashkenazim in other areas, especially
North and South America and Israel.

Curiously enough, the opposition Sephardi/Ashkenazi has given rise to a
certain confusion that dates from the end of the nineteenth century and has
religious, or rather, liturgical origins. The growing Ashkenazi emigration to
Palestine created the need for a chief rabbi for the Ashkenazim, parallel to the
Sephardic chief rabbinate that had existed for many years. An immediate consequence of the increasing impact of Ashkenazi culture in the area of Palestine
that later became Israel was to include under the authority of the Sephardic
rabbinate all matters that were not Ashkenazi, even those that had no connection to the Jews of Spanish origin. And so Sephardim became the name
not only of the descendants of the Jews expelled from Spain in the fifteenth
century but also of all those who came from Arab and Eastern countries, be
they the Jews of Cochin (India), the Yemenites, or the black Jews from
Ethiopia.

Throughout this book, we will use the term *Sephardi* in its narrow meaning
to refer to those who share the following characteristics:

They are descendants of the Spanish Jews who were expelled from the
Iberian Peninsula in the fifteenth century or have assimilated to them socio-
culturally. This excludes not only the Ashkenazim and Jews of other ethnocultural branches but also those who lived in the Iberian Peninsula before the
expulsion (whom we prefer to call Spanish Jews, and whose culture, when
expressed in Hebrew, is Hebreo-Spanish or Hispano-Hebrew). Outside this
classification too, is the first generation of those expelled, who more accurately might be considered Spanish Jews in exile than true Sephardim, because their sociocultural milieu had not yet produced the changes derived
from having lived isolated from the Iberian Peninsula. And, of course, we do
not consider as Sephardim those Jews who converted and remained in Spain,

sometimes practicing Judaism in secret (converts, crypto-Jews, or Marranos[10] during Spain's Golden Age,[11] Portugal's *cristãos novos* or Mallorca's *chuetas*).

They have retained Hispanic cultural characteristics, and especially the Spanish language in their own dialect—Judeo-Spanish. Therefore, we only consider marginally the Jews of Spanish origin who, throughout the centuries, have assimilated culturally to the countries that received them, losing the Spanish language (as happened in France, England, or the Low Countries, for example). Although it may be repetitive, remember that merely speaking Spanish (for example, being from Spain or Latin America, or as a result of having studied the language) is not sufficient to automatically identify a Jew as a Sephardi. Only the Spanish-speaking Jew who is also the descendant of Spanish Jews in exile is a Sephardi.

SEPHARDIC JUDAISM

The Sephardim, therefore, are Spanish Jews. The brief historical outline with which this chapter begins explains how they are Spanish. We will now consider what their Judaism is like, speaking—again briefly—about the Spanish influence on cultural, social, folkloric, and traditional characteristics of the practice of Judaism. This is not, of course, an attempt to give an exhaustive description of the very complex religion of the Jews but rather to offer the reader the information necessary to understand what is discussed in the rest of this book.

Religion and the Written Word

Judaism, since its birth as a religion, has been characterized by its absolute veneration of the written word. Christianity and Islam, the other two religions that together with Judaism constitute what the Muslims call "people of the book," are not based on Judaism without reason. These three great religions are based on written revelation.

Jewish veneration of sacred writings goes to the extreme of also considering the supporting texts sacred. Thus, the rolls of parchment on which the Pentateuch (or Torah)[12] are written are kept in the most sacred spot in the synagogue and must be made of materials created according to strict ritual instructions. Those charged with writing the scrolls must be pious men who

10. A Spanish term of contempt, meaning "swine."
11. Spain's Golden Age is generally the sixteenth and seventeenth centuries. In contrast, the Golden Age of Jewish culture in the Iberian Peninsula is the ninth and tenth centuries.
12. That is, the five books of Moses—the Old Testament.

purify themselves before beginning the task. The rabbi does not touch the sacred scroll during the synagogue reading but uses a pointer (*yad* or *moré*) to follow the written line.

In addition, when any religious text becomes damaged or defective, it is never unbound or burned. Rather, it is put in the *genizah,* a repository in the synagogue where unusable texts are stored temporarily. In fact, the discovery of a forgotten *genizah* in Cairo gave scholars the opportunity to read and study some very valuable Hebrew religious texts that otherwise would have been lost. When the synagogue's *genizah* is full, its contents are taken to the cemetery where they are buried. In some communities, funeral honors were accorded the books. Michael Molho describes such a ceremony among the Eastern Sephardim:

> The Jewish population of the city formed a procession. At the head, marking a slow and religious pace, walked the two wardens of the synagogue, carrying the sacks that contained the *genizah*. Then came the rabbi of the community and the members of the community council. During the procession, they sang religious songs. . . . In Salonika, a few old men used to go to the Jewish homes to collect old holy books, singing a special song in Judeo-Spanish to the accompaniment of a tambourine. (*Usos,* 198)

What were these holy books to which such honors were given? They were religious texts, written by great rabbis, and, of course, also included the Bible.

The Christian Bible differs somewhat from the Jewish one in both organization and content. For example, the Christian canon includes books such as Judith and Tobias, considered apocryphal or extracanonic by Jews. Judaism refers to its complete Bible as the *Tanach,* a combination of the initials of the three parts into which it is divided: *Torah, Nevi'im,* and *Ketubim.*

a) The Torah, or Law, is the basis of Judaism. It is made up of the five books called the Pentateuch, which are known in Hebrew by their first words. Thus, Genesis is *Bereshith* because it begins with that word, meaning "in the beginning." *Shemoth,* Hebrew for "names," is Exodus; Leviticus is *Vayikra* (Hebrew for "and he said"); Numbers is *Bamidbar,* "in the desert"; and Deuteronomy is *Devarim,* "words." The Torah is written on parchment scrolls and kept in sumptuous covers or cases in the *aron* [ark] of the synagogue, and reading it forms the central part of public services. The reading is divided into fifty-four parts, called *parashot* (singular *parasha*), and is completed within one year.

b) The books called *Nevi'im* [prophets] are divided into *Rishonim* [first] and *Aharonim* [last]. The first group includes the books that Christians consider historical: *Yehoshua* [Joshua], *Shofetim* [Judges], *Shemuel* [Samuel], and *Melahim* [Kings]. The second group is made up of the strictly prophetic books: *Yeshaya* [Isaiah], *Yirmiya* [Jeremiah], *Yehezkiel* [Ezekiel], and *Tere'asar*—the twelve minor prophets.

c) The most heterogeneous group is the *Ketubim* [writings], including (1) the five *megillot* [scrolls]: *Shir Hashirim* [Song of Songs], *Ruth, Ehah* [Lamentations], *Kohelet* [Ecclesiastes], and *Esther;* (2) the poetic-sapiential books: *Tehilim* [Psalms], *Mishleh* [Proverbs], and *Iyob* [Job]; and (3) some historical books, such as *Ezra, Nehemiah* and *Divre Hayamim* [Chronicles].

These books make up the Bible or Jewish written law. But throughout the centuries the rabbis elaborated on oral law through their advice and teachings, which was not written down until much later. Part of it is collected in the Mishnah, writings that, together with their commentary, or Gemara, form the Talmud, an extensive body of work treating the most varied aspects of Jewish life, from celebrations, matrimony, and family life to liturgy, work, and detailed legal and ritual regulations. The corpus of the Talmud was definitively established between the fourth and sixth centuries B.C.E. in two different versions: the Talmud Yerushalmi reflects rabbinic traditions of Palestine whereas the Talmud Babli is based on those of Babylonia.

Another kind of rabbinic literature is the Midrash. In contrast to the Talmud, which is, above all, a legal and prescriptive code, the Midrash is a general term used for commentaries on the biblical books. It includes a great deal of hagiographic and legendary material and, because of its rich imaginative fund, it is an inexhaustible source for Jewish literature. The Midrash will be discussed in the section on patrimonial Sephardic literature.

Dietary Laws

Perhaps one of the characteristics that most distinguishes Jews from other peoples has been their charge to observe specific dietary laws. Dietary restrictions are not exclusive to Judaism; most religions have norms for the feeding of the faithful. Recall, for example, the strictures in Christianity on abstaining from meat on specific days, or the prohibition in Islam of pork and alcohol. Nevertheless, Judaism is much more detailed in this matter, because the precepts in the Bible, quite restrictive in themselves, have been expanded over the centuries by interpretation and practice, and have become obligatory. Today only the strictly observant comply with such detailed regulations, which are very difficult to follow, especially for those who live in predominantly non-Jewish areas. Still, they have played an important part in Jewish life and customs in general and, naturally, were important to the Sephardim.

Food prepared according to Jewish dietary laws is called kosher [clean, appropriate]; its opposite is *tref* or *trefáh* (and, among medieval Spanish Jews, *trifá*), which originally meant "torn," for reasons which will be explained later. Whether an item is kosher or not depends not only on its condition but also on how it was prepared. In other words, a dish can be *tref,* or impure, either because it is prohibited or because, although permitted, it was not prepared according to the prescribed norms.

The Bible establishes a list of *tref* and kosher foods: for example, the consumption of the flesh of ruminating mammals with split hoofs is permitted, as indicated in Lev. 11:1–3. The Sephardic Ferrara Bible,[13] in its peculiar archaic language, translates that section thus:

Y habló [Adonay[14]*] a Moseh y Aarón por dezir a ellos: Hablad a hijos de Israel por dezir: esta es la animalia que comeredes de toda la qatropea que sobre la tierra: toda uñán uña y hendién hendedura de uñas alçán rumio en la qatropea, a ella comeredes.*

[And the Lord spoke unto Moses and Aaron, saying to them: Speak unto the children of Israel, saying: These are the living things which ye may eat among all the beasts that are on the earth. Whatsoever parteth the hoof, and is wholly cloven-footed, and cheweth the cud, among the beasts, that ye may eat.]

Fish with fins and scales are also permitted, according to Lev. 11:9–11.

A este comeredes de todo lo que en las aguas: todo lo que a él ala y escama en las aguas, en los mares y en los arroyos, a ellos comeredes; y todo lo que no a él ala y escama en los mares y en los arroyos, de todo romovible de las aguas y de toda alma la biva que en las aguas, abominación ellos a vos.

[These may ye eat of all that are in the waters: whatsoever hath fins and scales in the waters, in the seas, and in the rivers, them may ye eat. And all that have not fins and scales in the seas, and in the rivers, of all that swarm in the waters, and of all the living creatures that are in the waters, they are a detestable thing unto you, . . .]

All fowl is permitted as well, except those mentioned in Lev. 11:13–19:

Y a estos abominaredes de la ave, no sean comidos, abominación ellos: a la águila y al açor y al esmerejón. Y al milano y al buytre a su manera. A todo cuervo a su manera. Y a hija del autillo y al mochuelo y a la cerceta y al gavilán a su manera. Y al halcón y a la gavia y a la lechuza. Y al calamón y al cernícalo y al pelícano. Y a la cigueña la ensañadera a su manera. Y al gallo montez y al morciégalo.

[And these ye shall have in detestation among the fowls; they shall not be eaten, they are a detestable thing: the great vulture, and the bearded vulture, and the ospray;

13. [AN] Unless otherwise indicated, biblical citations in Judeo-Spanish are from the Ferrara Bible, ed. Salomón Proops (Amsterdam, 1762). The original spelling is retained, but punctuation and accentuation have been modernized. Citations in English, unless otherwise noted, are from *The Pentateuch and Haftorahs,* ed. J. H. Hertz, 2d ed. (London: Soncino Press, 1966).

14. One of the Hebrew names for God.

and the kite, and the falcon after its kinds; every raven after its kinds; and the ostrich, and the night-hawk, and the sea-mew, and the hawk after its kinds; and the little owl, and the cormorant, and the great owl; and the horned owl, and the pelican, and the carrion-vulture; and the stork, and the heron after its kinds, and the hoopoe, and the bat.]

On the other hand, it is forbidden to eat all kinds of insects and reptiles (Lev. 11:20 and 11:41). Thus the prohibition extends not only to pork but also to the flesh of a number of other mammals, such as the horse and rabbit; fish is permitted but seafood—shellfish and mollusks—are *tref;* and, of course, all kinds of reptiles and amphibians, such as the frog and turtle, are forbidden.

Consumption of blood is also forbidden, according to Lev. 17:12: *"Por tanto dixe a hijos de Israel: toda alma de vos no comerá sangre"* ["Therefore I said unto the children of Israel: No soul of you shall eat blood"]. This prohibition includes the blood contained in meat, so that it affects the means of slaughtering the animals meant for consumption, as we will see shortly. Also prohibited is the fat of animals, even if they are kosher. The combination of meat with milk and dairy products is also forbidden, according to Exod. 13:19 and 34:26, and Deut. 14:21.

As has already been noted, food is kosher not only because of what it is but also because of how it is prepared. Especially important are the regulations on the means of slaughtering animals whose flesh is destined to be eaten. The slaughtering of cattle is called *shehita,* and in all Jewish communities there is a *shohet,* an official slaughterer, who knows those norms. It was specifically for these *shohetim*[15] that the first books of *dinim* [ritual prescriptions] were translated into Judeo-Spanish (see chapter 4).

The animal to be slaughtered must be healthy, with no physical defects, and it must be slain in a nonviolent and painless manner that permits the blood to be drained (to avoid its consumption). Eating the meat of any animal killed by violence (for example, by hunting) is strictly forbidden. The word *tref* originally meant "torn" and refers to an animal killed violently by plunderers, the consumption of which was prohibited.

Unlike the Muslims, the Jews are not forbidden from the use of alcoholic drinks. On the contrary, wine—also prepared according to specific regulations—plays a very important part in communal and religious life. There is even a special benediction (*kiddush* [sanctification]) recited over a glass of wine during the ritual meals of religious festivals or life-cycle events, and at

15. Plural of *shohet.*

the Sabbath dinner. Sabbath is the day of the week dedicated to God. At the Passover seder one is supposed to drink several glasses of wine while reading of the exodus of the Jews from Egypt. Wine has its place in the ceremonies of the life cycle as well: a few drops are brushed on the lips of a male infant when he is circumcised; at a wedding, the bride and groom drink from the same glass as a symbol of their unity.

Prayer and Religious Practice

The synagogue is the house of prayer for Judaism as the church is for Christianity and the mosque is for Islam. Its basic parts are the nave where the worshippers (the males wearing a *kipa* or skullcap and a white *tallith* or prayer shawl) gather, the *aron* or ark in which the Torah scrolls are kept, and the *teba* or pulpit from which the Torah is read and where the rabbi (or anyone over the age of thirteen) directs the service.[16] There are three daily services, or *tefilot: shaharit* in the morning, *minha* in the afternoon, and *arbit* or *ma'ariv* when night falls. On holidays, there are also set readings or specific ceremonies.

Not all Jewish religious practice takes place in the synagogue, however. As important as public liturgy (and sometimes even more important) are the private celebrations that take place at home and in the family for religious holidays. At all of the celebrations, there is a family dinner (*se'uda*) at which, in addition to eating special foods (many of which have symbolic meanings), the family recites benedictions and prayers, and sings songs appropriate to the holiday.

Before describing the various Jewish religious celebrations, I will examine the calendar and the way the Jews measure time in order to place those celebrations chronologically.

The Calendar

The Jewish calendar begins to count from the supposed year of the creation of the world, which is calculated by adding the ages of the different generations mentioned in the Bible. According to this computation, 1990 was the year 5750 since the creation of the world. The Jewish year can be calculated by adding 3,760 to the Christian year or, alternately, by subtracting 240 from

16. In orthodox synagogues, the men and women are seated separately, and only a male may lead the services. Conservative and Reform synagogues, especially in the United States, do not have separate seating, and both denominations now also have female rabbis. Sephardic synagogues tend to be traditional and orthodox.

the Christian year and adding 4,000. Thus, the year 2000 will be (2000 − 240) + 4000 = 5760.

The Jewish year, like the Christian year, is solar, but its months are lunar. Consequently, every two or three years a leap month is added to keep the lunar months in accord with the solar year. The year begins in the autumn with Rosh Hashanah [the head of the year] and consists of twelve months of twenty-nine or thirty days each, beginning with the new moon (*rosh hodesh* [head of the month]). The months are: *Tishrei* (coinciding with September or October), *Heshvan* (October–November), *Kislev* (November–December), *Tevet* (December–January), *Shevat* (January–February), *Adar* (February–March), *Nisan* (March–April), *Iyar* (April–May), *Sivan* (May–June), *Tamuz* (June–July), *Ab* or *Av* (July–August), and *Elul* (August–September). Leap month, when it occurs, is added after *Adar* and is called *Veadar* or *Adar Sheni*.

The Jewish week begins on Sunday and ends on Saturday, the Sabbath, the day consecrated to God. The new day does not begin at dawn but rather at sunset the previous day. Therefore, the Sabbath does not start on Saturday morning but at sundown on Friday.

Holidays

Shabbat (Sabbath)

The sanctification of the Sabbath is not only the holiest obligation of the Jew but also the one most characteristic of Judaism. Not only pious Jews but even those who are not orthodox commemorate that day, even if only because of its traditional and family significance. Orthodox Judaism requires a cessation of work and of carrying out specific activities that might be considered "work," such as setting out on a trip or kindling a fire. The latter prohibition gives rise to the need for preparing the Sabbath dinner the previous afternoon— a fact that has had a significant impact on Jewish eating habits. This is the way Molho describes it, referring to the Sephardim in Salonika:

> The housewise prepared . . . the *pastel* [pastry] or an essentially Jewish kind, filled with chopped meat or cheese in the winter, puree of squash, eggplant, zucchini, spinach, mixed with cheese in the other seasons. . . . She did not skimp on firewood, since the fire had to last through midday of the following day so that, despite the prohibition against lighting a fire on the holy Sabbath day, hot meals could be served. This was called *hamin*. (*Usos*, 205)

And José Benoliel describes *adafina*, the typical Sabbath dish in Morocco, which is cooked slowly on the embers:

A stew, destined for Sabbath lunch and prepared the previous afternoon, it consists of meat, calf feet, whole eggs, chick peas, potatoes, a meat or rice filling—sometimes stewing hens—and spices. During the night and part of Saturday, this stew, along with that of many other families, is kept in a closed oven, above the embers. (Benoliel, "Hakitía" 15 [1928]: 52)

On Friday night the festivity is celebrated in the synagogue, but the real celebration has always taken place at home. The housewife, at sunset, lights two ritual candles or an oil lamp while reciting a blessing; the family dines together after the father says the *kiddush* over a cupful of wine. The evening used to end with pious readings and joyous songs sung by the family, as David Menaché describes:

. . . *la mesa estava preparada sovre un masero, blanco como la ñeve, con dos bujías apuntadas con dos candelabros color del oro y posados uno de cada lado . . .*

Con grande solemnidad nuestro padre nos invitava a sintir el quiduz y todos nos rodeávamos al torno de la mesa, y él, tomando el copo de vino en la mano, y transportado de alegría, cantava con su boz hermosa el Yom Axixi; bivia un sorbo, y pasava el copo a mi madre, la cuala a su turno lo pasava a nosotros sigún las idades. Comíamos y después de comer io meldaba la peraxa de la semana fin xeni, cantava la aftara, y después de un chico intervalo, cantávamos todos juntos ciertos pismonim, como "Yoduja Rajiona, Omar l'adonai majsi", etc., y en último "Pazare ajora y veré la tierra santa de Tevaria". (Menaché, "Suvenires," 119–20)

[. . . the table was set on a tablecloth, white as snow, with two candles lit in two gold-colored candlesticks set at either end . . .

Very solemnly our father invited us to hear the *kiddush* and we all got around the table and he, taking the cup of wine in his hand, and transported by happiness, sang in his beautiful voice the *Yom Hashishi* ("sixth day"—beginning of a Sabbath psalm). He took a sip and passed the cup to my mother who, in turn, passed it to us in the order of our ages. We ate and, after eating, I read the first three parts of the Torah portion for the week, sang the *Haftorah* (the section of the Prophets read after the Torah portion) and, after a short while, we all sang certain hymns together, such as *Yoduha Rahiona, Omar l'Adonay Mahsi* (Sabbath hymns: "May my thoughts praise you"; "I speak to God, my refuge"), etc., and, last, "I will go and see the holy land of Tiberias" (the refrain of a neo-Zionist Judeo-Spanish poem praising the city of Tiberias, on the shore of a lake with the same name).]

During the Sabbath, relaxation continues until the first three stars announcing the end of the day appear. Then the *Havdalah,* a blessing that marks the end of the Sabbath and the beginning of the new week, is recited over wine and several aromatic spices. The Sephardim also generally sang allusive songs, such as the one that begins "El Dio alto con su gracia": ["God on high with His grace"], or another that expresses good wishes and hopes for prosperity for the coming week:

Buena semana nos dé el Dio	May God give us a good week
alegres y sanos.	with happiness and health.
A mis ijos bien decir	For my children, a blessing that
que me los deje el Dio vivir.	God may let them live.
Buena semana.	A good week.
Para fadar y cercucir,	To name [girls] and circumcise [boys],
para poner tefel.lín:	to put on *tefillin:* [17]
Buena semana.	A good week.

(Cancionero, IB8)

The Annual Liturgical Cycle

The annual liturgical cycle is divided among: (1) solemn holidays, (2) major holidays, (3) minor or commemorative holidays, and (4) fasts.

1) The solemn holidays are called *yomin nora'im* [days of awe]; their celebration has connotations of austerity and penitence. They start with the beginning of the year, or Rosh Hashanah, and continue to Yom Kippur [the Day of Atonement].

2) The major holidays (*yomim tovim* [good days, festive days]) are the three great pilgrimages that were made to the temple in Jerusalem in biblical times: Passover (Pesaḥ), the Feast of Weeks (Shavuot), and the Feast of Tabernacles (Sukkot). To these holidays one should add Simḥat Torah, or celebration of the Law, at the end of Sukkot.

3) The minor or commemorative holidays recall some historic occurrence of the Israelites (Hanukkah, Purim), or a cycle of nature (Tu-b'shevat).

4) Of the various fasts, only the fast of Tisha b'av, in remembrance of the destruction of the first and second temples in Jerusalem, will be discussed here because it is the fast most often mentioned in Sephardic literature and folklore.

Now to explain each of these holidays, following the order of the Jewish calendar.

Rosh Hashanah

As its Hebrew name "Head of the Year" indicates, Rosh Hashanah is the beginning of the Jewish year, celebrated on the first two days of the Hebrew month of *Tishrei* (September–October). Unlike other new year observances, for Jews the beginning of the year is not a time for rejoicing but a time of

17. Small square leather boxes with attached straps containing parchment slips inscribed in Hebrew with four scriptural passages. They are worn, one on the left arm and the other on the forehead, by males during morning weekday prayers as reminders of the obligation to keep the Law.

repentance for sins committed in the previous year and of expressing good intentions for the coming year. People shake clothes over the ocean, a river, or a well to symbolize the sins being thrown to the waters. This spirit of renewal also appears in some popular customs, such as wearing new clothes or getting new furniture at this time of the year.

Yom Kippur

Also called the Day of Atonement, Yom Kippur is the most solemn celebration in the Jewish calendar. It takes place on the tenth day of *Tishrei* and marks the culmination of the ten days of penitence that begin with Rosh Hashanah. On that day, all Jewish adults (over thirteen years of age) are to abstain completely from eating, drinking, wearing any leather, using perfume, and having sexual relations.

The entire day is dedicated to prayer and asking for pardon for sins committed. The first prayer in the synagogue is the famous *Kol Nidre* [Aramaic, all vows], in which God is asked to forgive vows that were not fulfilled and promises that were not kept during the previous year. The beginning of Yom Kippur is consequently often called *Kol Nidre* because of this prayer. Other prayers follow *Kol Nidre;* the Sephardic liturgy includes a good number of poems by great Hispano-Hebrew medieval poets, such as Shelomo ibn Gabirol or Yehuda ha-Levi. The Sephardim generally also read or sing verses in Judeo-Spanish to remind man of his own insignificance and the uselessness of material goods.

Sukkot

Sukkot is Hebrew for "booths," and the holiday is also called the Feast of Tabernacles. It is celebrated for eight days, from the fifteenth to the twenty-second of the month of *Tishrei,* and it commemorates the time during which the Israelite people wandered through the desert after leaving Egypt. In contrast to Rosh Hashanah and Yom Kippur, which are essentially religious and austere in nature, Sukkot is a festive celebration. This air of rejoicing has created some very picturesque folkloric customs. Originally one of those festivals in which primitive agricultural peoples (in this case the Hebrew people) celebrated the wheat and fruit harvest, the message of Lev. 23:42–43 caused the commemoration of the wanderings through the desert to be superimposed on this holiday, whose key characteristic is the construction of a *sukkah* [booth] in which the family gathers for meals during the eight days of the celebration. Here is how Enrique Saporta y Beja describes it.

la suka no deve de estar debacho de alguna pare or tejado. Por esto se eskojia fazerlo sovre los balkones o las tarrasas. Segun la tradisyon se deve de dechar avyerturas entre las kanyas del tejado para ke se vea el syelo.

Se empesa en fazyendo una armatura de palo. Despues atando masas de kanyas entre eyas se faze las paredes i el tejado. Kuando todo esto esta montado, las mujeres se okupan de moblear el interyor. Sovre las paredes de ramas i de fojas se espanden savanas blankas. Tenidas por alfinetes unas flores amariyas yamadas flores de suka (gravina de las indyas) forman ermozos dizenyos sovre la blankura de la hase. La puerta esta aserrada por un tapet enkolgando, ke se alevanta para pueder entrar. De kada parte, a los dos lados de la puerta ay dos tyestos de plantas. La mas parte de las vezes son tyestos de finojo (fenouil). (Saporta, Torre, 203)

[the *sukkah* should not be under any wall or roof. Therefore, one chose to construct it on balconies or terraces. According to tradition, one should leave openings between the reeds of the roof so that the sky can be seen.

First a wooden skeleton is erected. Then the walls and the roof are made by tying reeds together. When this is all put together, the women are in charge of furnishing the interior. White sheets are spread over the walls of branches and leaves. Held by pins some yellow flowers, called *sukkah* flowers (gravina of the Indies), form beautiful designs on the whiteness of the cloth. The doorway is closed by a hanging rug that can be raised to enter. On both sides of the door, there are flowerpots. Generally, they contain fennel.]

The agricultural character of the holiday is shown in the ornamentation with branches and flowers, and in the required presence of other plants.

kada manyana se bendize la suka, en yevando a los kuatro kantones un buketo fetcho de ramas de tres plantas diferentes: un ramo de "lulab" (palmera), uno de "araba" (saule) i uno de "hadase" (myrte) a las kualas se adjunta un fruto: el "etrog" (sidra). (Ibid., 204)

[every morning the *sukkah* is blessed, carrying to each of the four corners a bouquet made up of three different plants: a branch of palm, one of willow and one of myrtle, to which is added a fruit: the citron.]

The items used in Jewish ceremonies usually have great significance, and these plants are no exception. Some say that each item here represents one of the sins for which man should ask pardon; according to others, each plant represents a part of the body, all of which should be used in the service of God; still others consider that the assortment represents the variety of individuals and personalities that make up the people of Israel. Whatever the symbolic meaning attributed to them, the use of plants is a clear indication of the agricultural origin of the holiday.

There are also Hebrew and Judeo-Spanish songs associated with the holiday, as Michael Molho describes:

We ate and drank our fill. Then, at dessert time, songs were heard . . . the whole
city sang. . . . The men at the top of their voices . . . singing topical songs. . . .
The women kept silent while the singing was in Hebrew, but when, after each
melody, the Judeo-Spanish translation was sung, they immediately joined the men.
(*Usos*, 220)

Simḥat Torah

This festival, which means "the happiness of the Law" is celebrated at the end
of Sukkot. It takes place on the twenty-third day of the same month of *Tishrei*, and it is, as its name indicates, a celebration of the joy of the Law revealed
by God to his people. As I previously mentioned, the Torah readings are
divided into fifty-four sections, one for each week of the year. Simḥat Torah
is celebrated precisely when the last section is read and the cycle begins again.

In Ashkenazic Judaism, this is the holiday characteristic of Hasidism [He-
brew, pietism], a mystical movement that advocates the zealous love of God
and His Law, a love whose joyful, public expression is song and dance. For
the Sephardim, too, the holiday has a good deal of that joy, mysticism, and
excitement. In contrast to the austerity and politeness that habitually reign in
the synagogue, on Simḥat Torah there are demonstrations of joy that might
be considered scandalous. Candy and candied almonds are thrown at the
people called to read the Torah; the scrolls of the Law, and even the worshippers themselves, are sprinkled with rosewater; and, most important, the
Torah scrolls are passed around the synagogue seven times to the accompaniment of songs in Hebrew and Judeo-Spanish. People dance as well.

Each community had its own special customs, some very picturesque and
even shocking. In some of the Eastern communities, people drank *raki* (a
strong Turkish alcoholic drink) during the Torah reading; in others they gave
gifts to the faithful, held collective meals, or played games and told risqué
stories that, except for their festive character, had little to do with the celebration of the day.

The lack of female participation is noteworthy in these ceremonies that
took place in the synagogue and its surroundings; they seemed to be an exclusively masculine demonstration of love of the Law. The central characters
were the *ḥatan Torah* [Hebrew, bridegroom of the Law] and the *ḥatan Bereshith* [bridegroom of Genesis], that is, the two men in the community who
read the last and the first sections of the Torah respectively. The very name
"bridegroom" expresses that almost erotic love for the Torah, which is considered the bride of the people of Israel, as is indicated in paraliturgical verses
that used to be sung on that holiday.

Hanukkah

This holiday takes place at the end of the month of *Kislev* (November–December) and lasts for eight days. It commemorates the purification of the temple in Jerusalem after the victory of the Maccabees over Antiochus Epiphanes, the Greek governor who had prohibited the practice of Judaism in an effort to assimilate the Hebrew people to Greek culture. A holiday with nationalist overtones, it is no coincidence that centuries later many Zionist groups adopted names related to the Maccabean revolt because of their symbolic connection to the ideas of cultural and political independence. In Sephardic literature, the theme of Hanukkah, at first present only in a religious sense in some paraliturgical verses, began to appear at the end of the nineteenth century in many plays, poems, and even in the names of Zionist newspapers.

According to the legend, when the Maccabean revolt broke out, the supply of oil for the temple lamp, which always must remain lit, was sufficient for only one day. But, miraculously, the lamp remained lit for the eight days it took for the rebels to triumph. In remembrance of that miracle, candles are lit in a *hanukkiya* (eight-branched candlestick, often called a menorah) in Jewish homes. Each night an additional candle is lit; on the eighth night all of them are lit.

On a more folkloric and secular level, the Sephardim generally invited guests to celebrate the festival, and gave gifts, especially to little children. It also became the custom to organize collections for the poor and, in more recent times, to present school plays on the theme of Hanukkah.

Tu-b'shevat

Another of the minor Jewish holidays, Tu-b'shevat is celebrated on the fifteenth day of *Shevat* (January–February). It is also called *Rosh Hashanah Lailanot* [New Year of the Trees], since it celebrates the reawakening of nature after the winter. The celebration was basically a family meal served at a table adorned with flowers at which several kinds of fruit were blessed and eaten. Here is how Molho describes the custom among the Sephardim from Salonika:

> In the center of the table were watermelon and muskmelon, carefully preserved for several months by the head of the family. Apples, pears, dates, dried figs, almonds, hazelnuts, walnuts, chestnuts, medlar, etc., beautifully displayed on platters or trays by the housewife, were a delight both to see and taste. After the meal, the head of the

household pronounced the blessings for the fruits, and for red and white wine. With the contentment that comes from good food and drink, seasonal songs were sung. (*Lit.,* 154)

Among these "seasonal songs" were the verses of the *Debate of the Flowers and the Debate of the Fruits,* which will be discussed in chapter 4.

Purim

Purim, the most joyful and festive Jewish holiday, falls on the fourteenth, and sometimes also the fifteenth, of *Adar* (February–March). It commemorates the story told in the biblical book of Esther, that is, how Esther, a young Jewish woman who was married to the Persian king Ahasueros, intervened to save the Jews from death. Their execution had been planned by the cursed Haman, Ahasueros's minister and mortal enemy of Esther's uncle Mordehai.

The only distinguishing feature of the religious celebration is the reading of the *megillah* [scroll] that tells the biblical story of Esther. It is at home and in public that the real celebration takes place, a celebration similar to the Christian Mardi Gras in its festive atmosphere and the custom of wearing disguises. It was (and continues to be) the rule to eat (especially sweets), to drink, to celebrate, and to exchange platters of delicacies, which the Eastern Sephardim called *platicos.* It was also traditional to give a gift of money (*purimlik* or simply *purim*) as well as clothing and gold and silver objects. The children also received money, presents, or, especially in the East, figurines and toys made of sugar. And, of course, there were special sweets for Purim: maraschino cherries and especially *folares,* sugared replicas of the gallows on which the accursed Haman died. These replicas later took on many other forms. Here is how Gina Camhy describes these customs.

> *In un ermozu platu pintadu o di plata si mitia a un piasu di techpechti, di torta, di biskutela, un fular forma korazon o forma estreya.*
>
> *Il platu si kuvria kun tuvajika lavrada kun dizenyu di Magen David i si mandava esti platu a la famiya i a lus amigus akompanyadu kun bindisyonis iskritas. . . .*
>
> *Estus mandamyentus di "platikus" duravan il dia interu di Purim i la notchi de la seuda. Era tambyen la uzansa di resivir "purimlik" ki es dadiva in moneda.* (Camhy, "Purim," 38–39)

[On a beautiful plate with a design, or of silver, was put a piece of *teshpeshti,*[18] of cake, cookies, a cookie shaped like a heart or a star.

The plate was covered with a cloth with an embroidered Jewish star on it, and this platter was sent to family members and friends, along with written blessings. . . .

18. A sweet pastry containing pieces of dough and nuts, all covered with honey. *Teshpeshti* is very similar to Ashkenazi *teiglach.*

This exchange of *platicos* lasted the entire day of Purim and the night of the holiday dinner. It was also customary to get a *purimlik,* which is a gift of money.]

Games of chance and theatrical presentations are also customary. The evil person in the story is the object of all kinds of jokes and insults. As Arcadio de Larrea Palacín points out:

Formerly, an effigy of Haman was made, which was hanged and burned after being dragged through the streets. Many fireworks were set off, even at the synagogue, when the name of Ahasueros's favorite was read, and children were given a wooden toy in the shape of Haman, with two hammers placed so that they would hit him.   (Larrea, *Rituales,* 173)

Pesaḥ (Passover)

Pesaḥ is celebrated from the fifteenth to the twenty-second of *Nisan* (March–April) in commemoration of the exodus of the Jews from Egypt under the guidance of Moses. It is one of the preeminent festivals of Judaism, especially in the family celebration.

On Pesaḥ, even more than on other holidays, the most important ceremony is not the synagogue service but the one that takes place in the home—the *seder* [Hebrew, order] of the first two nights of Passover. At the *seder,* the family eats together and reads specific religious texts.

Before Pesaḥ can be celebrated correctly, however, it is first necessary to carry out a meticulous ritual cleaning of the home, kitchen implements, and clothing. This cleansing serves to eliminate any trace of *hametz* [leavening], that is, of food that is fermented or contains yeast. The Bible recounts that the Jews left Egypt so quickly that their bread had no time to rise, and this is the reason why on Passover only a special type of bread, that has not risen and does not contain any yeast (matzah), is eaten. Any leavened food must be avoided. What cannot be thrown away is held during Passover in a special room and is sold by the symbolic sale of the key to that room. Also, all kitchen implements are immersed in boiling water, or special dinnerware (called "Pesaḥ china" by the Sephardim) is used during that time.

The housewife's labor in carrying out this ritual cleansing has become almost a literary topic among the Sephardim. For example, the excessive zeal of these *balabayas* (from Hebrew, *ba'al habayit* [master of the house]) is satirized in a short theatrical work in verse[19] that describes how, in order to eliminate the most minute traces of leavening, the whole family had to eat in the street and even put their very health at risk:

19. The name of the play is *Ocho días antes de Pésaḥ.*

A la većina cale ver,	You must see the neighbor lady,
que ella con su saber	for with her knowledge,
al marido y su hijo	her husband and child
te los quitó al cortijo.	she has thrown out on the patio.
Ya escapó su rijo	She completed her task
según ella quiso:	as she wished:
arenó bien las puertas,	she cleaned the doorways well,
ya adobó dos camaretas	she readied two rooms,
no dejó zapatetas	she didn't even leave slippers
que no fregó las soletas.	without scrubbing their soles.

(In Romero, *Teatro,* 2:966)

All of the work was forgotten, however, at the beginning of Passover, when the whole family gathered around the table to participate in a ritual over a thousand years old, one that is celebrated today with almost no changes and in which every element has a beautiful and profound symbolic sense.

Everyone joins around the table, at which there is a place set for the supernatural guest, Eliyahu Hanavi [the prophet Elijah], the herald of the messianic era. He is given a seat and a glass of wine.

The ritual elements for the dinner are placed on a special tray: three *matzot* [unleavened bread] covered with a white cloth; the shank bone of a lamb to represent the strength of God's arm when He took His people out of Egypt; a roasted egg, which represents the fleeting nature of life (for that reason the *seder* is a typical funeral meal) and which here also refers to the pain of the destruction of the temple in Jerusalem; the *maror* or bitter herbs (usually lettuce), which symbolizes the bitterness of slavery; and the *haroset,* a paste made of dried fruit, cinnamon, and honey, to represent the mortar with which the Jewish slaves made bricks for the Egyptians. Next to the tray there is a bowl of salt water and vinegar, in which the bitter herbs are dipped, to recall the waters of the Red Sea that the Hebrews had to cross in their flight from Egypt.[20]

And so begins the ceremony, in the course of which four cups of wine are drunk and the *Haggadah,* the story of the exodus from Egypt, is read or chanted:

Este pan de aflegisión que comieron nuestros padres en tierra de Egipto; todo el que tenga hambre, que venga y coma; todo el que tenga menester pascual, que venga y pascue; este año aquí, al año el vinién en tierra de Israel: éste aquí, siervos; al año el vinién en tierra de Israel hijos horros. (Larrea, *Rituales,* 221)

20. Some of these items are different among the Ashkenazi Jews. For example, Ashkenazi *haroset* is usually made with apples, nuts, cinnamon, and Passover wine.

[This is the bread of affliction which our ancestors ate in the land of Egypt. Let all who are hungry come and eat. Let all who are in need come and celebrate Passover. This year we are here: next year in the land of Israel! This year we are slaves: next year, free men!][21]

The youngest member of the family asks the head of the household the questions of the *Ma nishtana* [how is it different]:

Cuánto diferente la noche la ésta más que todas las noches: que en todas las noches no nós entieniente tampoco una vez una y en la noche la ésta dos veces; que todas las noches nós comientes yebdo o seseña, y la noche la ésta todo seseña; que en todas las noches nós comientes las demás verduras, y la noche la ésta lechuga; que en todas las noches nós comientes y bebientes, tanto asentados y tanto rescobdados, y la noche la ésta todos nós rescobdados. (Larrea, *Rituales*, 221)

[Why is this night different[22] from all other nights? On all other nights, we can eat bread or *matzah:* why, tonight, only *matzah*? On all other nights, we can eat any kind of herbs: why, tonight, bitter herbs? On all other nights, we don't dip the herbs we eat into anything: why, tonight, do we dip twice? On all other nights, we can eat either sitting up straight or reclining: why, tonight, do we all recline?]

The whole family, in response, explains why this night is so different, reading the complete story of the flight from Egypt. It is a ceremony that unites commemoration with learning, as the meaning of the holiday is explained to the youngsters. After the *Haggadah,* other texts may be read, such as the Song of Songs or the Proverbs of Solomon. The Sephardim may sing songs in Judeo-Spanish, including several ballads. And everyone wishes everyone else to celebrate Passover "el año el vinién en Yerushalayim" ["next year in Jerusalem"].

Shavuot

Shavuot is celebrated on the sixth and seventh of the month of *Sivan* (May–June), seven weeks after Pesaḥ. That fact explains the name of this holiday, for *shavuot* means "weeks" in Hebrew. In the New Testament, it is called by the Greek name Pentecost [fifty days].

In Judeo-Spanish, Shavuot often becomes *Sabuó* or *Sebó* and, on occasion has been called the *Fiesta de la Recolta,* a calque of the French *Fête de la Récolte* [harvest festival], because it originally celebrated the end of the harvest season. A commemoration of God's giving the Ten Commandments to Moses

---

21. Translations from the Passover *Haggadah* are taken from *A Feast of History,* ed. Chaim Raphael (New York: Simon and Schuster, 1972).
22. The actual translation of the first words is "How different this night is . . ."

on Mount Sinai was superimposed onto this original agricultural sense. Consequently, the holiday is also the celebration of *Matan Tora* [giving of the Law].

Among the Sephardim, the holiday preserves this double function: they read the book of Ruth, which takes place in an agricultural setting during the harvest, and they sing verses praising God for having given the Law to his people. (Some of these verses are also appropriate for Simḥat Torah.) Aside from these religious or paraliturgical customs, some communities also used to picnic in the country at this time.

Tisha b'av

This holiday takes place, as its Hebrew name indicates, on the ninth of the month of *Av* (July–August). The epitome of mourning, it commemorates the greatest misfortune ever to have happened to the Jewish people—the destruction of the temple in Jerusalem and the subsequent dispersion of the people of Israel across the face of the earth. To this initial cause for mourning have been added the memories of all of the misfortunes visited on the Jewish people collectively—the expulsion from Spain, persecutions, murders, and pogroms—and on each individual—the death of a loved one, a family misfortune.

Among the Sephardim, the holiday is known colloquially as *Tesabeá* (deformation of the Hebrew *Tisha b'av*); in Morocco it is sometimes called the *fiesta verde* [green holiday] as a euphemism to avoid mentioning such an evil date. Its celebration includes numerous picturesque details in which religious statutes are combined with tradition and even popular superstitions.

The holiday begins with a dinner consisting of foods considered traditional for that day: lentils and hard-boiled eggs, both of which are typical foods of mourners. The meal is followed by a strict twenty-four-hour fast.

In the synagogue services, sad texts were entoned in Hebrew and in Judeo-Spanish: the lamentations of Jeremiah, the book of Job or various *kinot* [dirges] (singular *kinah*). The women would generally meet in a home, often the home of a family member who had suffered some misfortune that year. They would spend the day there, neither eating nor drinking, singing dirges and sad, mournful ballads that would provoke the compassion of everyone present. Even the children sang dirges, imitating their elders. They played macabre games, such as holding pretend funerals or making clay figurines before which they cried and mourned as if those figurines were dead bodies.

Tisha b'av, which was not originally as important in the Jewish calendar as Pesaḥ or Yom Kippur, thus acquired great meaning and a wealth of folklore among the Sephardim. The abundance of refrains about *Tesabeá* in Sephardic proverbs illustrates its significance. Specific traditional songs have become so linked with this day that it is considered bad luck to sing them except during mourning. Superstitions regarding the day have also proliferated such as not going near any bodies of water because evil spirits were said to be there on Tisha b'av.

Religious Life-Cycle Ceremonies

Circumcision

Circumcision is one of the fundamental precepts of Judaism without which no male may be considered a member of the people of Israel. The measure is referred in various biblical passages, most especially in Gen. 17:10–12, where God commands Abraham to circumcise all the males of his house:

This is My covenant, which ye shall keep, between Me and you and thy seed after thee: every male among you shall be circumcised. And ye shall be circumcised in the flesh of your foreskin; and it shall be a token of a covenant betwixt Me and you. And he that is eight days old shall be circumcised among you, every male throughout your generations, he that is born in the house, or bought with money of any foreigner, that is not of thy seed.

In Hebrew the ceremony is called *b'rit mila* [covenant of circumcision], a phrase the Sephardim abbreviate as *mila* or *berit* or deform into *beri* or *berin*. Circumcision takes place eight days after the birth of a male infant and is performed by the *mohel* [circumcisor], a member of the Jewish community with special training. During the ceremony, the infant is given his name. In addition to the parents, the *sandak* (a man honored with holding the baby during the ceremony), relatives, and friends attend, since the circumcision is a cause for celebration. Naturally, the prophet Elijah is also invited; a seat is reserved for him, just as it is during the Passover *seder*. After the circumcision, those in attendance have a glass of kosher wine, a few drops of which are also put on the infant's lips during the ceremony.

More for folkloric than religious reasons, the Sephardim generally kept watch over the new mother and her son the night before the circumcision to prevent evil spirits from harming either of them. This vigil was called *shemirah*, "vigil, guard" in Hebrew, or *noche de viola* in Judeo-Spanish. During this time, the people involved would drink, eat sweets and, of course, sing, as Enrique Saporta describes:

La notche antes del dia del berin de su fijo, Avram resivyo algunos paryentes i amigos. Era la "viola" tradisyonal. Los vijitores venian a ver el parido i la parida.

Segun la kostumbre avia un "tchalgi" ke djugava muzika turka i kantes sefardis en espanyol. El tchalgi estava komponido de una "kimane", un "lut" i un "kanun" . . . ke sonavan la mizma koza.

El kantador akompanyando su kante en aharvando sovre su pandero, etchava un "mekan" i los invitados lo ritmavan en dando palmadas. . . .

Bona la tanyedera empeso la primera, kantando una kantiga klasika i tradisyonal de viola . . . (Saporta, *Torre*, 27–28)

[The night before the circumcision of his son, Avram hosted some relatives and friends. It was the traditional vigil. The visitors came to see the new father and mother.

As is customary, there was a small band that played Turkish music and Sephardic songs in Judeo-Spanish. The band was made up of a violin, a lute and a zither . . . all playing together.

The singer, accompanying himself by striking the tambourine, sang a song and the guests accompanied it with rhythmic clapping. . . .

Bona, the tambourine player, began, singing a classical and traditional vigil song . . .]

None of these ceremonies accompanies the birth of a girl. There is only the *fadamiento,* or *las fadas,* more social than religious in character, during which she is given her name.

Bar Mitzvah

Bar Mitzvah [son of the covenant] marks the attainment of religious adulthood, celebrated by Jewish males at age thirteen. From that time on, they can participate actively in religious ceremonies like any other adult and, most important, can be counted as part of the *minyan,* or group of ten men, the minimum number required for public services. Consequently, to indicate that a boy had already become a Bar Mitzvah, the Sephardim said that he had "already formed a *minyan.*"

The ceremony is also referred to popularly as "putting on the *tefillin*" or simply "*tefillin,*" because during the ceremony the boy wears his *tefillin,* or phylacteries, for the first time. The *tefillin* are small leather cases that contain folded pieces of parchment bearing various passages from the books of Exodus and Deuteronomy. They are held to the forehead and the left arm by leather straps during morning prayers, symbolizing the fact that the Jew always has the Law of God present, both in thought and deed. By analogy to the Christian celebration, the Sephardim in Morocco and the Jews living in Spain sometimes refer to the Bar Mitzvah ceremony as "first communion."

Today, in the more modern communities, girls go through a similar ceremony, called the Bat Mitzvah [daughter of the covenant], although they neither wear *tefillin* nor form part of the *minyan*. It is a ceremony that marks their religious maturity rather than their integration into public religious services.

Marriage

The Jewish wedding ceremony, called *kiddushim* or *kiddushin,* is especially rich and complex. It consists of two parts: the betrothal and the marriage itself. The two stages used to be separated by months, even years, but at least since the nineteenth century the two ceremonies have become one. Before that time, though, the *esponsales* or *espozorios* [betrothal] was more a social ceremony, one at which the marriage was arranged.

> *El dia de los kortes de espozoryo, se azia un akto kontenyendo las kondisyones del kaza-myento. I estas se dizian en primero de boka delantre de los testiguos. La seremoniya se pasava ande la espozada. El haham azia djurar al mansevo i despues a la mansevika sobre las kondisyones de la boda.* (Benbassa, 33)

> [On the day of the betrothal, a document was written up containing the conditions of the marriage. And these were first declared orally before witnesses. The ceremony took place in the home of the bride-to-be. The rabbi made the future groom, and then the bride, declare under oath what those conditions were to be.]

The future groom generally gave his fiancée a piece of jewelry. From that time on, the bride-to-be, with the help of the women in her family, began to prepare her trousseau, which was put on display several days before the wedding. That allowed relatives and friends to see it, and the *preciadores* [assessors] to insure that its value fulfilled the conditions of the marriage contract. In Morocco, the showing of the trousseau was carried out on the so-called *jueves de la tufera* [Thursday of the unbraiding], when other festive ceremonies of great symbolic content were held.

> This word [*tufera*] designated the tresses of the bride . . . and the festivity revolved around the ceremony of unbraiding her hair and chanting *ulalé.* . . . The groom would send the bride a tray with raisins, *alconfites* [candies] and almonds, a ribbon and candles. The raisins and candy symbolized sweetness, and the almonds, which represented purity, were shared by the guests. Then the women retired with the bride, unbraided her hair, tied it with the ribbon, and covered it with a *meherma,* or silk cloth. At nightfall, the boys and girls would leave the house with the candles lit, preceded by one member of the family who held a large candle and another with a kettle of whitewash to leave brush marks on the doors of friends' houses as a good omen. Accompanying them as well was the *guisandera,* who played the *sonaxa* [tambourine]. In this fashion, and shouting *ulalé, ulalé,* they went to the groom's house. (Larrea, *Rituales,* 14–15)

It was also the custom, a few days before the wedding, for the bride to have a sort of farewell to the single life, when her female relatives and friends would join her to sing, dance, drink, and eat sweets.

Among the religious rites celebrated before marriage is the bride's ritual bath, carried out as an obligatory sign of purification. The Sephardim surrounded this ceremony with many popular and festive activities.

> In the Middle East, it acquired a solemn and sometimes raucous form. Musicians of both sexes accompanied the bride to the *hammam* [Turkish bath]. Her mother, sisters and aunts accompanied her, carrying the cleaning utensils sent over the previous night, or the night before that, by the groom. For the occasion, the bride wore luxurious clothing and a great deal of jewelry. . . . The bride's "toilette" took several hours. After having made good use of all of the objects and ingredients in the package sent by the groom, his future wife had to go through the triple immersion [*tebilah*] ordered by rabbinic law.   (Molho, *Usos,* 22–23)

During the course of the entire ceremony, and especially during the trip to the bathhouse and when the bride came out of the water, allusive songs were sung.

> *A la salida del banyo se komia kozas de orno i se bevia raki en kantando i baylando en el hamam. En vezes esta seremoniya del banyo tomava lugar un dia antes de la boda . . . i se puede dizir ke era una fyesta de mujeres i de grande emportansa.*   (Benbassa, 34)
>
> [On leaving the bath, they ate baked goods and they drank *raki* while singing and dancing in the bathhouse. Sometimes this bathing ceremony took place the day before the wedding . . . and it can be said that it was a ceremony for the women, and of great importance.]

In Morocco, the groom's mother played an important part in the ceremony.

> The groom's mother gives the bride, completely nude, to the *bañera,* or the woman charged with assisting her, who enters the bath with the bride, making sure that the water covers her completely, that her body does not touch the walls of the pool, and says the purification prayers. . . . It is the mother of the groom who puts the chemise on the bride, and the other women in the groom's family dress her in the rest of her clothing, which is white, so that the life she is about to begin will be bright and happy. (Larrea, *Rituales,* 16–17)

The wedding itself may be celebrated in the synagogue or in a home, normally that of the groom. Under the *huppa,* or nuptial canopy, there is a *tálamo* [bench] on which the bride and groom sit, and before which two candles are lit. The officiating rabbi blesses a glass of wine, from which both bride and groom drink to symbolize their obligation to share everything.

Then the groom places a gold ring on the bride's finger, saying the Hebrew words: *Arey at mekudeshet li betaha at tsot kedat Moshe veYisrael* [Be thou consecrated to me by this ring, according to the law of Moses and Israel]. Then the Aramaic text of the *ketubah* [marriage contract] is read, specifying the obligations of both the bride and the groom, and the dowry (which is only symbolic today). Then the *shevah berahot* [seven blessings] are recited and the groom stamps on a glass, breaking it as a reminder of the painful destruction of the temple in Jerusalem.[23]

After the ceremony, the bride is led in a procession to her new husband's home, accompanied by music and song. In Morocco, this procession used to take place the day before the wedding and, to guarantee chastity, the future mother-in-law slept with the bride-to-be. In other times, the consummation of the marriage and proof of the bride's virginity were announced by hanging out the bloodstained sheet and sending sweets and candy to friends and relatives.

After the marriage was consummated, the bride and groom had to practice celibacy for seven days, although the celebration continued.

Los otchos dias ke seguian la boda se yamavan la semana de la hupa. En estos otcho dias el novyo no lavorava i devia de kedarse al lado de su mujer. De las puertas i ventanas avyertas de las kazas de los kosuegros se oyia kantes y bayles. El tchalgi no kedava de tanyer. La mandolina i el pandero akompanyavan estos pasatyempos. Mujeres aedadas kantavan romansas en espanyol. . . . (Benbassa, 36)

[The week following the wedding was called the week of the *huppa*. During that week the groom did not work and was to stay with his bride. From the open doors and windows of the homes of relatives songs and dances were heard. The band did not stop playing. The mandolin and tambourine gave accompaniment to these pastimes. Old women sang ballads in Judeo-Spanish. . . .]

On the Saturday after the wedding (*Shabbat del tálamo*), the groom received the honor of doing the public reading in the synagogue. The following day, or sometimes two or three weeks after the *Shabbat del tálamo*, there was a wedding reception at the bride's parents' home.

Death and Mourning

There is a complex cycle of ceremonies for a year after a death. All Jewish communities have a society called the *hevra kadishah*, whose members wash

---

23. For other interpretations of breaking the glass at the end of the wedding ceremony, see Isaac Jack Lévy, *Jewish Rhodes: A Lost Culture* (Berkeley, Calif.: Judah L. Magnes Museum, 1989).

and shroud the body according to very specific statutes, after which it is placed in a simple coffin. The closest relatives make a small tear in their clothes as a sign of mourning. At the cemetery, after the body has been buried, the closest male relative (preferably a son) pronounces the *kaddish,* or mourners' prayer.

But the ceremonies do not end here; they continue for at least a year. During the first week of mourning the close relatives abstain from working. Among the Sephardim it was also customary during that time to eat seated on the floor as a sign of grief, and friends of the mourning family would provide food for those days and visit them to help assuage their grief. Typical mourners' food, as has been noted previously, was hard-boiled eggs.

After this period of strict mourning, there is a time of semi-mourning, which lasts for thirty days, during which time festive occasions are avoided and the tear in the clothing is retained. The Sephardim call the Saturday before the end of this thirty-day period *cortadura del mes* [end of the month], and it is spent again in strict mourning. Close relatives, nevertheless, are supposed to continue pious practices to honor the memory of the deceased for an entire year. Males are required to say the *kaddish* for the deceased daily.

At the end of this year, coinciding with what Middle Eastern Judeo-Spanish calls the *cortadura del año* [end of the year], the important ceremony of placing the gravestone (in Morocco, the *fraguanza*) takes place. Before that time the grave has a temporary marker. The survivors also have the pious duty of visiting the graves of loved ones, especially on each anniversary of the death, as well as on Yom Kippur and other holidays.

Around these statutes, valid for all Jews, the Sephardim developed a traditional ritual involving death in which it is sometimes difficult to distinguish between pious practice and superstition. Thus, there are many beliefs about the *malah hamavet* [angel of death], identified with Huerco or Güerco (a phonetic descendent of Orchus, the Roman god of Hades), who is the personification of death.

Of still greater consequence has been the custom—shared with other Oriental and ancient peoples—of the *planto* [public mourning], that is, gathering around the body to show one's grief at the death by shouting, crying, and injuring oneself. During this ceremony, it was not unusual for people also to sing dirges referring to the unhappy occurrence or to the deceased's qualities. Those in charge of performing the ceremony were always women. Some of them were members of the family; others were professional mourners who were paid a salary for their labors, as Enrique Saporta describes:

A parte la famiya, i sus amigos ke tenian una verdadera pena de la pye-drita . . . , otros venian para onorar su memorya . . . i las yoraderas, las karpideras, las endetchaderas lo fazian, pagadas, para ke kon sus djestos i reskunyos, karpyendo i enguay-ando dyeran mas importansya a la memorya del muerto. (Saporta, *Torre,* 189)

[Aside from the family and their friends, who were truly grieved by the loss . . . , others came to honor the deceased's memory . . . and the professional criers, scratchers, dirge singers did it for pay, so that by their gestures and scratches, wailing and keening, they might enhance the memory of the deceased.]

In Morocco, the mourning is accompanied by shouts of *¡uo!, ¡uo!,* the sound of sadness, and *oyinaderas* [professional mourners] are hired.   (Alvar, *Endechas,* 20)

RECOMMENDED READING

On the history of the Jews in Spain, one might consult the valuable summary by Luis Suárez Fernández, *Judíos españoles en la Edad Media* (Madrid: Rialp, 1980), and Yitzhak Baer's much more detailed *History of the Jews in Christian Spain,* trans. Louis Schoffman et al., 2 vols. (Philadelphia: Jewish Publication Society, 1961 and 1966), or its more recent Spanish translation from the original Hebrew, *Historia de los judíos en la España cristiana,* trans. José Luis Lacave, 2 vols. (Madrid: Altalena, 1981). Also useful are the relevant chapters in the monumental history of the Jewish people edited by H. H. Ben-Sasson, originally in Hebrew, but translated into English as *A History of the Jewish People* (London: Weidenfeld and Nicolson, 1976), and into Spanish as *Historia del pueblo judío,* 3 vols. (Madrid: Alianza, 1988). Various concrete aspects of the history of the Jews in Spain are treated in the collection *Encuentros en Sefarad. Actas del Congreso Internacional "Los judíos en la historia de España,"* ed. Francisco Ruiz Gómez and Manuel Espadas Burgos (Ciudad Real: Instituto de Estudios Manchegos, 1987). For the situation of the Jewish communities in Spain at the time of the expulsion, consult Lacave, "Los judíos en la época de la Expulsión," in *Los sefardíes: Cultura y literatura,* ed. Paloma Díaz-Mas (San Sebastián: Universidad del País Vasco, 1987), 35–48. Those curious about Jewish vestiges in Spain will find useful Juan G. Atienza's *Guía judía de España* (Madrid: Altalena, 1981), or, in English, Manuel Aguilar and Ian Robertson, *Jewish Spain: A Guide* (Madrid: Altalena, 1984).

For information on terms related to Judaism, see the *Encyclopaedia Judaica,* 17 vols. (Jerusalem: Keter Publishing House, 1971–72).

On the Jewish religion, see Meyer Waxman, *Introduction à la vie juive* (Paris: Albin Michel, 1958); Pablo Link, *Bases del judaísmo* (Buenos Aires: n.p., 1948); and Erna C. Schlesinger, *Manual de religión judía: Principios, ritos y costumbres,* 3d ed. (Buenos Aires: Instituto Judío Argentino de Cultura e Información, 1955). Useful for the layperson is Mario Muchnik's informative and almost journalistic *Mundo judío: Crónica personal* (Barcelona: Lumen, 1983). A good summary of the most important Jewish rites and festivals, relating them to Sephardic customs and folkways, is Díaz-Mas, "El judaísmo: Religión y cultura," in *Los sefardíes: Cultura y literatura,* 23–34.

The only monograph on Sephardic ethnography and folklore to date is Michael

Molho, *Usos y costumbres de los sefardíes de Salónica* (Madrid and Barcelona: Consejo Superior de Investigaciones Científicas,[24] 1950).

Iacob M. Hassán, in "Los sefardíes como tópico," *Raíces* 1 (Apr. 1986): 32–38, offers an essential clarification of general ideas about the Sephardim. See also his synopsis, "Los sefardíes: Concepto y esbozo histórico," in *Los sefardíes: Cultura y literatura,* 11–22.

24. Hereafter abbreviated CSIC.

T W O

HISTORY OF THE SEPHARDIM

THE HISTORY OF the Sephardim from their expulsion from Spain in 1492 to the present day can be divided into three basic stages separated by two catastrophes. The first and third of these stages can be characterized as an opening to the outside world marked by emigration; the middle phase is one of internal development when the communities concentrated on their own activities.

The first stage runs from the expulsion in 1492 to the middle of the seventeenth century, and was basically a search for a place to settle. The exiled Jews and the converts who fled the Iberian Peninsula after the expulsion formed settlements in Christian (Catholic and Protestant) and Islamic (the Turkish Empire, North Africa) areas. In the latter, the Sephardim found circumstances most favorable for their continued existence.

The period ended with a crisis provoked by the followers of the false messiah Shabbetai Zvi, giving rise to the second stage, which took place during the eighteenth and a good part of the nineteenth centuries. During this time, the Jewish communities, which were now quite stable, concentrated on themselves and their own environment.

A new crisis—political, economic, and cultural—that began toward the end of the nineteenth century and continued through both world wars pushed the Sephardim to seek new surroundings. This resulted in the so-called Second Diaspora. The effect of this upheaval was that the largest concentrations of Sephardim are no longer found in the areas with which they are traditionally associated; rather, they live in the Americas, Western Europe, and Israel.

Sephardic history developed somewhat differently in the various areas of settlement: in Christian countries, in the Ottoman Empire, in North Africa, and in the settlements of the Second Diaspora.

EXILE TO CHRISTIAN COUNTRIES

Many of the Jewish exiles took refuge in nearby European countries where, for a century or two, they were able to retain their cultural distinction and their language. Both were subsequently diluted in greater or lesser degree by the influence of their surroundings.

Among the Catholic countries, many Sephardim chose Portugal, where some Jewish communities already existed. But just a few years later, when Princess Isabel of Castile married King Manuel (1497), Jews were also forbidden from living in Portugal. The majority of them chose to become baptized, although more than a few of these New Christians (*cristãos novos*) continued to practice the religion of their ancestors secretly. They thus formed crypto-Jewish communities that still survive today (especially well known is the area of Guarda).

Those who could emigrate—generally using their commercial activities as the pretext—headed for the Turkish Empire, North Africa, or the Low Countries where they founded prosperous colonies such as that of Amsterdam. A more permanent settlement was established by those exiles who headed to Italy in 1492. There they formed communities in Venice, Rome (where most of the Popes had Jewish physicians), Ancona, Padua, Pisa, Lucca, Florence, Leghorn, Ferrara, and so on. They were very well received in Naples by King Ferdinand, but that community wound up emigrating to other areas of Italy or toward the east, primarily because of a terrible epidemic of bubonic plague.

In Italy the Jews were mainly businessmen, and until the seventeenth century they maintained close relations with the communities in the East and in North Africa. Leghorn and Ferrara were especially notable because, in addition to great wealth, they were the centers of great cultural and editorial activity. Their presses printed a great number of books in Spanish in the Roman alphabet, among which is the famous Ferrara Bible. Nevertheless, the Italian Sephardim virtually lost the Spanish language during the seventeenth century, although some retained specific characteristics, such as the Sephardic liturgy.

Exiles also settled in cities in the south of France (Bayonne, Biarritz, Bordeaux, Perpignan, St. Jean de Luz, Toulouse, etc.), where nuclei of Jews of Spanish origin are still found today, but they quickly lost the Spanish language, preserved only in some of their liturgy.

Within Protestant Europe, the Low Countries received the greatest number of exiles, and that is where the European Sephardic communities showed their greatest vigor. In cities such as Rotterdam, The Hague, Utrecht, Leiden, and especially Antwerp and Amsterdam, the Sephardim were economic leaders, active primarily in banking, diamond merchandising, and import-export, all of which were carried out in cooperation with coreligionists in other lands (for example, the kingdom of Morocco).

During the sixteenth and part of the seventeenth centuries, the Dutch communities—like other diaspora communities—received a constant influx of Marranos (that is, crypto-Jewish converts) returning to the Law of Moses. Since many were people of means and culture, they helped to enrich, in all senses, the Jewish communities they joined. They were also the conduit through which Spanish cultural innovations reached the Sephardic diaspora. Consequently, these communities maintained an intense intellectual life in which singular figures within Jewish culture, such as David Pardo or Shelomo ben Verga, played a part. There were even figures of universal import like the philosopher Baruch Spinoza. It was not uncommon for the businessmen and bankers, Sephardic and Ashkenazi alike, also to be patrons of the arts. Consider, for example, the Ashkenzi Jacob Jacobsz Trip, who was Rembrandt's protector.

Given the economic dynamism and the high level of culture, it is not surprising that the Low Countries, together with Italy, would become an important center of Jewish publication where numerous books were printed in Spanish. Portuguese replaced Spanish, however, as the language of communication as early as the seventeenth century, due, of course, to the fact that many of the immigrants to the Dutch communities were from Portugal. Spanish was retained as a language for publication because of its greater cultural prestige, but even in the nineteenth century the Jews in the Low Countries spoke Portuguese.

These countries also served as springboards for the first Jewish settlements in America. From the mid-seventeenth century, groups of Sephardim, or of converts who had come back to Judaism, settled as Dutch citizens in Holland's American colonies—Guyana and Brazil.

From Holland, specifically Amsterdam, came the founders of the Sephardic community of London in Oliver Cromwell's time. At the very end of the seventeenth century, the size of the colony was enlarged by emigrants from Morocco; at the beginning of the eighteenth century, it increased again with the arrival of Sephardim from Italy, France, and Holland itself. The Sephardim were always a minority among English Jews, most of whom were Ashkenazim. Consequently, their cultural peculiarities (except in matters of liturgy) began to disappear quickly. However, note the Sephardic origin of some of the great Jews of nineteenth-century England, such as Sir Moses Montefiore or the conservative politician Benjamin Disraeli.

SEPHARDIM IN THE EAST
Settlement

Undoubtedly, it was in the Turkish Empire that the Sephardim were best received. It is widely accepted that Sultan Bayazit II (1481–1512), on hearing one of his courtiers praise the political wisdom of Ferdinand of Aragon, replied, "How can you consider intelligent a man who impoverishes his own reign to enrich mine?" Whether or not this story is true, it is true that the sultan, realizing that the Jews constituted an extremely important economic and human resource, gave them varied incentives to settle in his empire, and he sent a *firman* [Turkish, decree] to the governors, threatening death to those who maltreated the Jews.

The influence of the Ottoman Empire at that time extended through almost the entire southern and eastern shores of the Mediterranean as well as through a large part of the Balkans. The empire included, among other territories, modern Turkey—both European and Asiatic—Greece, Albania, Yugoslavia, Bulgaria, and part of both Rumania and Hungary. In the years following the arrival of the Sephardim, those areas were extended to include Palestine, Egypt, and several Mediterranean islands. In addition, Algeria, Tunis, and Tripoli were vassal states. As can be seen, the Ottoman Empire was a great power in the process of expansion.

Under the control of the Sublime Porte (as the Ottoman Empire was also known) were grouped peoples of various races, cultures, languages, and religions. The peculiar political and administrative system allowed each group to maintain its distinctions. Each region was governed by a *basha,* a delegate of the central government, who was entrusted with, among other things, imparting justice, collecting taxes, and recruiting soldiers. The *rayas,* or non-Muslim peoples, were allowed to retain their way of life, maintain their peculiarities, and even govern their own internal affairs in their own way, as long as they paid the numerous taxes imposed on them.

When they reached the Ottoman Empire, the Sephardim were thus able to retain the community organization and institutions they had brought from Spain. They continued to use their own rabbinic tribunals to resolve internal legal matters within each community. Community life was ruled by rabbinic orders [*haskamot*], and the Sephardim themselves elected their representatives to the government. Cultural hegemony within the Ottoman Empire also allowed them to preserve the folkways derived from their religion, their Spanish language, and the use of the Hebrew alphabet.

The majority of the new arrivals settled in urban areas, preferably in the larger cities, although some also remained in small population centers. Thus Sephardic communities soon developed in Constantinople (Istanbul), Adrianopolis, Izmir (Smyrna), Bursa, and towns such as Gallipoli, Magnesia, and Rodosto in Turkey; Athens, Salonika, Larisa, Serre, Kavala, Demotica, and Kastoria in Greece; Sarajevo, Belgrade, Monastir, and Skopje in modern-day Yugoslavia; Jerusalem and Safed in Palestine; Bucharest in Rumania; Sofia and Filipopolis (Plovdiv) in Bulgaria; and in other territories in which the influence of the Ottoman Empire was felt, such as Budapest, Rhodes, Cairo, Alexandria, and Vienna.

In the large cities the Sephardim tended to choose their quarters according to the areas from which they had come, so that those from any given area in the Iberian Peninsula lived in the same neighborhood. Thus, in Constantinople, where Sephardim were allowed to settle in the Balat area, there were forty-four synagogues, many of them with regional names: from Castile, from Aragon, from Portugal, from Cordova, from Toledo, from Barcelona, from Lisbon, and so on. The same thing happened in Salonika, where the Sephardim formed thirty different groups, each with its own synagogue: the *cal* (from Hebrew, *kahal* [community]) of Aragon, of Castile, of Mallorca (also known as the *cal Mayor* [major community]), of Evora and of Portugal (both composed of Portuguese emigrants), of Italy (made up of those who had spent time in that country), and so on. There was also the Ashkenazi *cal* for the Jews of Ashkenazi origin who wound up adopting Judeo-Spanish culture.

The arrival of the Spaniards constituted a true revolution for the Eastern Jewish communities, which until then had been made up of Romaniote (Byzantine) Greek-speaking Jews and some Italians and Ashkenazim. Those who came from Spain were not only numerous but also generally more highly cultured and more conscious of their own past. Consequently, although for the first few years the original Jewish community and that of the immigrants remained separate, as time passed the Jews of other origins adopted the liturgy, culture, and language of the Spaniards. A good illustration of this fact is the existence of the family name *Ashkenazi* among the Sephardim from Constantinople and Smyrna: it indicates, as one might imagine, an Ashkenazic family that has become completely "Sephardicized."

The Sixteenth and Seventeenth Centuries

The preponderance of Sephardim in the Eastern Jewish world is due in no small measure to the role they played during the sixteenth and seventeenth centuries in the political, cultural, and economic life of the Ottoman Empire. In fact, the presence of Jews in the court during that time was not rare, be it as physicians and interpreters for sultans and viziers or as advisers who came to exercise extraordinary power. A typical example is the Nasi family of converts who returned to Judaism and settled in Turkey.

The matriarch of the family, Doña Gracia (or Beatriz) Mendes (Méndez or Mendezia), was born in Portugal in 1510 and died in Constantinople in 1568. Doña Gracia descended from the illustrious Jewish Benveniste family. As a Christian, her name was Gracia de Luna; she married Francisco Méndez, a descendant of the Nasi family and a well-known banker in France and Flanders. Widowed at age twenty-five, she left Portugal with her sister, her daughter Reina, and several nieces and nephews. She went first to Antwerp, then to Venice, and finally to the Ottoman Empire, arriving with all the pomp described in *Viaje de Turquía* [Turkish trip]:

> She came to Constantinople with forty horses and four triumphal carriages filled with Spanish ladies and maids. Her household was no smaller than that of a Spanish duke, and she could do that because she is very wealthy, and she requested an audience. She arranged that from Venice with the Great Turk [Suleiman the Magnificent], for she didn't want other conditions in his lands except permission for her servants to not use headdresses like the other Jews, but rather caps and clothing in Venetian style. He allowed it, and would have permitted more if she had wanted it, for the sake of having such a taxpayer. (*Viaje*, 451)

Her nephew, Juan Micas, also returned to Judaism and married Doña Gracia's daughter:

> After a year, in 1554, there came to Constantinople a nephew of hers, who had great support in the court both from the Emperor and the King of France, and he deserved it all because he was a gentleman, well-trained in arms, well-read and a friend among friends. And there are few important men in Spain, Italy and Flanders who do not know him, to whom the Emperor had given nobility. His name was Juan Micas. And because that lady had only one daughter, whose dowry was three hundred thousand ducats, the devil deceived him and he was circumcised and he married her. His name is now Iozef [Yosef] Nasi. His gentlemen have now become Samuel, another one Abraham, and another Solomon. . . . When asked why he had done that, he answered that it was simply to avoid being subject to the Spanish Inquisition. (Ibid., 452–53)

To illustrate the power of this family, consider that it was able to cause the commercial boycott against the Italian port of Ancona in reprisal for its persecution of converts, and even succeeded in having Sultan Suleiman the Magnificent intercede in favor of some coreligionists who were jailed in that same city.

Suleiman's successor, Selim II (1566–74), made Yosef the Duke of Naxos; he granted him territory on the shores of Lake Tiberias, where his protégé rebuilt the city of the same name and established a silk-production industry. He even permitted an embargo on French merchandise in all the ports of the empire when France refused to pay a 150,000-ducat debt she had contracted with the banker. Beyond doubt, Yosef Nasi is the most outstanding of those Sephardim—educated, wealthy, intelligent, powerful, and capable business-men—who participated so actively in the politics and economy of the Otto-man Empire and who contributed to enlarging it, extending it (Nasi, for example, took part in the conquest of Cyprus), and unifying it.

But the great leaders were not the only ones to enrich the Ottoman Em-pire. The Sephardim who practiced craft industries, such as glassblowing and, especially, textile production, were equal contributors. Salonika was the ma-jor center for the production of woolens (and, to a lesser extent, silk and cotton goods) and of carpets until the nineteenth century, when the textile craft industries could no longer compete with industrializing Western coun-tries (England, France, Holland, etc.). The extent of these activities is illus-trated by the fact that the Jewish community paid a good part of its taxes in fabric used to make uniforms for the imperial troops. To protect the wool business, the rabbis established detailed orders [*haskamot*] regulating all phases of production, from the purchase of the raw material to the sale of the finished product.

Another notably Jewish profession was commerce, as much within the em-pire as on an international scale. A great part of the imports and exports passed directly through Jewish hands; at other times, the Jews served as in-termediaries between foreign merchants and the Turks, as testimony of that time indicates, although not without some scorn:

When a fresh merchant or factor comes to Constantinople, the first Jew that catches a word with him makes him his own, his peculiar property, calling him his merchant; and so he must be as long as he stays, and from this time, no other Jew will interpose to deprive him of his purchase. . . . If the merchant wants anything, be it never so inconsiderable, let him tell his Jew of it, and, if it be above ground, he will find it.   (In Benardete, *Hispanic Culture,* 126)

Jews also played a basic role in the distribution and manufacture of fire-arms. Much of Turkish artillery technique came from the Marranos who had returned to Judaism, as a traveler noted:

Likewise they have amongst them workmen of all arts and handicrafts most excel-lent, and especially of the *Maranes,* of late banished and driven out of Spain and Portugal, who to the great detriment and damage of Christianity have taught the Turks divers inventions, crafts, and engines of war, as to make artillery, harquebuses, gun-powder, shot and other ammunition; they have also there set up printing, not before seen in those countries, by which, in fair characters, they put in light divers books in divers languages, as Greek, Latin, Italian, Spanish, and the Hebrew tongue.   (Ibid., 69)

In fact, the Sephardim introduced printing to the Ottoman Empire and held a monopoly on the business until 1727, when the Turks were relieved of the prohibition (for religious reasons) against printing in their language. Fruit of this monopoly was the development of a flourishing printing indus-try whose most important centers were Constantinople, Smyrna, Salonika, and, later, Sarajevo and Vienna.

A major factor in the cultural superiority of the Sephardim during the sixteenth and seventeenth centuries was the contribution of the converts, who were generally from the upper and educated class, and often true intel-lectuals. Some had been educated in Spanish universities, such as Salamanca (especially in medicine); others owned rich libraries that they took with them into exile. There were outstanding names among printers, such as the Son-cino family (originally Italian), who settled in Constantinople toward the end of the fifteenth century. Writers expelled from Spain included Shelomo ben Verga, Abraham Zacuto, Yitzhak Aboab, and Yosef Caro; others were born in exile, such as Moses Almosnino, Israel Najara, and Elia Capsali; and there were whole families of intellectuals, such as the Abravanels and the Pardos.

One of the fields of Jewish culture that flourished at this time was Kabba-lah or mysticism, which had already been well cultivated in the Iberian Pen-insula. After the expulsion it had continued especially in the Palestinian city of Safed. Some of the greatest figures in Jewish mysticism arose there, such as Yosef Caro, author of the *Shulhan Aruh* [Hebrew, set table]; Isaac Luria and his successor, Haim Vital, author of *Etz Hayim* [Hebrew, tree of life], and others.

Perhaps this interest in mysticism set the stage for a phenomenon that ultimately proved disastrous for Hebrew culture in the Sephardic world—the appearance of messianic movements, the most famous of which was that of Shabbetai Zvi. Shabbetai was born in Smyrna in 1629, during the sultanate of Murad IV. Dedicated to the study of Kabbalah from a young age, and with an attractive personality to which his good looks and pleasant voice contributed significantly, by age twenty he had already become a teacher with his own followers. The rabbinic school of his city began to suspect the orthodoxy of his teachings and excommunicated him, but the young rabbi had already discovered an apocryphal prophecy that spoke of a "Mordehai Zvi" with a son named Shabbetai who "was to save Israel and kill the dragon." Because of the coincidence of names, the young man believed himself to be chosen by God and began to proclaim the arrival of the messianic era.

Preaching the good news, he traveled through Salonika, Athens, Jerusalem, and Cairo, where he was protected by the wealthy kabbalist Rafael Yosef Chelebi. With Chelebi's approval, Shabbetai contracted a second marriage (he had repudiated his first wife without cohabiting with her) with a woman named Sarah, whose story was even more fantastic than his own. A Polish Jew whose parents had been killed by the cossacks, Sarah was taken into a convent at the age of six. She later fled, first to Amsterdam and then to Leghorn. In Italy she became a prostitute, declaring that she had to reach the depths of degradation to better fulfill her sacred mission—being the wife of the messiah.

This exalted couple armed a true revolution in the Jewish world. People came from all parts of the Mediterranean and central Europe to listen to Shabbetai's preachings, to participate in frenzied processions celebrating the Torah, and to follow him in his planned pilgrimage to the Holy Land where the reign of Israel would be restored. There were authentic cases of collective hysteria. Some went into rapture on hearing preaching and melodies in the messiah's sweet voice.

Shabbetai's popular support gave him enough power to remove several rabbis who opposed him from their posts. The Jewish world, especially that of the Eastern Sephardim, experienced moments of true messianic fervor under the skeptical and alarmed watch of Turkish authorities, who saw potential danger in that fanaticism. The king of Morocco shared those misgivings, as will soon be seen.

The delirium reached its end abruptly. The authorities decided to intervene; Sultan Mehmet IV had the false messiah brought to him and said that he would have to undergo a test to prove his status. His soldiers would shoot several poisoned arrows at him, certain that they would not cause any injuries. Terrified, Shabbetai confessed that such a test was beyond his powers, and finally acceded to the Sultan's pressure, converting to Islam. He took the name Mehmet Efendi. Converting along with him was not only his wife

Sarah but also many followers in the Turkish Empire as well as in North Africa, Italy, Germany, and Poland.

That group gave rise to a crypto-Jewish group within Islam, the Dönmes or Maaminim, who, almost to the present day, have retained Jewish characteristics in their religious practice and have maintained Judeo-Spanish as their religious language for several centuries (without, however, understanding it). To give an idea of the number of these converts, one century later there were five thousand Dönmes just in Salonika, as compared with twenty-five thousand Jews. Their number steadily decreased, but they still contributed quite a bit to Ataturk's reform of Turkey at the beginning of this century, and there are still remainders of the sect in Constantinople and Smyrna.

The Eighteenth Century

The Eastern Sephardic world emerged from the Shabbetaian adventure damaged. Rabbinical authorities, fearing new messianic outbreaks, girded themselves in the strictest orthodoxy, which resulted in the impoverishment of intellectual life and Hebrew literary production. Other messiahs proclaimed themselves nonetheless, such as Frenk Leibowitz, an Ashkenazi Jew brought up in Salonika. In 1754 he proclaimed himself to be God's chosen one, eventually converting to Islam and then to Christianity, only to wind up practicing alchemy after having wandered through half of Europe.

The cultural decline was accompanied by the political and economic decadence of the empire, which was to continue throughout the following century. Adverse circumstances all seemed to come together. The corruption and venality of the Turkish administration created political instability, which led to rebellions such as the one in 1703 that deposed Sultan Mustafa II, or the attack of the Serbs in Belgrade (1787) in reprisal for the Turks' conquest of Crimea. There was an economic crisis because of ruined harvests and increases of up to 50 percent in the price of wool, a raw material essential to the textile industry. The plague decimated the largest cities (in Salonika, where it was endemic into the nineteenth century, there were outbreaks in 1679, 1687–89, 1697–99, 1708–9, 1712–13, 1718–19, 1724, 1729–30, and so on until 1814–16). There were fires, either accidental or deliberate, in the Jewish sections of centers such as Salonika (1754, 1788) and Constantinople (1756); earthquakes, such as the one in Safed (1758), caused more than a hundred fatalities and destroyed two thousand homes. In addition, there were frequent abuses by the Janissaries.

The Janissaries (Turkish, *yeniçeri* [new guard]), created by Sultan Orhan in 1334, were originally an elite corps whose members were Christian boys recruited from among conquered peoples (Albanians, Bosnians, Serbs, Bulgarians, Greeks, or Armenians). They were circumcised and converted to Islam, and were given careful military and religious training. As of 1591, the troops were no longer drawn from Christians but composed of Turks and the sons of Janissaries. The organization degenerated to the point of becoming a sort of corrupt praetorian guard in which positions were inherited or sold, and whose sheer numbers allowed it to exercise tyrannical control over the monarch and exploit the people.

The Jews, like the Armenians or the Greeks, were a frequent target of its abuses. Arbitrary contributions were demanded, in money or in kind, and the soldiers led frequent assaults on the Jewish quarters: in Salonika alone there were attacks in 1703, 1721, 1730, 1747, 1751, 1758, and 1789.

The Janissaries were also involved in the first known accusation of ritual crime against the Eastern Sephardim. In 1633, two of their soldiers killed a child in Constantinople and left his body at the entrance to the Jewish quarters, accusing the Jews of having sacrificed him to use his blood in the preparation of the Passover unleavened bread. In that instance the truth was discovered and the matter ended favorably for the Israelites. Subsequent accusations of the same type throughout the nineteenth century had more tragic consequences.

In the midst of this political and economic decadence, and despite the impoverishment of Hebrew letters, the Eastern Sephardic world saw an extraordinary flourishing of literature in Judeo-Spanish, such that the eighteenth century is generally considered the Golden Age of Sephardic letters. The extensive encyclopedia of rabbinic knowledge, the *Me'am Lo'ez*, was composed during that time; many religious books were published. And the *coplas*, the most characteristically Sephardic poetic genre, flowered. All this will be discussed in chapter 4.

The publishing industry also continued to develop. Two Ashkenazi printers, Yona ben Ya'acob and Besalel Halevy, headed the publishing centers of Constantinople and Salonika respectively. A standardized system for writing Judeo-Spanish in Hebrew characters was developed. It has endured to the present and will be discussed in chapter 3. Sponsoring the publication of books—whether by paying for the typesetting, the paper, or the labor—and participating in the process of preparation, composition, or printing was considered a pious work, since publication would spread God-inspired knowledge. Thus a system of patronage by the wealthy was established, to the immense benefit of the publishing industry. Great families such as the Gazes, the Cuencas, the Abravanels, the Ardittis, the Menashes, the Hasons, and many others sponsored editions of books for the educated and also for the masses.

One of the most important publishing centers (along with Salonika, Constantinople, and Smyrna) was Vienna, where a Sephardic community had been founded at the beginning of the eighteenth century by several Jews from Constantinople and other parts of the Turkish Empire, among whom were Abraham Camondo, Aaron Nisan, and Nephtali Esquenazi. Its first president was the Marrano Moshe Lopez Pereira (as a Christian, Diego de Aguilar), whom Charles VI of Germany had given the title of baron. The signing of treaties between the Turks and the Holy Roman Empire allowed the citizens of one country to live freely in the other, thus enlarging the Sephardic community in Vienna, which was an important center for the Eastern Sephardim, despite the fact that the Jews of Spanish origin were a minority within a basically Ashkenazi Jewish community.

The Nineteenth Century

One of the most important events in the Turkish Empire during the first half of the nineteenth century was the dissolution (or perhaps, more accurately, the extermination) of the Janissaries by Sultan Mahmud II (1808–39). I have already noted how this military corps became a threat to the government and a danger to the people, who were forced to bear their continual abuses. The matter came to a head in 1826, when the sultan decided to impose discipline on the Janissaries, 140,000 strong at that time. They rebelled, and the sultan recruited volunteers to combat them. The result was a horrible massacre in which nearly fifty-thousand Janissaries died (some eight thousand perished just in the siege and subsequent fire at the quarters in Constantinople) and the guard disappeared forever. The death, under mysterious circumstances, of the Sephardic banker from Constantinople, Chelebi Behor Carmona, seems to have been related to the Janissary rebellion. He was ordered throttled by the sultan a month after the revolt.

The Carmonas, along with the Gabays and the Ayimans, were among the most influential Jewish families of the time. Yehezkiel Gabay was a banker from Baghdad who settled in Constantinople and granted loans to the Sublime Porte. As a protégé of the court favorite, Hallet Efendi, he exercised great power, which gained him the enmity of the Armenian bankers (especially of Cazas Artun, or Aretin), who were then beginning to compete with the Jews in commerce and banking.

The Ayiman dynasty was founded by Meir Ayiman, succeeded by his descendants Ya'acov, Baruch, and Yeshaya. They were also bankers, treasurers for the army, and quartermasters for the Janissaries. All met violent deaths: Meir was assassinated by a Janissary, a former protégé of his; the others were executed by order of the sultan.

The Carmona fortune came from textiles, although the family later became bankers. The founder of the dynasty, Moshe, also obtained a monopoly on alum imports and was an adviser to Sultan Selim III.

Mośé Carmona se hiźo atirar la atención del sultán Selim III, que lo recibió en audienza y le manifestó su favor imperial. Él era llamado al palacio en momentos difíciles y el poderośo soberano lo llamaba babalik, *porque Mośé Carmona era aedado de 80 años cuando el sultán lo conoció por la primera vez.* (Tópicos, 73)[1]

[Moshe Carmona attracted the attention of the Sultan Selim III, who received him in court and granted him his imperial favor. He was called to the palace in times of difficulty and the powerful sovereign called him *babalik* (grandpa), because Moshe Carmona was 80 years old when the sultan first met him.]

He was succeeded by his grandson Behor, since his son Eliyahu had died young.

Bajo el reino de Maḥmud II, Bejor Yiśḥac Carmona goźaba de una grande influenza. El soberano lo nominó el saraf o banquiero de su hermana la princesa Asma. Cada vez que el goberno tenía menester de contractar un préstimo, él se aderezaba en primero a Carmona; fue Carmona que aḥasteció los fondos necesarios para construir las fábricas del departamento de la artilería (tophané). En recompensa de este servicio la familla Carmona fue declarada exenta . . . de todo impuesto. (Ibid., 73–74)

[During the reign of Mahmud II, Behor Yitzhak Carmona enjoyed great influence. The sovereign named him *saraf* or treasurer for his sister, Princess Asma. Whenever the government needed a loan, it went first to Carmona. It was Carmona who provided the funds necessary for the construction of the buildings for the artillery department (*tophane*) (the Janissary quarters). In return for this service the Carmona family was declared exempt . . . from all taxes.]

Partially because of his relations with the Janissaries, partially because of the machinations of the Armenian banker Cazas Artun (the one who had confronted the Gabays), and partially because of the debts that the government had contracted with him, the powerful banker fell into disfavor. He was ordered executed by the usual procedure of the times—strangulation.

Reprisals also affected the Carmona family. Their possessions were confiscated, and they were issued an order of exile, which was subsequently re-

1. [AN] The text of this quote and the following one is from a biography of Behor Carmona published by the Sephardic newspaper *El Tiempo* [Constantinople], 20 July 1920, 655–57.

voked. Two details will provide an idea of the national and international repercussions of the death of the banker and, indirectly, of the power of the Carmona family in Jewish society of that time. First, the Sephardim in Constantinople considered the event a national disaster. To honor Carmona they composed a long eulogy, which even a century later was still sung on Tisha b'av, the day of mourning. Second, one of the banker's sons appealed to the British Jewish philanthropist, Sir Moses Montefiore, who managed to have Queen Victoria of England intercede in defense of the family. As a result of the queen's intervention, Sultan Meyid, the successor of Mahmud II, granted a type of indemnity and a lifetime pension to Behor Carmona's descendants.

Other misfortunes jolted the Eastern Jewish communities during the nineteenth century: fires in the Jewish quarters; cholera epidemics from 1832 to 1913; several earthquakes, such as the one that destroyed Tiberias and Safed in 1837, or the one in Salonika in 1856; and numerous accusations of ritual crime (1840 in Damascus and Rhodes; 1862 in Beirut; 1864 in Smyrna; 1866, 1868, 1870, and 1874 in Constantinople; 1872 in Edirne, Smyrna, Marmara, and Janina; 1874 in Magnesia; 1875 again in Smyrna, etc.). Added to this situation were the economic crisis of the end of the century and the political decline that allowed nationalist movements to develop in the Balkans.

In the midst of the nineteenth century the East fell into a great crisis from which it was to emerge renewed. Little by little new inventions appeared, precursors of a technological revolution. New political ideas arose as well: the first Zionist groups emerged. The Zionists were constantly confronted by others who upheld socialist ideology; the socialists, in turn, were opposed by the conservatives. A great number of these changes became possible thanks to extensive educational reform.

The growing interest in the West by the Eastern world inspired the establishment of Western educational centers in various parts of the Turkish Empire. "Dante Alighieri" Italian schools were founded in several cities. English and Scottish Protestant missions were established in places like Smyrna and Salonika: they provided educational and welfare services but attempted to gain converts among the Sephardim (they even published a Judeo-Spanish Bible, which attained wide circulation). Several European Jewish magnates became concerned about their Eastern coreligionists. Moses Montefiore traveled from London to Turkey at least eight times between 1829 and 1875; the Vienna Rothschilds created "Camondo" schools in Constantinople (sponsored by their colleague, the Sephardic banker of the same name), which certainly aroused the ire of conservatives in matters of religion.

But the greatest work was done by the Alliance Israélite Universelle, a French institution for Jews founded in Paris in 1860. In 1865 the Alliance opened its first school for Eastern Sephardim in Salonika with the aid not only of Sephardic leaders such as Yehuda Nehama, Shelomo Fernandez, and Moshe Allatini, but also a Protestant minister named Grosby. In 1868 a school opened in Larisa (Greece), in 1870 in Shumen (Bulgaria), in 1873 schools in Smyrna (Turkey) and Ruse (Bulgaria) opened, and so on, until there were a total of 150 Alliance schools in the Mediterranean area. More than forty thousand students received their education there in French—Jews, Greeks, and Armenians. Through the initiative of the Alliance, farm schools were also created near cities such as Jaffa or Smyrna.

At first the Alliance angered those who wanted traditional education at all costs. This education was to be fundamentally religious, taught in Judeo-Spanish, and available almost exclusively to boys. In their eyes, these secular schools—where the teaching was done in French and some of which accepted female students—constituted heresy. Several rabbis excommunicated the backers and teachers of the Alliance; in some cities the reaction was so strong that religious groups managed to have the schools closed.

Little by little this new kind of education became acceptable to the wealthier classes, and the traditional schools were left for the poor. Jewish intellectuals thereafter came out of Alliance classrooms, which resulted in profound cultural changes in the Sephardic world.

The Alliance schools were not just places for the Spanish Jews to learn a trade or study. They were something more: a vehicle for progress and modernization through which the Sephardim became acquainted with Western culture. Western customs, styles, and behavior became fashionable. Women began to receive an education that previously had been reserved for men. Traditional clothing was gradually replaced by European styles. Guidelines for social relations changed. Young people abandoned traditional trades. French literature became known, as did English and Russian literature through translations into French. Jews wrote works in genres they previously had not used—theater, novels, autograph poetry, and especially journalism. French works were translated into Judeo-Spanish. Even the language changed as a large number of Gallicisms were added, giving rise to Judeo-Fragnol, which will be discussed in chapter 3.

The process, which started in the mid-1800s among the upper classes, reached its zenith in the 1920s, by which time it had spread to the children of the lower middle class (small businessmen and artisans) and to the newly formed Sephardic proletariat (such as the workers in the tobacco factories).

The Twentieth Century

Significant political changes occurred at the beginning of the twentieth century. In 1908 the Young Turks' revolution dethroned the last sultan, Abdul Hamid. The movement was headed by Enver Bey; in his ranks was a young man who was to create the most profound changes in Turkish society—Mustafa Kemal, subsequently known as Ataturk [father of the Turks].

Before these changes came about the old Ottoman Empire was partitioned. The support of European powers for Balkan nationalist movements in the middle of the previous century gave rise to a series of wars beginning in 1912, resulting in the birth of new countries in territory that previously had been part of the Ottoman Empire. Southern Greece had seceded from the empire already. During those wars Jews were recruited for the first time. They previously had been exempt from military service, paying a tax instead.

This situation, combined with internal political instability, economic crisis, natural catastrophes (cholera epidemics from 1911 through 1913, another fire in Salonika in 1917), and the outbreak of World War I almost immediately afterward, pushed many of the Sephardim toward emigration. Their preferred destination was America especially North America, although many went to South America or Europe (Paris, London, the Low Countries, and even Spain) as well. Those who decided to stay had to adjust to the changing circumstances. In the newly independent Balkan countries, Sephardim had to join the mainstream of national life in all aspects, even educationally and linguistically, thus giving up the cultural and legal autonomy that they had enjoyed in the Ottoman Empire. The Jews in Turkey also had to adapt to the considerable reforms undertaken by Ataturk, which on the one hand tended to Westernize the country and on the other to eliminate the peculiarities of the different national minorities. The result was the loss or deterioration of many specifically Sephardic characteristics, among them the language, because of the intense campaign to make Turkish the universal language of the entire population.

World War II, which had disastrous consequences in the Balkans, was the coup de grace for the Eastern Sephardim, who were either exterminated or resettled. The only sizable Sephardic community left within the old Ottoman Empire today is in modern Turkey.

Sephardim in Morocco
Settlement

In 1492, when some of the exiles went to North Africa, they did so knowing that they would find Jewish communities there. All of North Africa was then under Turkish influence except for Morocco. Living in that area were both Berber- and Arabic-speaking Jews, whom the Muslims had allowed to practice their religion and maintain their institutions in exchange for the payment of a special tax. This was not the first time that the North African Jews had received coreligionists from the Iberian Peninsula: in the ninth century Jews had fled there from Al-Andalus [southern Spain] to escape the revolts against Caliph Al-Hakam I. The murders and persecution of 1391 also sent a good number of Spanish Israelites into exile, the majority of whom also went to North Africa.

More than a century later, a huge wave of refugees came to North Africa. In 1492 almost forty thousand people came directly from Spain. Later, when forced conversions were being carried out in Portugal, those who had been allowed to leave that country for commercial reasons arrived. Over the course of the next hundred years North Africa received crypto-Jews who returned to Judaism on leaving the Iberian Peninsula.

The road to safety was not an easy one. For example, consider the hazards faced by the twenty ships that left the port of Santa Maria in 1492, bound for Arcila. Three of them sank during the crossing; the captains of other ships returned to Spanish ports, where the passengers found themselves in such danger that more than five hundred chose conversion to save their lives. Those who were successful arrived at Arcila, a Portuguese garrison, only to encounter the intransigence of the military leaders, who refused to receive them. They finally managed to head overland to Fez but were attacked en route by highwaymen. The fear did not end even when they reached their destination: there they found overcrowding and shortages caused by the sudden population increase. Epidemics broke out, and in 1493 a devastating fire leveled the Jewish quarter.

It is estimated that nearly half of the refugees who went to North Africa perished as a result of the hazards of the journey, pillaging, illness, and natural catastrophes. In addition, the existing Jewish communities—submerged at the time in great material and cultural poverty—did not give these newcomers a cordial reception. The new arrivals were more highly cultured and educated, and therefore were viewed as possible rivals and competitors. Nev-

ertheless, the Moroccan sharifs allowed the refugees to settle in the largest
cities, especially in Fez.

That is how the Holy Communities of Those Expelled from Castile were
founded. For more than four hundred years they maintained their own synagogues and cemeteries, and their own style of community organization.
Their members were known as Castilians, pilgrims, speakers of Moorish
Spanish, Persians (because they did not speak Arabic), or Megorashim [He-
brew, refugees] to distinguish them from the native Jews, who were called
Toshavim [Hebrew, residents], Palestinians, or strangers (which they were
from the viewpoint of the Spanish Jews). Because the Megorashim were
more highly cultured and better educated than their Berber- and Arabic-
speaking coreligionists, it is no surprise that they soon gave a new character
to Jewish life in Morocco.

Fez was the refugees' original spiritual center. After the first moments of
confusion and the terrible conflagration in 1493, they began to organize their
community. They formed other communities in such places as Alcazarquivir
and, most especially, in Tetuan, definitively established in 1530 with the intervention of Hayim Bibas, the rabbi of Fez. Because they were people of the
Book, the sharif granted the communities complete judicial and legislative
autonomy, except in criminal matters or where one of the affected parties was
a Muslim. It consequently became necessary to establish internal community
legislation. As a basis for that, the "Castilians" used rabbinic law from their
home country. The so-called *Castilian Taqqanot* [regulations] were composed, a body of legislation that regulated marriage, divorce, and inheritance,
and that today is a document of great historical and social interest. The first
of these *taqqanot,* written in Spanish, was enacted in Fez just two years after
the expulsion from Spain. Three years later the second *taqqanah* [singular of
taqqanot] was drawn up, and the third in 1545. Throughout the sixteenth
century, the *New Taqqanah* (1593) and the *Later New Taqqanah* (1599) were
composed; additions were made through 1755. While the first ones were
written in Spanish, the extension of these Hispanic law codes to the Toshavim required later documents to be in Judeo-Arabic, Berber, or Hebrew.
These codes governed the Moroccan Jewish communities through the twentieth century.

Especially interesting was the procedure (now known as parliamentary)
used for the proclamation of *taqqanot*. Each *taqqanah* was written by a group
of scholars and was read publicly in the synagogue on a holiday before being
put into effect. The men of the community would attend the reading,

and they could appeal or propose modifications before the legislation was enacted.

Community organization not only affected legal matters but every aspect of daily life. A ruling organization for each community had to be constituted—the community council, presided over by the *parnass* [Hebrew, administrator], who dealt with all civil matters. Community funds were instituted, supported by taxes on kosher meat, collections, individual contributions, and rental fees for community property. Those funds covered necessities such as elementary and rabbinical education, medical aid, lighting and care of the streets of the *mellah* [Jewish quarter], aid to the needy, support for the elderly, and the reception of strangers. Each community was represented to the sultan by a *sheh al-Yahud* [Arabic, head of the Jews]. A high rabbinic tribunal was founded in Tetuan to govern the communities of Tetuan, Tangier, Larache, Alcazarquivir, Arcila, Xauen, and later Ceuta, Melilla, and Gibraltar. The tribunal achieved great prestige.

This kind of community organization was instituted in practically all the Jewish communities in Morocco, including those of the Toshavim or strangers. In the communities in the north, where the Spanish element was in the majority (for example, Tangier or Tetuan), the language of the refugees came into general use as well, to the detriment of Judeo-Arabic. Other Jewish communities (such as Fez itself), made up mainly of Toshavim, adopted the Spanish legal system and community organization but retained Arabic or Berber as their language.

Role in the Economy and International Relations

The arrival of the Sephardim had a greater impact than just the modernization of the structure and internal organization of Moroccan Jewish communities. It also heralded great changes in the economy and politics of the country. Although some of the new arrivals settled in rural areas and became farmers, a much larger number preferred the life to be found in urban settings, as they did in the West. There they began to practice the trades they continued to the middle of this century: goldsmithing and the distillation of alcoholic beverages (both prohibited to Muslims for religious reasons), artisanry and small business.

The presence of Sephardic Jews as interpreters, physicians, or advisers in the court of the sharifian monarchs was common from the sixteenth to the eighteenth century. Sephardim also played an important role as intermediaries in commercial transactions with Christian countries, especially with the

Low Countries and England. Exports of cloth, copper, and pelts, for example, passed through Jewish hands, and payment for these goods took the form of promissory notes to the Jews, a factor that also contributed to strengthening Jewish banking in the Low Countries. Particularly important during the sixteenth and seventeenth centuries was the Jews' domination, almost as a monopoly, of various industries, such as the production of beeswax and rubber, the luxury of ostrich feathers, and, above all, sugar refining. They used a sugar-refining technique introduced by the Marranos in the sixteenth century, which was of great consequence for Morocco's balance of trade and its relations with England.

These commercial activities favored the Jews' participation in key positions in Morocco's international relations. As early as the sixteenth century, with the rise of the Sa'adi dynasty and its expansionist policies (confrontation with the European powers such as Spain and Portugal, which had military bases in the Maghreb; conquest of the Sudan in 1591; buildup of relations with England, France, and the Low Countries), Jews held important diplomatic posts. That was the case of the Palache family, one of whose outstanding members, Samuel Palache, signed the first treaty between Morocco and a Christian territory—the Low Countries—in 1610. He also served as an intermediary in relations with Spain, Italy, and England.

When Palache died in 1616, he was buried in the Portuguese cemetery in Amsterdam; his brother José continued his work as ambassador. The latter died in 1638. Throughout the seventeenth century other members of the same family (David, Moises, Yoshua, Isaac) had diplomatic roles representing the Moroccan sovereigns. In the eighteenth century there were still Sephardic names on the roster of Morocco's international politics, such as Jacob Benider, ambassador to London in the 1770s.

The Spanish, Portuguese, and English settlements on the Moroccan coast also used Sephardim as intermediaries with the monarchs. Portugal established bases on the Atlantic coast of Morocco at the beginning of the sixteenth century; groups of refugees settled in those cities, serving as interpreters and commercial agents between the Portuguese and the Moroccans. Families such as the Benzameros, Adibes, and Dardeiros were protected by the king of Portugal. Sephardim also played an important role in supplying food for the Spanish bases in Oran, Melilla, and Bujia. At the same time they set up commercial relations between the Maghreb and the Iberian Peninsula.

Tangier, where a few Jewish families lived at the beginning of the seventeenth century, was under English control between 1662 and 1684. During that time a stream of immigrants from all parts of Morocco arrived, among them Jews who merged with those from Italy and Holland. Within a few years the city had a large Sephardic colony. Some were of Spanish origin, such as the Pariente or Falcon families, who served as intermediaries between the English and the Muslims, and who developed relations between their new community and the most important Jewish communities of the country: Fez and Tetuan.

Something similar happened in Gibraltar, an English possession since 1704, whose Jewish community developed during the eighteenth century with the arrival of Moroccan Sephardim who founded the *Etz Hayim* [Hebrew, tree of life] synagogue in 1760, the oldest existing synagogue in Gibraltar. Immigration continued for more than 150 years (a large wave in 1860 was motivated by Spain taking Tetuan), during which time Maghrebi immigrants included not only simple workers but also rabbis and community leaders. Consequently, we may consider the Gibraltar Jewish community as a part of Moroccan Sephardic Judaism.

Jews also initiated and developed relations between Morocco and the Americas, relations that were very fruitful at times. The first Sephardic migrations to North and South America occurred during the seventeenth century. Most of these immigrants went to the New World to make a fortune and return to their home countries. Commercial and political relations between Morocco and America were promoted heavily in the eighteenth century by Isaac Pinto and Isaac Cardoso, the latter achieving the signing of a treaty between the two countries in 1787. Sephardic emigration to the United States intensified in the nineteenth century because of the severe economic problems in the Maghreb, aggravated by two terrible epidemics in 1799 and 1818. In the twentieth century, North and, particularly, South America became the destination for many of the emigrés, motivated by Moroccan independence and the subsequent Arabization of the country in the 1950s.

Cultural and Religious Life

During the sixteenth and seventeenth centuries, burgeoning commercial activity allowed the Sephardim to maintain substantial cultural and personal contacts with their coreligionists in other countries. This was true not only of the Marranos from Spain who had fled to Morocco to escape inquisitorial persecution and to return to the religion of their elders. North African Jews, too, visited communities in Italy and the Low Countries, or settled there for long periods while carrying out diplomatic and commercial missions. Books published in Leghorn, Ferrara, Ancona, and Florence circulated widely in Morocco over the course of two centuries. Close contact was maintained with the Sephardic communities in Turkey, Greece, and, above all, Palestine, a center that received Jewish settlers from all over the world.

But not all the movement was outside Morocco. The internal life of the communities was also especially active during the sixteenth and seventeenth centuries. A good number of influential intellectuals came out of the rabbinic academies; families such as the Abensurs, Almosninos, Uziels, Serfatis, Sereros, and Toledanos had among their members outstanding rabbis. The cultivation of Kabbalah and mysticism also found fertile ground in the Maghreb. Some important names are: Moses Ben-Atar, author of the mystic treatise *Or Hahayim* [Hebrew, light of life], and José Corcos.

The strongly rooted mystic calling in the country helps explain why the Shabbetaian movement would attract a large number of followers. According to Germain Mouette, a French Christian who had been kidnaped by pirates and was being held in the city of Sallee in 1671, that port city had become a center for spreading messianic propaganda as far as Amsterdam. Active participants in this movement were Marranos who had returned to Judaism only recently. The Moroccan Jews expected the messiah to come in 1672, and this hope produced a veritable rash of supposed apparitions and revelations, all of which failed when Shabbetai Zvi, the supposed messiah, converted to Islam. Yet this wave of messianic fanaticism created a series of persecutions against the Jews fostered by the first Alauite monarch, Mulay al-Rashid (1660–72).

Decadence, Difficulties, and Adversities

The death of Mulay al-Rashid's successor, Mulay Ismail (1672–1727) opened a period of instability and revolts that lasted thirty years, from 1728 to 1757. Needless to say, those uprisings had repercussions in the Jewish communities, whose rank and file were already in a precarious situation. Not all was economic prosperity, political power, and spiritual cultivation in Morocco's Jewish communities. Although specific families were enormously prosperous, the popular classes in many communities were living in poverty that was just this side of misery. At the same time as some Jews served as ambassadors to European courts, their Maghrebi coreligionists were required to pay special taxes, to live in the *mellah* [Jewish quarters], to wear specific kinds of clothes, to bare their feet when passing mosques, and to suffer insults and degradation at the hands of Muslims.

These conditions, along with the uncertainty and the anarchy of 1728–57, aggravated the situation. Many farmers took refuge in the cities. As a result, the Jewish quarters in Fez and Meknes became true slums where the new arrivals congregated in the streets. All of Morocco, and the Jewish communities in particular, started down the road of economic decay, a process that became increasingly obvious during the last third of the eighteenth century. The crisis greatly affected the flowering Jewish community of Tetuan, many of whose members left for Gibraltar or Tangier. Cultural decline accompanied the economic downturn, aggravated by the rigidity and aging of the rabbinic authorities who made up the intellectual class and were opposed to all innovation for fear of provoking another messianic movement. Thus,

teaching in Tetuan's rabbinic academies became fossilized. Their teachers, holding rigidly to doctrines and methods that had become obsolete, lost prestige. Foreign students no longer came there, and the native students were so badly educated that they could barely carry out the responsibilities of their ministries, despite the fact that they were in an environment of such ignorance that knowing how to read and write was considered the epitome of knowledge. . . . Such intellectual poverty was even worse in that it coincided with the exceptional intellectual vitality of the Jewish communities on the other side of the Mediterranean. (Vilar, *Tetuán,* 42)

The last decade of the eighteenth century was particularly difficult for Morocco's Sephardim. The Jews had supported the reigning sultan against his son, Mulay al-Yazid, who tried to take the throne. When the latter finally succeeded in 1790, reprisals were rapid. During the two years of his reign, there were attacks on the Jewish communities of Larache, Arcila, Alcazarquivir, Fez, and especially Tetuan, whose Jewish quarter was sacked and almost completely destroyed.

But these were not the only misfortunes to befall the Moroccan Jews. We have already noted habitual discriminatory legislation and the imposition of special taxes. Conflicts in strictly religious matters were less common, although not completely absent, as evidenced by the martyrdom of the young Sephardi woman, Sol Hachuel, in Fez. She was decapitated in 1834 for refusing to become a Muslim. The reasons are not entirely clear, but it seems that a young Muslim who was in love with Sol and a neighbor woman, also Muslim, were involved. Both attempted to convince her to convert and, when she refused, they denounced her to the governor, who had her executed. Her coreligionists considered her a holy martyr for Judaism, giving her the name of Sol *la ṣaḍika* [Hebrew, the saint], and they still remember her in a long folk song that tells her story and begins thus:

Cuando Tara levantó el enredo	When Tara started the trouble
sentenciaron a la hermosa Sol	they sentenced beautiful Sol
y la hicieron juramento falso	and swore falsely about her
en presencia del gobernado.	in the presence of the governor.

Any historical occurrence had direct and accusing repercussions in the Jewish communities. Sometimes there was a tragic outcome, as in the above-mentioned destruction of the *mellah* of Tetuan in Mulay al-Yazid's time. On other occasions, the Jewish community came out unscathed, as in the case of two local Purims the Moroccan Jews celebrated until recently.[2] One, the Purim of Christians or Sebastian's Purim, commemorated the Battle of Three Kings on the outskirts of Alcazarquivir in 1578, in which the Portuguese were defeated by the Muslims and King Sebastian of Portugal disappeared. The Moroccan Jews felt that a Portuguese victory would have had ominous consequences for them, and so from that time on they celebrated a holiday.

The other Purim, Purim of the Bombs, was celebrated exclusively in Tangier, recalling an episode in the nineteenth-century Franco-Moroccan War. French expansionist policy in North Africa brought about the conquest of Algier from the Turks in 1830. Between 1831 and 1834, France acquired control of other Algerian bases, such as Oran and Bujia. The emir sought help from Abd-al-Rahman, Sultan of Morocco, who answered his request. War broke out, and on August 6, 1844, France bombarded Tangier from the sea, producing massive damage and the loss of many lives. The Jews of the city were unaffected because the French avoided hitting the southeast part of the city where the Jews and the majority of foreigners lived. The Sephardim wrote a *megillah* narrating their "miraculous" salvation, and from that time on they celebrated the Purim of the Bombs.

The Presence of Foreigners

The Purim of the Bombs illustrates, among other things, a constant phenomenon in Moroccan politics: the activity of foreign powers in the Maghreb. As already noted, between the sixteenth and eighteenth centuries several Christian countries (Portugal, Spain, and England basically) established military bases or commercial ports in the country. Foreign influence became more serious in the twentieth century with the establishment of the Franco-Spanish protectorate.

2. [AN] The liturgical festival of Purim commemorates the salvation of the Jews from great danger (the extermination planned by Haman). By analogy, the name *Purim of* . . . is given to other festivals that recall the supposedly miraculous salvation of a Jewish community.

Throughout the nineteenth and twentieth centuries, this intervention by foreign nations in North African politics affected the Jews in four areas: (a) the system of consular protection; (b) the intervention of European Jewish personalities in favor of the Moroccan Jews; (c) the presence of French culture through the schools of the Alliance Israélite Universelle; and (d) the taking of Tetuan by the Spanish.

a) Through the system of protection, individual Moroccan subjects could seek the protection of foreign consulates and thus achieve a legal status that granted specific advantages (such as the exemption from some taxes) and immunities. The concept was introduced in the Maghreb by an agreement between Morocco and England in 1856, and Spain adopted it almost immediately in deed, although not officially until 1861. Their example was followed by France and the United States.

A good number of those protected were Jews who sought exemption from certain special taxes and the discriminatory treatment of which they were the object (for example, the charge to live in special neighborhoods and to wear distinctive clothing). The foreign powers occasionally used these protected individuals to intervene directly in politics in the Maghreb, a situation that, needless to say, increased the hostility of the Muslims toward the North African Jews.

b) The presence of foreign powers in the Maghreb also provided an opportunity for the great Jewish personages of the time to become more interested in their nearly forgotten brethren in North Africa. Thus in 1857 the banker Solomon Rothschild visited Tetuan and was so affected by the backwardness and poverty in which the majority of the Jews lived that, on his return to Europe, he founded the Relief Fund of Morocco, a philanthropic organization to help Moroccan Jews supported by the Jews of London.

Sir Moses Montefiore also visited Morocco, in 1863, during one of his voyages to study the situation of Jewish communities in various parts of the world. A year later he arranged an audience with King Muhammad, at which the king signed a declaration promising favor and protection to the Jews. The declaration, however, had little practical effect.

c) A constant in French foreign policy has been to leave the cultural impression of France on the areas and countries in which France has intervened in one form or another. In the case of the Sephardim, France left its mark through the Alliance Israélite Universelle. In Morocco as in the East, its schools, placed in strategic locations, brought the Sephardim an air of modernity, development, and Europeanism that would take them out of the cultural and material poverty in which they were immersed. This is what the Spaniard Manuel Ortega said—not without some envy—of the Alliance in 1919:

> The great work of the schools of the "Alliance Israélite Universelle" is what has most influenced the intellectual progress of the North African Hebrews in modern times. We should not avoid giving it our well-deserved praise.
>
> In 1860 this worthy association was founded in Paris, and two years later it opened its first school in Tetuan, following that [in 1865] with one in Tangier. The Larache school was established in 1902.
>
> Today they educate 1,859 boys and 1,139 girls in Morocco. Half of them receive the education at no cost. . . . At first the Moroccan rabbis opposed the establishment of these teaching centers for fear of their orthodoxy, and they excommunicated the founders. Later they accepted them. . . . The centers receive endowments from the Jewish communities of each locality, and they accept no economic support from any government. . . . The Alliance is universal in character . . . but its official language is French, its teachers are trained in Paris, its libraries contain only French works, and the maps and Ten Commandments that cover the walls of the schools are written in French.   (Ortega, 1919, 265–66)

d) I have deliberately left for last the war in Africa and the Spanish taking of Tetuan, which was to have great repercussions on the Sephardic communities in Morocco and on Spanish public opinion. The so-called African War was of only the slightest international importance. Despite the heroic and patriotic fervor that it produced in the Spain of Isabella II, it was no more than a ruinous skirmish that produced many human and material losses but very few practical results. The dispute amounted to a disproportionate response to the constant harassment of the Spanish garrison by the Kabyles[3] in Anjera. After several diplomatic incidents, Spain declared war on Morocco in 1860 and, with a courageous but disorganized army, undertook a march to Tetuan. At that time the city had some thirty-five thousand inhabitants, of whom six thousand were Sephardim living in the Jewish quarter under conditions of extreme poverty, subject to various types of discrimination (special taxes, requirements to dress in a specific manner, prohibitions against holding public office or receiving honors, curfew in the Jewish quarter, etc.).

The knowledge that the Spaniards were getting ready to lay siege to Tetuan met with varying Jewish reactions. Some chroniclers of the conflict report that the Sephardim helped the Spanish troops to enter the city and received them joyfully. The majority must have had their doubts, more as a result of the arrival of the fanatic Kabyles, who were coming to participate in the "holy war" against the invading infidels; as was to be feared, the Kabyles

---

3. A tribe of Bedouins or Berbers.

wound up attacking the Jewish quarter. But there were also those who chose to flee from the danger and sought refuge in Tangier, Oran, Gibraltar, and even the cities of southern Spain. In Gibraltar the large number of refugees created a serious health problem because of the precarious conditions in which they lived, crammed into tents.

On February 4, 1860, the Muslim troops surrendered to the Spaniards and left the city along with a large number of civilians. The Kabyles went into the Jewish quarter and began to plunder it and to massacre the inhabitants. The looting and killing did not end until February 6 when the Spanish army entered Tetuan. The exact number of Jewish fatalities is unknown, but some estimate it at about sixty people.

The Spaniards occuppied the city for slightly more than two years (until May 1862), but in that short period some significant changes took place, among both the Spaniards and the Jews. The Spaniards "discovered" the existence of the forgotten Sephardim. Documents written by the chroniclers of the campaign include observations and opinions about the recently discovered Jews, ranging from surprise to curiosity, from sympathy to repulsion, from sensitivity to anti-Semitism. I will discuss these matters in chapter 5.

The Jewish community also underwent change when Tetuan was taken. Respecting the preexisting community organizations, such as the high rabbinic tribunal or the community council, the Spaniards in turn installed a new kind of administration with a mixed city government including Christians, Jews, and Muslims. They also undertook urban and administrative modernization in which the Sephardim participated actively. They gave new life to the city. Spanish-language newspapers began to appear, and a modest theater was even built, to the delight of the inhabitants. The presence of the troops stimulated business in the city, which benefited Muslims as well as Jews. Contact with Spaniards reinforced the process of re-Hispanization of Moroccan Judeo-Spanish, which will be analyzed in chapter 3.

In short, when the Spaniards left Tetuan, the Jewish community had undergone a series of changes and could no longer return to its previous way of life.

From the Protectorate to the Present

As I have already indicated, European intervention in Morocco culminated with the institution of a protectorate system. By virtue of the agreement in Fez in 1912, France and Spain divided Morocco into two protectorate zones, leaving Tangier as a free city. Jews were generally favored by this system, which gave them greater freedom than the old regime of the sultans. If the

Europeanization that led to the protectorate favored the Jews, however, the
process of Arabization accompanying the independence attained by Muhammad V in 1956 was to their disadvantage. Among other things, Jews were
forbidden to hold official posts, and Zionist organization activities were prohibited. Those organizations had been channeling a constant migration to
the national Jewish homeland since the creation of the state of Israel in 1948.
After Moroccan independence, most of the Jews in Morocco emigrated to
America, Israel, France, or Spain.

The Second Diaspora

If anything characterizes Sephardic history in the twentieth century, it is what
has been called the Second Diaspora—a vast migratory movement in which
the Sephardim left their lands for younger countries (and, to a lesser degree,
western Europe). Large Sephardic communities are no longer found in Morocco nor in the eastern Mediterranean, but rather in the United States, Spanish America, and Israel. Needless to say, this geographic change also implies
a change in community characteristics and in Sephardic culture in general.
So, for example, the Judeo-Spanish of the elderly has gone through a process
of leveling and a loss of dialectal differences as Jews of different origins and
social classes have come together. The youth are on the way to losing their
Sephardic identity as they join the mainstream of the countries in which
they live.

North America

America, especially North America, was the first to receive the flood of Sephardic emigrants who came from the Levant[4] and, to a lesser degree, Morocco between the end of the last century and the beginning of this one. But
these were not the first Jews of Spanish origin to arrive in the New World.
In the seventeenth century some descendents of the converts who had re-
joined Judaism in the Low Countries became American colonists. That is the
case of twenty-three Sephardic Jews who in 1654 settled in the Dutch city of
New Amsterdam (later to become New York). They were granted "the right
to practice their own religion, the right to live in Manhattan, the right to
fight in the militia, and the right to engage in all economic activities in which
the Dutch Calvinists work. . . . These four rights were denied to Quakers,
Catholics and Anglicans" (*Actas,* 151).

4. A general term for Eastern Mediterranean countries. Hence Eastern Sephardim (from
Greece, Turkey, Bulgaria, Yugoslavia, Egypt, and Israel) are often called Levantine Sephardim.

These colonists founded the first Jewish congregation in North America, Shearith Israel [Hebrew, remnant of Israel]. Somewhat later communities were formed in Newport, Rhode Island and Savannah, Georgia. Although there are reports of Sephardim in Canada as early as the seventeenth century, the first community was not founded until the mid-eighteenth century in Montreal, a community that has grown substantially since 1956 with the arrival of Moroccan Jews. But it was mainly the Ashkenazi Jews who emigrated to America.

The first contemporary Sephardic emigrants came from Morocco, a country that had maintained close diplomatic and commercial relations with North America through Jews since the seventeenth century. During Mulay Suleiman's reign, the dreadful epidemics of 1799 and 1818 drove many Jews to the New World. It was a temporary emigration of individuals who were leaving to become wealthy, intending to return to their home countries after a few years. This movement intensified during the last quarter of the nineteenth century. According to Juan Bautista Vilar,

it was never quantitatively important, although qualitatively it was. We find individuals who, in the majority of cases, had been given an excellent education in the schools opened in Morocco by the "Alliance Israélite Universelle," a philanthropic organization based in Paris, which worked fruitfully with the American legation in Tangier; a very dynamic organization aimed at the Hebrew element.   (Vilar, "Emigrantes," 22–23)

Given their high cultural level and the Anglo-Saxon presence in Morocco, the Moroccan Jews did not find the language problem too serious; it was, indeed, a stumbling block a few years later for their coreligionists from the Levant.

In Tangier and Tetuan, where British cultural centers have existed for a long time, and whose Hebrew congregations have maintained close commercial contacts with Gibraltar and the United Kingdom since the eighteenth century, the English language, if not common, has at least been widely known in Israelite sectors . . . for many years the "Anglo Jewish Association" and the "Board of Deputies" held English classes in the Moroccan "Alliance" schools.   (Ibid., 23)

However, the largest contingent of Sephardim to come to the United States at the beginning of this century was from Turkey and the Balkans. The Young Turks' revolution, the subsequent Balkan wars, the generally unstable situation, and the economic and political crisis drove a good number of Jews to follow the road their Muslim compatriots had opened a generation earlier: emigration. It is estimated that between 1890 and 1907 more than twenty-seven hundred Sephardim came over from the Levant. Even more came between the Young Turks' revolution (1908) and World War I (1914)—over ten thousand. Nearly ten thousand more came between the end of World War I and 1924. In 1925 a restrictive immigration quota was imposed in the United States, thus not even 150 Sephardim came over in that year. In all, from the beginning of the century through 1925, at least twenty-five thousand Sephardim who declared themselves as such settled here. To that number must be added many others who came over as citizens of their respective countries without revealing their Jewishness. Some estimates put the total as high as seventy thousand.

The majority of the Sephardim settled in New York, a city with one of the largest Jewish populations in the world. Communities were also founded in Seattle, San Francisco, Atlanta, Rochester, Portland, Chicago, Indianapolis, Los Angeles, Cincinnati, and Montgomery.

When the Jews were expelled from Spain in the fifteenth century, people from the same area settled together and they founded synagogues "from Toledo," "from Aragon," "from Evora," and so on. In like manner, the recent arrivals in the New World tended to settle where there were people who had come from the same area. Those from Rhodes established their own synagogues and welfare societies in Los Angeles, Atlanta, and Seattle. There were only forty Jewish families in Seattle in 1910, but they were divided into two groups, each with its own institutions: those from Rhodes and the "Turks." It is easy to see that in New York, the major Sephardic center, there were not just two groups but many more: Monastir, Castoria, Dardanelles, Rhodes, Gallipoli, Rodosto, and other Levantine cities, each group with its own institutions. Such fragmentation, obviously, did not help the newcomers to adapt to their new surroundings.

The beginning was by no means easy. In the first place, the majority of the Sephardim were severely lacking in education, which channeled them to the most menial jobs. Also, many of them knew no English, which left them defenseless in an unknown environment. The late Mair José Benardete, Sephardic professor and publicist who came to the United States as a boy in 1910, describes the situation of the immigrants in Cincinnati:

Low wages, long hours, periods of idleness, ignorance of the language, unfamiliarity with the customs of Ashkenazic Jews as well as of Gentiles, gave the tiny group an unenviable status. Since I belonged to the second contingent that arrived in 1910, I remember other aspects of the social milieu in which the Hispano-Levantines found themselves in Cincinnati. As a mere lad in his early teens I had the advantage of going to the American public schools. A few Sephardic boys and I unwittingly served as connecting links between the Sephardic factory hands and the institutions of the city. . . . While still a high school student, I, with a very imperfect knowledge of the English language, was the only person available to guide the young men and married workers employed during the day at exhausting jobs. (Benardete, *Hispanic Culture*, 163)

To make matters worse, the Sephardim, so proud of their heritage, discovered that not even the American Jewish world received them cordially:

Arriving in America, the Sephardim found a society where the cultural and religious norms of Judaism had already been set by the very numerous Ashkenazim who had come to the United States from central Europe beginning in the second half of the nineteenth century. The Sephardim found that the culture, the rites, the customs and even the food of the central Europeans were already considered the only authentic Jewish manifestations in North America. Placed in doubt was the very Judaism of these exotic Sephardim, whose rites were different, who did not speak Yiddish and who knew nothing at all about the complex of cultural traits that characterized and united the Ashkenazic Jews. (*Actas*, 281–82)

José Estrugo, a Sephardi from Smyrna, felt the same way:

After spending a few years in the Jesuit school in Cairo, I emigrated to the United States in 1911, and among my difficulties I remember how complicated it was to explain my background to Americans. I told them that I was from Turkey, but since my name was not Mustafa, nor did I speak Turkish, they didn't believe me, and they could never understand that people who spoke Spanish and had Spanish surnames came from Turkey. Nor were they convinced that I was Jewish. There, to be a Jew, one must speak Yiddish and have a German surname (even Jesus Christ himself . . .). When we were heard speaking among coreligionists and they asked, we told them that we were Sephardim. Another inexplicable mystery to them. We could have told them that we were from Neptune! We finally told people that we were Spaniards (although from the Levant), and that simplified matters. (Estrugo, *Retorno*, 32)

The result of all these circumstances was that, at least at the beginning, the Sephardim formed a kind of spiritual ghetto within American Judaism. Perhaps as a form of self-defense they tried to perpetuate their form of Levantine life in the New World. In New York there were many small Turkish coffee shops, which were viewed with suspicion by the authorities and the object of frequent police roundups.

The scattered, individualistic communities, societies, and clubs that people joined according to their place of origin were difficult to integrate into broader associations that could combine efforts and resources to attend to their coreligionists' needs for education, religious services, community life, and material and moral support. The first attempts, such as the Federation of

Oriental Jews and the Sephardi Community, created in New York in 1912 and 1917 respectively, ended in complete failure. Until 1928, with the creation of the Union of Sephardic Congregations, American Sephardim had no stable, unifying organization. The Union was succeeded by other institutions that helped American Sephardism take on form.

At the same time, media for expression of Sephardic groups began to appear, giving rise to fruitful journalistic activity. The pioneer in this field was the weekly *La América,* published from 1910 to 1923. It was followed by other newspapers such as *La Voz del Pueblo* [Voice of the people], *El Lucero Sefardí* [Sephardic splendor], *La Luz* [The light], *El Progreso* [Progress], and, above all, *La Vara* [The staff], which was published in New York from 1922 to 1948 and achieved wide circulation.

With the passage of time, other institutions were established, from homes for the aged to centers for Sephardic study, such as the Foundation for the Advancement of Sephardic Studies and Culture, created in 1969 by a group of learned Judeo-Spaniards. In 1964, the orthodox Yeshiva University introduced in its curriculum a program in Sephardic studies, which will be discussed in chapter 6.

Although still in the process of becoming integrated into American life and culture, today the Sephardic community of the United States is one of the largest Sephardic settlements in the world.

Latin America

Hispanic Jews no doubt began coming to Latin America very early. Converts emigrated during the era of Spanish colonization, evading the prohibition against their going to the New World.

> To achieve their purpose they resorted to any procedures we may imagine: registering in Seville under assumed names, falsifying documents of purity of lineage, traveling as stowaways, hiding in the service of important dignitaries or undertaking the trip in ships of smugglers, pirates and privateers.   (Vilar, "Emigrantes," 21)

In the seventeenth century, Dutch colonies in South America—like those in North America—accepted Jewish colonists of Spanish origin coming from the mother country. Commercial relations between the Low Countries and Morocco encouraged settlements of North African Sephardim in Guyana, Brazil, and the Antilles. The same thing happened in Jamaica because of commercial exchange with England. Special mention should be made of the Jewish colonies in Surinam (Guyana), Pernambuco (now Recife, in Brazil) and Curaçao (the Antilles).

More important was the migration from North Africa, which took place in the mid-nineteenth century because of the demographic explosion in Morocco, the Hispano-Moroccan war, the Westernization of the Sephardim, and the exodus of Jews from the interior of the country to Atlantic coastal cities that served as jumping points to America. As in the case of the United States, this was a temporary emigration to "make a fortune," and it aimed for the most productive countries. Consequently Brazil, with its rubber and coffee plantations, was one of the preferred destinations. Argentina, Venezuela, Uruguay, Chile, and Peru also received waves of Sephardic immigrants. Emigration to Mexico, Central America (especially Santo Domingo, Panama, and Costa Rica), and Cuba came somewhat later.

In Venezuela the first Jews to settle in the east (Barcelona, Carupano, Cumana) in the mid-nineteenth century, who dedicated themselves to supplying cloth and provisions, assimilated completely into the rest of the population because of their inability to organize into true communities and the necessity for them to marry non-Jews. For that reason today one finds among the Christians in the country family names that are of unmistakable Jewish origin: Benchimol, Cohen, Levy, Sananes, and so on. At the end of the nineteenth and beginning of the twentieth century, Jews settled in the center of the country and in Caracas, forming sizable communities. But the first synagogues were not established until the 1930s, the pioneer of which was in the Conde district of Caracas. Today that city forms a true "reservation" of Hispano-Moroccan Judaism.

Jews from Morocco began to arrive in Buenos Aires by 1875 and in 1891 the Latin Israelite Congregation was founded. After the Balkan wars, Levantine Sephardim also came over, surpassing in number those from North Africa; they settled in Buenos Aires and provincial cities (Rosario, Santa Fe, Cordova, Tucuman, etc.). Even so, the Levantine and North African Jews constitute just a small minority within Argentine Jewry, which is mainly Ashkenazi.

Moroccan Jews began to arrive in Peru at the end of the nineteenth century, most by way of Brazil. Some Peruvian colonies—like Iquitos, which had three hundred members in 1910—took on the glow of El Dorado in the mind of the Moroccan Sephardim, despite the fact that living conditions were quite harsh. Business and the exploitation of rubber allowed a number of North Africans to make a fortune for some years, and these people encouraged their coreligionists from across the seas.

Here is how Vilar describes the basic characteristics of Moroccan-Jewish emigration to Spanish America:

The emigrant was usually well received at his destination and did not take long to prosper, due to his education, industriousness and perseverance. Once he was situated, however modestly, he sent for some of his relatives, preferably young bachelors. If there were none in his family, he wrote to school directors or rabbis in the town, asking them to send the right people for his purpose, and he promised to place them, advancing them the money for the trip. Moroccan colonies soon formed in the major Hispano-American centers, which, far from breaking ties with home, happily proceeded to strengthen them, even lending aid when needed by the home country. Remember, for example, the generous participation of Jacob Bendahan, president of the Latin Israelite Congregation, based in Buenos Aires, in the restoration of the original, grandiose Castilian Cemetery in Tetuan. . . . Numerous families, especially the elderly, lived on the money sent to them by relatives across the sea.   (Vilar, "Emigrantes," 24)

The flow of Levantine Sephardim was small at first, except to Argentina. This group preferred going to the United States. Only when that country imposed restrictive immigration quotas (as in 1925 and during World War II) did they go to Spanish-speaking America.

Israel

While historic Palestine was under Ottoman control there continued to be Jewish communities, mainly Sephardic, and there was a Sephardic chief rabbi in Jerusalem. Only in 1836 did the Ashkenazim begin to organize their own community, and in the middle of the last century an Ashkenazi chief rabbinate was created. Until the fall of the Turkish Empire and during the English protectorate, emigration to Palestine intensified, encouraged by Zionist organizations. Sephardim (especially from Salonika and Bulgaria) came, but the Ashkenazim took the most active part in founding the first kibbutzim and in the "illegal immigration" during the British mandate, so that the latter were more prominent.

World War II and Nazi persecution provoked massive flights of European Jews to Palestine, a flow that increased when the state of Israel was established in 1948. Among these Jews were a good number of Levantine Sephardim, from countries such as Greece, Yugoslavia, Bulgaria, and Rumania. Jews of other origins, especially Moroccans, arrived after 1956.

This twentieth-century emigration completely upset the social and cultural balance between the Sephardic and Ashkenazic communities in favor of the latter group. Many Ashkenazim came from advanced Western countries and were of a high sociocultural level. Some were intellectuals, liberal professionals, or university faculty who had been dispossessed completely during the war; others felt themselves incapable of continuing to live in their home countries after having experienced such horror and savagery. By comparison, many Sephardim from Eastern or Islamic areas were much less cultured and educated.

The situation got even worse with the arrival of Jews from the Arab and Levantine countries, many of which were truly underdeveloped. These immigrants were officially identified with the Sephardim and placed under the Sephardic chief rabbi. Israeli society was divided into two classes: the leaders, Ashkenazi and highly educated, and the followers, less educated and cultured, of whom the majority of Sephardic and Oriental Jews formed a part. As Ovadia Camhy points out, it was not so much a question of racial segregation as it was of class difference:

> No se trata aquí de racismo, no es menester hablar de ello: delantre de las leyes, delantre del Estado no hay ningún racismo. . . . No se trata si es sefaradí o no es sefaradí, si es del Asia o si es del Africa; esto no es emportante. Lo importante es que hay dos fracciones: una fracción no tiene el poder porque vino de lugares probes, de logares atrasados; y otros están viniendo de logares adelantados y tienen el poder de pagar las escolas.   (Actas, 431)

> [It is not a question here of racism, there is no need to talk about it. Before the law, before the State there is no racism. . . . It is not a question of whether or not one is Sephardic, from Asia or from Africa. This is not important. What is important is that there are two factions: one faction does not have power because it came from poor places, from backward places; and others are from advanced places and can pay for schooling.]

Recently there have been indications that the situation can be remedied. Due to mixed Sephardi-Ashkenazi marriages and the birth of *sabras* (native Israelis), there are Jews who no longer feel linked to one or the other tradition of their parents, but permeated by Israeli culture. Also, the activity of Sephardic personalities and institutions have begun to help the Sephardim recover their tradition, value their own culture, and attempt to raise the social and educational level of Sephardic and Oriental Jews.

Europe

Reference should be made in passing to Europe as a target for the Second Diaspora. When the wave of emigration of the Levantine Sephardim took place at the beginning of the century, some chose to settle in European countries rather than venture to faraway America. As would be expected from the presence and prestige of the French element in the Levant, France (and most especially Paris) was one of the chosen destinations. The nearby communities of Belgium and Holland also received some reinforcement from their Eastern coreligionists. Others went to England, joining the London Sephardic community, which had begun in the seventeenth century.

Also because of World War II, Sephardim took refuge in those European countries where Jews were not persecuted: France (later occupied by the Germans), England, or Spain itself, as we shall see in chapter 5. Nevertheless, few stayed there after the war; the majority went to America or Israel.

Finally, political changes in North Africa in the 1950s drove some Sephardim to France or Spain. The European communities, however, are not as important for Sephardism today as the ones in America and Israel.

RECOMMENDED READING

It should be noted here that a great deal of momentum has been given to studies of Sephardic history recently by several Israeli research teams. Unfortunately for those who do not read Hebrew, the results of their research are published in that language. I have not included those works in my bibliography, because it is limited to works accessible to the interested lay reader. One of those works, however, has been translated into English: Hayim J. Cohen, *The Jews of the Middle East, 1860–1972,* trans. Z. and L. Alizi (New York: Wiley [1973]).

Among general panoramic works covering Sephardic history, see Haïm Vidal Séphiha, *L'agonie des judéo-espagnols* (Paris: Entente, 1977) 9–15 and 23–69, and Mair José Benardete, *Hispanic Culture and Character of the Sephardic Jews,* 2d ed. (New York: Sepher-Hermon Press, 1982). It is worth noting the relatively recent, somewhat disordered compendium by Nissim Elnecave, *Los hijos de Ibero-franconia: Breviario del Mundo Sefaradí desde los Orígenes hasta nuestros días* (Buenos Aires: La Luz, 1981), in which some interesting data may be found.

For the history of the Levantine Sephardim, the classic is a late nineteenth-century work (1897) that recently has been reprinted: M. Franco, *Essai sur l'Histoire des Israélites de l'Empire Ottoman depuis les Origines Jusqu'a nos Jours* (Paris: Centre d'Études Don Isaac Abravanel, 1981). On Salonika, see Joseph Nehama, *Histoire des Israélites de Salonique,* vols. 1–4 (Paris: Durlacher, 1935–36); vol. 5 (London: World Sephardi Federation, 1959); vols. 6–7 (Salonika: Communauté Israélite de Thessalonique, 1978). On Rhodes, see Marc Angel, *The Jews of Rhodes: The History of a Sephardic Community* (New York: Sepher-Hermon Press, 1978), and Isaac Jack Lévy, *Jewish Rhodes: A Lost Culture* (Berkeley, Calif.: Judah L. Magnes Museum, 1989). For other Turkish communities, there are works that tend to be unsystematic but rich in information, especially Abraham Galanté's *Histoire des Juifs d'Istanbul depuis la prise de cette ville en 1435, par Fatih Mehmed II, jusqu'a nos jours* (Istanbul: Hüsnütabaiat, 1942) and *Histoire des Juifs de Rhodes, Chio, Cos, etc.* (Istanbul: Société Anonyme de Papeterie et d'Imprimerie [Fratelli Haim], 1935). Specifically on the Shabbetaian movement, its development and implications, see Gershom Scholem *Sabbataï Sevi: The Mystical Messiah,* trans. R. J. Zwi Werblowski (Princeton, N.J.: Princeton University Press, 1973), also translated into French as *Sabbataï Tsevi: Le messie mystique (1626–1676)* (Paris: Verdier, 1983).

The bibliography on Moroccan Sephardic communities is somewhat more modern. See the well-documented book by H. Z. (J. W.) Hirschberg, *A History of the Jews in North Africa,* vol. 2 (Leiden: Brill, 1981). Spanish and French influence on the Moroccan Jews in the nineteenth century is analyzed by Sarah Leibovici, *Chronique des juifs de Tétouan (1860–1896)* (Paris: Maisonneuve et Larose, 1984).

For the effect of the Alliance Israélite Universelle on the Sephardim, see Michael M. Laskier, *The Alliance Israélite Universelle and the Jewish Communities of Morocco, 1862–1962* (Albany: State University of New York Press, 1983), and Aron Rodrique, *French Jews, Turkish Jews: The Alliance Israélite Universelle and the Politics of Jewish Schooling in Turkey (1860–1925)* (Bloomington and Indianapolis: Indiana University Press, 1990).

A series of essays dealing with the Jews' relationships with the Dutch can be found in Jonathan Irvine Israel, *Empires and Entrepots: The Dutch, the Spanish Monarchy, and the Jews, 1585–1713* (London and Roncevert, W. Va.: Hambledon Press, 1990).

The problems faced by Sephardic immigrants to the United States are well illustrated in Angel, *La America: The Sephardic Experience in the United States* (Philadelphia: Jewish Publication Society of America, 1982).

T H R E E

LANGUAGE

Jewish Languages and the Speech of Spanish Jews in the Middle Ages

IN CENTURIES PAST, the Jews lived in physical isolation (confined in special areas) from their non-Jewish compatriots. Most of the time this isolation was not only physical; it also implied social, cultural, and, of course, linguistic isolation. It led the Jews to develop their own ways of speaking, due as much to their cultural peculiarities as to a need for self-defense, to communicate without the *goyim*, or non-Jews, being able to understand them. Thus were born what modern scholars have come to call Judeo-languages, variants of the language of the dominant culture that the Jews use in their social and family life.

For example, even in the times of the Roman Empire, the Jewish community of Rome spoke Latin with special characteristics. In the Ashkenazi world, the universal Judeo-language is Yiddish, derived from German. There also exist (or existed) Romance Judeo-languages parallel to medieval French, Italian, and Provençal (*šuadit*). The Jews in the Maghreb spoke a special variety of Arabic. Judeo-Spanish, of course, the language of the Sephardim, is another of these Judeo-languages.

A point of contention has been whether the Jews in the Iberian Peninsula before the expulsion spoke a Spanish that was different from the Christians' language. The study of documents and literary works indicates that Jewish Spanish did not differ from that of the other inhabitants except in a very few dialectal variations established especially for religious reasons. *El Dio,* for example, replaced *Dios,* whose final *-s* seemed to signal plurality, incompatible with the strict notion of monotheism. Other variants include use of the Arabic word *alḥad* to replace the Christian *domingo* [Sunday, etymologically "day of the Lord"]; use of the term *meldar* to mean "pray," "read religious texts," and later simply "read"; and use of Hebrew-Aramaic terms to designate certain realities of religious life. A further characteristic is the conservation of some Arabisms in forms closer to the original than in non-Jewish Spanish because Hebrew and Arabic both had a laryngeal sound [similar to German /ch/], that did not exist in the Spanish of that time.

EXILE

When the expulsion took place, Jews from different areas of the Iberian Peninsula scattered through Europe, the Eastern Mediterranean, and North Africa. Due to continuous travel and interchanges among the communities in different areas of the peninsula, and to the frequent links of Jews to the court, the majority of Jews (including those from Galicia, Catalonia, Navarre, and Aragon) must have known and frequently spoken Castilian prior to 1492.

Some scholars have tried to compile a hypothetical linguistic map of dialectal varieties of Judeo-Spanish based on the place of origin of the Jews who settled in each area. Such a project, however, has proven infeasible whenever the characteristics of the speech of a given diaspora city do not coincide with those of any specific peninsular area.

Continual communication among exile communities through rabbis, businessmen, and traveling craftsmen; relations with Spain through converts during the entire sixteenth and part of the seventeenth centuries; and the influence of works printed in Salonika, Constantinople, and Smyrna, which were distributed throughout the Sephardic world, helped to eliminate regional differences and to create a type of *koiné* or linguistic community in which without paying much attention to precise isoglosses, there coexisted a mixture of varied characteristics and dialectal forms sometimes very different from one another, but which all speakers understood. For example, in a single work published in Constantinople, and in very close proximity to each other within the text, both the forms *hijo* and *fijo* for *hijo* [son] are used. This detail makes it impossible to ascribe the archaic conservation of initial Latin *f-* to any specific Judeo-Spanish-speaking area. Many examples of this type could be cited, since polymorphism, variation of forms, is one of the outstanding characteristics of Judeo-Spanish. The Sephardim never settled on a unified linguistic norm, and the language continued to evolve independently of the normalization taking place in Spain. No matter what the initial distribution of the exiles, the speech of New Castile and Andalusia—the most innovative dialect, known by almost all since before the expulsion, and the dialect with the most sociocultural prestige—tended to dominate not only among the Spanish Jews (including those from Galicia and Catalonia) but also among the Portuguese. More surprisingly, it also dominated among the Greek, Italian, and Central European Jews who lived in Sephardic areas (especially in the Levant) and who abandoned Greek, Italian, and Yiddish in favor of Spanish.

In the sixteenth century the exiles' Spanish differed little from that of the Spaniards, as is indicated in Gonzalo de Illescas's oft-repeated remark about the Jews in his *Historia Pontifical y Catholica:*

> They took from here our language and they still retain and use it gladly, and it is certain that in the cities of Salonika, Constantinople, Alexandria and Cairo and in other commercial cities and in Venice they do not buy or contract business in any language but Spanish. And I met in Venice many Jews from Salonika who spoke Spanish, despite their youth, as well or better than I.   (Wagner, *Caracteres,* 14)

As their relations with Spain became more and more infrequent, Spanish-speaking Jews found themselves isolated in an environment where the language spoken was not Spanish but Arabic, Turkish, Greek, Italian, French, or Flemish. In some of these areas Spanish gave way to the other languages, as it did in France, Italy, the Low Countries (where Portuguese, nevertheless, was preserved longer), modern Tunis, and Algeria. In Egypt and Syria the only remains of Spanish are some expressions used in card games, numbers, and certain religious terms. In other areas, such as modern Morocco or the lands of the then-flowering Turkish Empire, sociocultural and economic circumstances were more favorable and there was less influence of other refined languages, so the Sephardim maintained the language that was their own—Spanish.

THE NAMES OF THE LANGUAGE

The fact that the Sephardim spoke the language of Spain is shown in names that they gave to their own language: *Espanyol, Espanyolit, Espanyol Ladino, Franco Espanyol,* and *Romance Espanyol.* Also, keeping in mind that *Sepharad* means Spain, they called the language *Sephardi, Sepharadi, Lešon Sefaradim* [Hebrew, language of the Sephardim], and *Lingua Sefaradit.* At times the dominant idea was speaking a Romance or Frankish language, as can be seen in the names *Francés, Frenkiš, Levantino, Lingua Franca, Portugal,* or *Romance.* Other times, they considered that the language was something other than Hebrew: *Lešon La'az* [Hebrew, foreign language] as contrasted with *Lašon Hakodeš* [Hebrew, holy language].

If it is certain that the Sephardim were very conscious that their language came from Spain, it is no less clear that they retained it not because it was a souvenir of Spain, the Spain that (do not forget, because they did not) had

thrown them out, but because they believed it was an identifying and distinguishing characteristic, one that made them stand out from the peoples who
surrounded them. Consequently they also gave the language names that indicated that its speakers were Jews: *Judezmo* (literally, Judaism), or simply
Judio or *Jidio* [Jewish]. Many examples are cited of the Jews' identification
with Spanish, such as the case of a Levantine Sephardi who, on hearing a
Spanish priest speak Spanish, exclaimed, "a Jewish priest!" There is also the
story Estrugo tells, which shows very clearly how closely, even at the beginning of this century, the older generations identified being Jewish with speaking Spanish:

> A Spaniard living in Constantinople had sought the hand of a young Sephardic girl
> with whom he was in love. The girl's father, who was a religious man, opposed the
> marriage because the young man was Catholic. But the girl's grandmother could not
> understand, and she kept saying, "How can James be a Christian? He speaks Spanish!"
> A few years later, when the girl married an Ashkenazi, her grandmother was indig-
> nant. Throwing over a Spaniard and marrying a German. What an embarrassment! It
> was a dishonor to the family.   (Estrugo, *Retorno*, 55–56)

The Sephardim were conscious of the fact that the language they spoke
came from Spain but what they emphasized was that it was theirs, the inalien-
able heritage of their people. This almost sentimental tie to their own language becomes clear in the name that the Moroccan Sephardim gave to their
dialect—*Haketia*. The etymology of the word is uncertain, but some take it
to be a derivative of *Haquito*, the diminutive of *Itzhak* [Isaac], with the ge-
neric meaning of "Jew." Others derive it from the Arabic word *hekaya* or
hakaita [clever saying]. In either case, it is an affectionate term with humorous connotations, and so it reflects very well the attitude of the Sephardim—at least in times past—toward their language.

LADINO

Some observations must be made about the word *Ladino,* derived from the
Spanish *latino* [Latin], applied to any medieval Moor or Jew who spoke Romance, the Christian language. Although the Sephardic language has sometimes been given this name (and it is known as Ladino today in Israel),
Ladino is really a calque-language of Hebrew, used to put Hebrew liturgical texts into Spanish words. It was never a real language for everyday
communication.

Ladino is not the only language of this type. It forms part of a group of
what have come to be known as *calque hagiolanguages* [holy languages], used
to "translate" religious texts in holy languages into the vernacular. These

calque hagiolanguages are not peculiar to the Jews. There is, for example, an Islamo-Persian calque that was used to translate the Koran word by word from Arabic into Farsi. Ladino is not the only Jewish artificial language of this type; other examples are calque Judeo-German, Judeo-Italian, and Judeo-Greek. Like the others, Ladino or calque Judeo-Spanish is faithful to the Hebrew source text in a completely literal fashion, as shown by the following features:

a) Syntax: For example, Gen. 37:14, in which Jacob sends his son Joseph to see how his brothers are, is "translated": "y diJo *a el* anda agora vee *a paz de* tus hermanos y *a paz* de las ovejas" ["And he said to him: Go now, see whether it is well with thy brethren and well with the flock"]. The italicized words reproduce Hebrew constructions literally. Another type of syntactic calque is repetition, such as *recelar recelé* (for *hube de recelar* [I should have suspected]) or *tomar tomarás* [you are to take]. Also, because there is no present tense, the function of that tense is taken over by the active participle, and those participles, either complete, as *comientes* [those who are eating], or apocopated, as *temién* (for *temientes*) [those who are afraid], have the value of present tense.

b) Morphology: For example, the word *vidas* [lives] is always in the plural because the Hebrew word *ḥayim* has the *-im* plural ending. The same thing happens with *mayim,* which is always translated as *aguas* [waters].

c) Lexicological derivation: Words are created by calque of the Hebrew, such as *acuñadear* [to act like a brother-in-law] from Spanish *cuñado* [brother-in-law] to express the fulfillment of the law of levirate, according to which a man is to marry his sister-in-law if she should become widowed.

d) Semantics: For example, in the biblical text cited above, the word *paz* [peace] is used with the same semantic field as in Hebrew, in which *shalom* means "peace" as well as "abundance" or "state of health."

e) Selection of Spanish words that sound like the Hebrew words they are translating: Thus, the Hebrew *namer* [tiger] is translated as *añámere* rather than the common *tigre*.

Such literalness produces a completely artificial language, one that is often unintelligible if the reader does not know the Hebrew source of the "Ladinized" passage.

The origin of this kind of translation is not known, but it probably dates to the Spanish Middle Ages. Although few medieval Ladino manuscripts have been saved, the tradition of Ladino translation is reflected in the first books Jews printed after their expulsion from Spain, during the sixteenth century. In these books, the editors occasionally allude to an "old" tradition (doubtless from the Iberian Peninsula during the Middle Ages) they are following. Here is how the Ferrara Bible states it: "fue forçado seguir el lenguaje que los antiguos Hebreos españoles usaron . . . y los ladinos tan antiguos y sentenciosos entre los Hebreos ya convertidos en naturaleza" ["it was necessary to follow the language that the old Spanish Hebrews used . . . and the Ladino texts so old and sententious among the Hebrews, already changed in nature (i.e., from Hebrew to Ladino)].

In summary, the Sephardim regularly called their spoken language *Judezmo* or *Español* to distinguish it from Ladino, the calque-language. However, Ladino has lately come to be used as a synonym for Judezmo. The name *Judeo-Spanish* is a recent scholarly creation. All of these distinctions of terminology are well summarized in the following words of Baruh Uziel, a Sephardi living in Israel and a native speaker of Judezmo:

> No es que últimamente que llaman al idioma sefaradita ladino. Ladinar *ande nośotros es sólo 'haćer la traducción española de la Biblia'. Mośotros meśmos, el pueblo, llaman a muestro idioma simplîcemente (semplamente)* español. *Los entelectuales lo llamaban más tadre* judeoespañol; *ma mi agüelo, y los de su ǵeneración, la llamaban* judeśmo, *que quiere dećir 'lingua judía'; "hablar en* judeśmo" *era 'hablar en español', como entre los aškenaźim llamaban a su propio idioma* yiḍiš *que también es 'lingua judía'.* (*Actas*, 322)

[Just recently has the Sephardic language been called *Ladino. Ladinoize* among us means only "to do a Spanish translation of the Bible." We ourselves, the people, call our language simply *Spanish.* Intellectuals later called it *Judeo-Spanish;* but my grandfather, and his generation, called it *Judezmo,* which means "Jewish language"; "to speak Judezmo" was "to speak Spanish," as among the Ashkenazim they called their own language *Yiddish* which is also "Jewish language."] [1]

Judeo-Spanish: A Fossilized Language?

Juan Pujol recounts how, on one of his trips through the Levant, he heard from the lips of a Sephardi living medieval Spanish, like a mummy that had found its wandering soul after many centuries of rest.   (Ortega, 1919, 219)

That savage ballad, that Spanish medieval poem had been alive in Xauen for centuries. . . . The language, mummified in that dungeon, the language was still young, but free of contamination, preserved in that hole in the wall like the flower of a soul.   (Borrás, 157)

The first Spaniards who, in the late nineteenth or early twentieth century, came into contact with the nearly unknown Sephardim had the same impres-

---

1. There is a great deal of disagreement among Sephardim themselves over the use of the term Judezmo for this language. It seems to have been a matter of regional preference. In the words of a Sephardi from Rhodes, "In all my travels I never heard of it [the term Judezmo for the language], and I spoke to hundreds of Sephardim."

sion: the Spanish that the Sephardim spoke sounded to the Spaniards' ears like a stammering infantile language, as if the first cry of Spanish had been frozen in time and was being offered to them miraculously revived. And so arose the commonplace that Judeo-Spanish was an archaic and fossilized language (that "mummy" that both Ortega and Borrás mentioned so often) that had been retained practically unchanged since the fifteenth century. That idea has caused many to forget that a language cannot endure without changes, without evolution.

Of course, the speech of the Sephardim presents archaic characteristics due to the conservatism of a language that has existed for centuries in isolation. But, like the living language that it is, it has also undergone a process of transformation throughout its history. As mentioned previously, the progressive isolation of the Sephardic communities among themselves and with respect to Spain produced the division of Sephardic Jewry into two large blocks: the Levantine and the North African. Needless to say, the language developed differently in each area.

JUDEO-SPANISH IN THE LEVANT

One difficulty becomes apparent immediately in looking at Levantine Judeo-Spanish: the oral texts recently collected reflect only the most popular speech, as it was only the common folk who had preserved the dialect fully when Western scholars first became interested in it at the end of the nineteenth century and especially during this century. Yet there are many printed texts from the eighteenth through the twentieth centuries that, aside from their being nearly inaccessible to Hispanists because they are written in Hebrew characters, reflect especially educated speech or literary style.

In other words, there is abundant documentation, but it is quite varied in terms of dates and language registers. It is virtually impossible to reconstruct the characteristics of Levantine Judeo-Spanish using documents that range from ballads and folktales collected during this century to scholarly rabbinic prose, in addition to Spanish poetry from the eighteenth and nineteenth centuries, translations of the Bible that follow medieval tradition, popular sayings, plays translated from French, and the remedies of folk medicine. That is tantamount to attempting to define the characteristics of Iberian Spanish based on a comedy by Lope de Vega,[2] Ripalda's catechism,[3] the text of the Constitution of 1812, the lyrics of several popular songs, a copy of yesterday's

2. A sixteenth-century playwright.
3. A Spanish Jesuit writer, 1536–1618.

newspaper, a novel by Sender,[4] a conversation among young people in a suburb, and a bad translation of an American best-seller. Is there any doubt that these texts will only represent, in part and at random, basic characteristics of Iberian Spanish? One would not know whether to identify other characteristics as part of the general system of the language, as typical of a specific group, or as stylistic peculiarities of a specific author or genre. It would also be nearly impossible, and worse, deceptive, to try to describe the current state of the language on the basis of texts from such varied time periods.

Nevertheless, the assorted Sephardic documentation available illustrates some common characteristics: (a) The basis of the dialect is Castilian-Andalusian speech of the fifteenth and sixteenth centuries, with the retention of certain archaic features (in phonetics, morphosyntax, and vocabulary) and the appearance of other features specific to the dialect; (b) some non-Castilian Hispanic elements (Catalonian, Aragonese, Leonese, Portuguese, etc.); and (c) numerous non-Hispanic components added, especially in vocabulary.

a) In regard to the conservation of archaic characteristics, the retention of the medieval phonetic system is the most noticeable feature. The following phonemes, no longer part of modern Spanish, are found in Levantine Judeo-Spanish:

/š/, voiced prepalatal fricative (like French *ch* or English *sh*),[5] which has become laryngeal in Spanish, except when followed by /k/, where it has become /s/: *pášaro* [bird], *jabón* [soap], *jarope* [syrup], *tejer* [knit, weave], *cašca* [shell], *cuešco* [pit (of a fruit)].

/ž/ (like the *s* in *pleasure*),[6] which has also become the Spanish laryngeal fricative: *mujer* [woman, wife], *ojo* [eye], *hijo* [son].

/ў/ (like the *j* in *jelly*),[7] which has also evolved into the laryngeal fricative in Spanish: *juntos* [together], *joya* [jewel], *ĝente* [people].

/z/ (like the *s* in *rose*):[8] *caśa* [house], *faćer* [to make, do], *cośa* [thing].[9]

Aside from these phonemes, lost in modern Spanish, Judeo-Spanish retains other archaic phonetic features:

4. A Spanish novelist, 1902–82.
5. [AN] Our transcription system represents it as *č, ĵ, š,* or *ž*.
6. [AN] It is represented as *ĝ, ĵ, ś, ŷ,* or *ź*.
7. [AN] It is represented as *č, ĝ, ĵ, ŷ, ź,* or *ž*.
8. [AN] It is represented as *ć, ś* or *ź*.
9. Although this sound continues to exist in modern Spanish, its distribution has changed: the *s* is no longer voiced between vowels; it is voiced only when followed by a voiced consonant, as in *mismo* [same].

The phonological distinction between occlusive and fricative /b/ is often realized by pronouncing the fricative as a labiodental /v/ (as in English).[10] Thus, the Sephardim distinguish between *ḥaver* [Hebrew, companion] and *ḥaber* [Turkish, piece of news].[11]

In some areas, such as Salonika and part of Bosnia and Macedonia, the word-initial Latin *f-* is retained.[12]

Up to this point, we have examined the conservative characteristics of the dialect. In other areas, however, Judeo-Spanish contains innovations associated with southern dialects (such as Andalusian, Canary, or American Spanish), for example, the pronunciation of the *ll* [/ly/, as in *million*, in modern Spanish] as /y/, which also occurs in Andalusia, areas of Castile, and Latin America (*llamar, llorar,* and *caballo* [call, cry, and horse] are pronounced as /yamar/, /yorar/, and /kabayo/). Peculiar to Judeo-Spanish is the disappearance of the /y/ in the diminutive ending *-illo/-illa,* producing forms such as *estrea* (for *estrella* [star]), *famía* (from *familla,* derived from Sp. *familia* [family]) or *maravía* (for *maravilla* [wonder]).

Judezmo also concurs with other southern dialects in the pronunciation of the /th/—written as *z* or as *c* before *e* or *i* in modern Spanish—as unvoiced /s/. As in Andalusia, the Canary Islands, and Latin America, *cielo* [sky, heaven] is pronounced /sielo/ [rather than /thielo/], *caza* [s/he hunts] is /kasa/ [rather than /katha/], *mazo* [mallet] is /maso/ [rather than /matho/], and so on.

Other phonetic features characteristic of the dialect include:

The pronunciation of multiflap /r/ with a single flap, so that word-initial *r-* [which is normally a double flap] in *rosa* [rose], *rico* [rich], or *rama* [branch] is pronounced as a single flap, as well as *guerra* [war] and *perro* [dog], which are pronounced as though they were *guera* and *pero.*

The metathesis of *rd* to *dr: cuerda* [cord, rope], *guardar* [guard, keep], *verdad* [true, truth] respectively are pronounced as /kuedra/, /gwadrar/, /vedrá/.

Notable among morphosyntactic archaisms is the retention of *-b-* in the imperfect endings of *-er* and *-ir* verbs: *quería* [I/he/she wanted] is /keriba/. Also the present-tense forms *voy* [I am going], *doy* [I give], *estoy* [I am] are realized as /vo/, /do/, /estó/.

A morphological feature peculiar to Judeo-Spanish is the ending *-í/-imos* for first-person singular and plural preterites of all verbs. This occurs by anal-

10. [AN] Represented as *b* or *p* in word-initial position, and as *ḇ* or *p̄* in intervocalic position.

11. Both have an identical fricative /ḇ/ in modern Spanish.

12. That sound generally evolved, first to aspirated /h/ and then disappeared (although it is still written as *h-*) in modern Spanish.

ogy to second- and third-conjugation verbs [that is, those whose infinitives end in *-er* or *-ir*], so that the first-conjugation verb *topar* [to meet, find] shows the forms *topí, topimos* instead of the Spanish *topé, topamos,* or *ordenar* [to order] has the forms *ordení, ordenimos* rather than the expected *ordené, ordenamos,* and so on.

As for pronouns, it is worth noting the use of *mos* [we, us] coexisting with the modern Spanish *nos: mos espartimos* [we're going] or *escucharmos* [listen to us].

There are words in the Judeo-Spanish vocabulary that have maintained their medieval Castilian form (*agora* [now], *avagar* [slowly], *adobar* [arrange], *cavśo* [cause], *mercar* [sell, buy], etc.), used along with words not of Castilian origin and, in some cases, not from Spain, as will be seen later.

b) The existence in Judeo-Spanish of non-Castilian Hispanic elements can be explained by the various points of origin of the refugees: they included not only Castilians and Andalusians, but also people from Catalonia, Valencia, Aragon, the old kingdom of Leon, Asturias, Galicia, and Portugal. Although the Castilian-Andalusian norm was adopted in general, some terms were retained from other dialects or other languages in Spain.

For this reason some areas have kept the initial *f-,* as Asturian and Leonese do, in words like *farina* [flour], *faba* [bean], *fijo* [son]. Also the Latin cluster *-mb-* remains in words like *palomba* [dove, pigeon], *lamber* [lick], and *lombo* [loin] where standard Spanish would use the forms *paloma, lamer,* and *lomo.* This feature coincides with Galician or Portuguese.

The expression *cale* or *cale que* [it is necessary, one must], used in sixteenth-century Castilian and preserved in contemporary Catalonian and Aragonese, is very common in Judeo-Spanish in such phrases as *cale que venga* [it is necessary for him to come] or *cale vivir a la moda* [one must live in style]. As in Aragonese, the typical diminutive suffix is *-ico.*

Other non-Castilian Hispanisms appear in the vocabulary: for example, *diada,* originally meaning "day of celebration," as in Catalan, and later "theatrical performance"; *birra,* meaning "anger, rage, fury," or *alfinete,* meaning "pin" as in Portuguese; *lonso* [bear] recalls Aragonese *onso;* *ĝinollo* [knee] is like Galician, Portuguese and Catalonian; *šamarada* or *šamalada* [call] look like Leonese.

c) Surprisingly, there are fewer non-Castilian Hispanic components in Judezmo than there are extra-Hispanic elements. Of the latter, three types may be distinguished: (1) Arabisms already in use in peninsular Spanish, (2) Hebrew-Aramaic elements, and (3) loan words from the languages of the old Ottoman Empire (Turkish and the Balkan languages).

1) Medieval Spanish contained a number of Arabisms, many of which have survived to the present. As indicated previously, Jewish speech has preserved some forms closer to the Arabic original than non-Jewish Spanish has, because biblical Hebrew (which the Jews knew as the language of their religion) contains the laryngeal spirant /ḥ/ also present in Arabic. So, for example, the Sephardic *ḥaroba* [carob], *alḥabaca* [sweet basil], *ḥaćino* [ill] more closely resemble the original Arabic words than the corresponding Spanish *algarroba, albahaca,* and *hacino* do.

In other cases, a similar Hebrew word (do not forget that Arabic and Hebrew are both Semitic languages) reinforced the Sephardis' retention of Arabisms, which are virtually forgotten in peninsular Spanish. That is almost surely what happened in the case of *almenara* (from Arabic, *manara* [lighthouse, beacon]), "lamp" in Judeo-Spanish, doubtless reinforced by Hebrew *menorah* [seven-branched candlestick].

These considerations are valid for the Arabisms in Moroccan Judeo-Spanish as well, but there the Arabic element is much stronger, as we will see shortly.

2) Although the majority of the Sephardim did not understand Hebrew and Aramaic—their liturgical language—very well (as Catholics generally do not understand Latin despite its having been their liturgical language until recently), they nevertheless understood these languages to some extent.

The only phonetic characteristics of Hebrew found in Levantine Judeo-Spanish are the *ŝ* (/ts/ or /tz/, pronounced like medieval Spanish *ç* or German *z*),[13] in specific Hebraisms (*maŝah* [unleavened bread], *ŝadik* [saint], etc.) and the retention of the Semitic guttural consonant *ayin*.

The most pervasive Hebrew-Aramaic influence, not surprisingly, is in vocabulary. It is only logical that some Hebrew-Aramaic terms would appear in Sephardic speech, especially in reference to phenomena related directly or indirectly to religious life. The names of the Hebrew months, for example, are used habitually, as are the names of religious objects (*menorah, kipa* [skullcap], *megillah*). Other examples are the names of ceremonies and festivities (*b'rit millah* [circumcision], *se'uda* [festive meal]), institutions and community authorities (*kehilah* [synagogue], *ḥevra* [first "association" and then "elementary school"],

13. [AN] Represented as *ŝ*.

ḥaḥam [wise person—a title given to rabbis]), the names of sins, vir-
tues, powers and moral attitudes (*zehut* [merit], *kavod* [honor], *avelut*
[mourning]). There are also terms refering to Jewish history (*beth
hamikdaš* [sanctuary], referring to the temple in Jerusalem, *Miŝrayim*
[Egypt]), or to the language itself (*lašon hakodeš* [holy language] to
refer to Hebrew, *la'aź* for any foreign language), or to being Jewish
(*goyim* [Gentiles, non-Jews]).

These Hebraisms frequently become Hispanized when Spanish morphemes are added to the Hebrew root. Thus, the Hebrew root *drš*
[preach] yields the verb *darsar* [with the Spanish *-ar* infinitive ending],
meaning "to preach publicly in the synagogue." The verb *diḥurear* is
formed from *diḥur* [speech], with the sense of "speak foreign languages". *Enheremar* [excommunicate] is built on Hebrew *ḥerem* [ex-
communication]; the phrase *ba'al haḥayit* [owner of the house] becomes
balabay in popular speech, from which the Judeo-Spanish feminine *ba-
labaya* [homemaker] is formed (plural, *balabayas*). Expressions containing both Spanish and Hebrew words are also common: for example,
tomar sar, "to become sad" [the first word is Spanish, the second is
Hebrew]. Others (with the Hebrew element in bold print) are **afilu**
que [almost], con **tenay** que [provided that], *haćer* **kavod** [to honor].
Hebrew elements, then, are not limited to literary language or religious
prose; they are also sprinkled throughout everyday speech.

3) The coexistence of the Levantine Sephardim with the Turks and
the Balkan peoples created a constant linguistic exchange for commercial, administrative, and social reasons. The majority of speakers of
Judeo-Spanish are, and have been, multilingual. Consequently, it is not
strange that Levantine Judeo-Spanish contains words from Greek, Bulgarian, Rumanian, Serbo-Croatian, and, above all, Turkish.

In some cases the introduction of loan words was caused by the birth
of nationalist movements and the subsequent compulsory integration
of minorities into national culture. It is no accident, therefore, that
many of the Bulgarian words in Judeo-Spanish refer to military life
(*polk* [regiment], *polkovnic* [colonel], *capral* [bullet]) or to secular education (*doskel* [teacher], *dictovka* [dictation]), as those terms entered the
language when those realities were imposed on the Jewish communities
in Bulgaria that previously had been culturally and socially independent. However, Judeo-Spanish already had taken on other Turkish and
Bulgarian elements.

If Hebraisms in Judeo-Spanish refer especially to religious life, Turkisms invade all areas of activity. Above all, though, they pertain to business, labor, and administration, because these were the areas in which the Sephardim had the majority of dealings with their non-Jewish neighbors. Among those words are *charší* [market], *maalé* [neighborhood], *midán* [public square], *hamal* [errand boy], *bakal* [grocery store], *parás* [money], and *hukiumet* [court]. The names of trades are indicated by the suffix *-ŷí* or *-chí,* thus the *boyaŷí* is the painter, *žaržavachí* is the vegetable man, and *estindakchí* is an inspector carrying out an investigation.

The elements of daily life, customs, and folkways that the Jews adopted from their Ottoman neighbors are also, naturally enough, named in Turkish: *hamám* is the Turkish bath; *chalgui* is a typical musical group whose instruments and musical modes also have Turkish names; *ŷežvé* is the special pot in which Turkish coffee is prepared; *rakí* is the very strong national alcoholic drink. There are many Turkish names for foods and sweets. Some forms of address are also Turkish: *chelebí* [sir] is used with a proper name as a sign of respect; the suffix *-achi* (with a corresponding Hispanic feminine *acha*) is affectionate, resulting in Behorachi, the affective diminutive of the Hebrew man's name Behor, or Isterulacha, for Esther.

Kitchen utensils and parts of a house form another semantic field for Turkish words: *filŷan* is a cup, *ŷan* is a window, the kitchen is *mutpak,* *tavan* is roof (sometimes used as a euphemism for "God"), a ladle is *tenŷere,* and so on. Given the dearth of Jewish vocabulary for elements of nature, many plants and animals are named in Turkish: *chichek* [flower], *konŷa* [rose], *bilbil* [nightingale], *kayesi* [apricot], *višna* [sour cherry], and *menekše* [violet].

Like Hebraisms—but more frequently—Turkish elements are fused with components from other languages. We have already seen two examples of the agglutination of a Hebrew name with a Turkish suffix in the cases of Behorachi and Isterulacha. Turkish words are also fused to Spanish suffixes: the plural of *bakal* [grocery store] is *bakales;* rather than calling a nightingale simply a *bilbil,* it is usually a *bilbilico* with the Hispanic *-ico* diminutive. Some words are created: the Turkish base *batak* [mud] yields the verb *embatacar* [to muddy, get dirty]; Turkish *fagfur* [porcelain] produces the noun *farfuria* with the same meaning, basis of the metaphor for certain white sweets that look like porcelain, called *farfulinis.* There are even some curious examples of the fusion of elements from three languages, such as the noun *purimlikes* [Purim presents], where the Jewish holiday of Purim has been given the Turk-ish suffix *-lik* and the Spanish plural ending *-es*.

To these non-Hispanic components of Judeo-Spanish must be added oth-ers from Romance languages such as French and, to a lesser extent, Italian from the end of the nineteenth century. The Alliance schools had a major role in introducing French terms as the Dante Alighieri schools did in introducing Italian. The arrival of Western culture to stratified Levantine Jewish society brought with it a new way of speaking. Logically, French and Italian supplied words for phenomena previously unknown. Just as the theater was new, the-atrical vocabulary was derived primarily from French: *rolo* [role], *jugar* [act], *jugador* [actor], and *vodvil* [vaudeville], with some Italianisms, such as *come-dia* (stressed on *-i-*). The new communication medium, journalism, also took its vocabulary from Italian and French, words that spread quickly from the printed page to everyday speech: people began to talk about *soĉeta* (Italian), *diplomacía* (probably a cross between French and Italian), *aferes* (French), *política*, and many other new realities that appeared in *gaĉetas* (French), *jur-nales* (French), or *jornales* (Italian).

Having been educated in Alliance schools, speaking French and being *à la page* [up to date] (never more appropriately said) became very desirable, the epitome of chic. The younger generation changed. The Jew who was *franco* or *franqueado* [Westernized] dressed and spoke *a la franca* [in Western style] and carried his *franquedad* [Westernness] to the extreme of *franquear la nom-bradía*, that is, of replacing his Hebrew or traditional Sephardic name with its French equivalent, more or less. Young women whose names had been Maźal Tov [Hebrew, good luck] or Clara started calling themselves Fortuné and Cler; young men were no longer Ya'acov or Abraham but Jac or Alberto. Of course, the speech of these *franqueados* was replete with words, phrases, and even syntax modeled on French. They were *muśiús* (French, *monsieur*) and *mamuaśeles* (French, *mademoiselles*) who no longer *se interesaban a* (French *s'intéresser à* as opposed to Spanish *interesarse por*) the same *aferes* (from French *affaires* rather than Spanish *asuntos*) as their *parientes* (French *parents* vs. Spanish *padres*) and their lives *deśvelopaban* (French *developper* vs. Spanish *desarrollar*) in a manner very different from the *tradicionel* (French *tradition-nel*, Spanish *tradicional*) so *regretada* (French *regretter*, Spanish *añorar* [pine for, miss]) by their elders; everything old *ǵenaba* (French *gêner*, Spanish *mo-lestar* [bother]) them and they did not *heśitaban* (French *hésiter*, Spanish *du-dar en* [hesitate]) to reject it.

This is how Levantine Judeo-Spanish became saturated with Gallicisms in the late nineteenth and early twentieth century, to the point where it was called Judeo-Fragnol, a derogatory word which, however humorous, is very revealing of its hybrid character: Judeo + French + Spanish.

ḤAKETÍA: MOROCCAN JUDEO-SPANISH

Distinguishing the characteristics of Ḥaketía, the Judeo-Spanish of Morocco, is quite difficult for two reasons: there are very few extant texts to tell us what the language was like before the nineteenth century; the dialect has practically disappeared in the twentieth century.

In the eastern Mediterranean there were large publishing centers—controlled entirely by Jews until the eighteenth century—so that there are a good number of divergent publications (literary, religious, community organization and, more recently, journalistic) that provide a considerable textual corpus in which Levantine Judeo-Spanish can be analyzed and its evolution traced. Morocco, on the other hand, had few publishing houses, and texts were transmitted primarily in two ways: as manuscripts for personal or family use and orally.

Relatively few manuscripts have been preserved, as is logical given the fact that they were single copies and meant to be short-lived. The oral texts (especially poetry) show some peculiar characteristics that make them questionable sources for linguistic documentation. It is generally known that linguistic devices in folkloric poetry are not exactly the same as the ones used in daily speech, and that orally transmitted texts retain obsolete language. For example, if in a ballad the expression *madre, la mi madre* [mother, my mother] appears, it is not appropriate to assume that the medieval use of the definite article [*la*] with the possessive adjective [*mi*] has remained current, as expressions of this type are to be found in all folkloric Hispanic poetry in which the language always tends to be archaic.

Those who study this dialect cannot put any faith in Spanish writers from the nineteenth and early twentieth centuries (Benito Pérez Galdós, Vicente Blasco Ibáñez, Tomás Borrás) who made contact with Sephardic reality and tried to reflect Ḥaketía in their novels. Their attempted reconstructions of the speech of Moroccan Jews are usually completely incorrect and conventional.[14] In addition, historical circumstances have worked against the preservation of the dialect in this century, so that there is little current documentation concerning it. Morocco was not isolated from Spain, whereas it was precisely

14. [AN] On the other hand, Angel Vázquez's modern novel *La vida perra de Juanita Narboni* (Barcelona: Planeta, 1976) reflects very charmingly some Ḥaketía expressions that form part of the confusing speech of the main character, a fiftyish woman from Tangier.

this isolation that helped preserve Levantine Judeo-Spanish. This is how Paul Bénichou explains it:

> The presence of peninsular garrisons [Spanish in Ceuta, Melilla, Vélez de la Go-mera, Larache and Oran; Portuguese in Tangier and Arcila] in Morocco continuously until Spain's occupation of the entire zone in the nineteenth and twentieth centuries suffices to suggest that the Spanish-speaking Moroccan Jews were not in a state of complete linguistic isolation in the seventeenth and eighteenth centuries, and that some knowledge of peninsular Spanish was preserved during that time. (Bénichou, "Observaciones," 242)

Such communication, nevertheless, could allow the preservation of a specific dialect, although not as distant from current Spanish as Levantine Sephardic speech. Additionally, however, the arrival in Morocco of soldiers, officials, and Spanish settlers in general from the middle of the nineteenth century caused a re-Hispanization of the Jews, similar to that produced in this century by the secondary emigration from the Balkans to Latin America. Iacob Hassán has made note of the situation:

> This contact has eroded the Ḥaketía dialect. Modern Spanish has invaded and destroyed several of its basic characteristics. Ḥaketía speakers have readapted their Judeo-Spanish to Spanish. Today the majority of the Sephardic population speaks normal Spanish. (Hassán, "De los restos," 2127–28)

Regarding how the recent contact with Spaniards has contributed to the destruction of the dialect, Bénichou's observation on Sephardic Ḥaketía speakers from Oran is very significant: "When speaking with Spaniards, everyone tried to make his language match modern Spanish, as he knew it, introducing many supplementary corrections into the native dialect" (Bénichou, "Observaciones," 218). The oldest compilation of data on Ḥaketía is the now classic study by José Benoliel. Published in several parts from 1927 to 1952, his text reflects the speech in Tangier at the end of the nineteenth century.

When Américo Castro visited the Jewish quarters in Morocco in 1922, the dialect was still apparently quite alive:

> I could not hide my surprise on hearing the Hebrews from Tangier, Larache, and Tetuan speak. Despite the proximity to the Iberian Peninsula, these people speak the same Spanish as the Levantine Jews. It was only natural to assume that the Hebrews in Tangier would speak the same way as those in Ceuta or Cadiz, and the same as those in Tetuan. But happily for the linguist that is not so. (Castro, "Entre los hebreos, 145)

French presence in North Africa and the schools of the Alliance Israélite Universelle also contributed to "cosmopolitanize" the Sephardim, leading them to abandon their dialect. As early as 1922 Castro mentioned that the young Moroccan Jews were imbued with French culture, even when the use of Haketía continued in the Jewish quarters:

> Since 1862 France has had a school in Tetuan, established through the Alliance Israélite Universelle, resulting in the fact that people younger than forty know French, in some cases perfectly. One of the strangest impressions for the traveler, among the many he has, is to hear in a *caleya* [alley] of the *mellah* [Jewish quarter] (along with very archaic Spanish words in perfect harmony with the general type of life in the city) young people speaking perfect French, with a good sense of modern life. All this without leaving Tetuan. (Ibid.)

Slightly more than twenty years later, Bénichou noted that "the dialect, or a large part of it, is now only a memory, which remains alive among people of the older generation" (Bénichou, "Observaciones," 209).

The adoption of peninsular Spanish (in its Andalusian variety) is practically complete today, except for a few dialectal traits. Nevertheless, the collected documentation points out some of the characteristics in the speech of North African Sephardim:

a) Regarding phonetics, Moroccan speech has not retained medieval phonemes lost in modern Spanish to the extent that Levantine Judeo-Spanish has:

There are no remains of the unvoiced dentoalveolar fricative /ŝ/ (ç in medieval Spanish).

The *j* is the modern Spanish velar rather than the prepalatal fricative /ž/ or /š/. Those sounds are preserved only in words that do not exist in modern Spanish, where the influence of the peninsular norm has been inoperative (for example, *peǰe* [fish], Verǰico, the name of a character in ballads), or in Arabisms (*aǰugar* [dowry]).

Voiced *s* (/z/) is very strong: *caŝa, hermoŝo*.

As in the Levant, the use of /s/ where peninsular Spanish uses /θ/ (*mansebo* for *mancebo, plasa* for *plaza,* etc.) and the pronunciation of *ll* as /y/ (*caye* for *calle* and so on) are general. Intervocalic *ll* is also lost in the endings *-illo, -illa: castío* for *castillo* and *Sevía* for *Sevilla.*

Word-initial *r* is a single flap, but there is a multiflap *rr* in medial position. Consequently, *rico* is pronounced with a simple /r/, but *perro* [dog] is differentiated from *pero* [but], which it is not in Levantine speech.

The labiodental *v,* which appears in the Levant, is not present in Haketía.

Phonetic characteristics specific to Haketía include:
Assimilation of *b/v* [both of which are pronounced as bilabials] or *g* before

the diphthongs *ua, ue, ui, ou: bueno* [good] becomes *ueno, fraguar* [build] is *frauar, antiguo* [old] is *antiuo*.

Confusion between *b/v* and *g* before *o* or *u: jubón* [jacket] becomes *jugón, agujero* [hole] is *abujero*.

Interdental articulation of voiced *s* before a vowel so that it sounds like the *th* in *then: sus horas* [his hours] sounds like *soothe oras*, for example.

b) In morphology, what stands out is the analogical extension of verb endings of one conjugation to another:

As in the Levant, the first-person singular and plural forms of the preterite tense end in *-í* and *-imos* respectively, which happens only in second- and third-conjugation verbs in Spanish: *gastí* [I spent] (for *gasté*), *despertí* [I awoke] (for *desperté*), or *tomimos* [we took] (for *tomamos*).

The second-person plural (*vosotros*) form of the future ends in *-ís* rather than *-éis: llorarís* [you will cry] instead of *lloraréis*, or *sacarís* [you will take out] in place of *sacaréis*.

The infinitive (and first-person singular of the future indicative) of third-conjugation verbs are formed like those of the second conjugation: *viver(é)* [(I will) live] rather than *vivir(é)*, *sirver(é)* [(I will) serve] for *servir(é)*, and *durmer(é)* [(I will) sleep] for *dormir(é)*.

There are other characteristic traits of verbs, such as frequent cases of first-person singular forms ending in *-oy* in the present tense: *tengoy* for *tengo* [I have], *vengoy* for *vengo* [I'm coming]. Also the verb *oír* [to hear] has the forms *oyer, oyo, oyis, oyeré*, for *oír, oigo, oyes, oiré; hacer, haciendo* [to do, doing] become *her, hendo*; and *ir* [to go] has *vay, vaite* in place of *vé, id* as imperatives.

Other morphological phenomena are the use of *le* for *lo* as a direct object pronoun, and of *la* as a feminine indirect object instead of the expected *le*.

c) In regard to non-Hispanic elements, it is worth pointing out that:

1) Gallicisms are not as common as in the later stage of Levantine Judeo-Spanish, as the contact with peninsular Spanish probably helped to maintain a clear difference between French and Spanish in the minds of the speakers. Consequently, the Franco-Hispanic hybridization that occurred in the Levant was prevented.

2) Contact between North Africa and Italy was almost nonexistent after the seventeenth century, so that the vocabulary does not include Italianisms. Of course, there are no loan words from Balkan languages or Turkish as there are in the Judeo-Spanish from the Ottoman Empire. On the other hand, there are occasional Anglicisms, such as *tippah*, from the English "tea pot," perhaps due to the influence of Gibraltar.

3) There is, naturally, the influence of Hebrew-Aramaic, the reli-

gious language, and certainly of Arabic, which the Jews spoke with
their Muslim neighbors.

Words from Hebrew are often from the areas of religious life, as
they were in the Levant: *šemá* (literally "listen")—the name of an important prayer, *kohen* [priest], *dinim* [norms, regulations], *megillah*
[scroll (of sacred text)], *galut* [exile] (normally in reference to the
Jewish diaspora), *goel* [redeemer], *mašiah* [messiah], *malah* [angel],
and *naví* [prophet]. Also, as in the Levant, there are many Hebrew
proper names: Miriam, Aḥašverós, Misrayim [Egypt]. There are also
set phrases that incorporate Hebrw words (indicated in bold type): *ser
un **sadic*** [to be a saint] or *echar hasta la **massá** de **Pésah*** [to be as sick as
a dog].

In many cases Hebraisms are distorted, generally according to Andalusian phonetics: the woman's name Maźal Tov is pronounced Ma-
saltó; *źehut* [merit] becomes *sehú; ta'anit* [fast] is *tanid*. In other cases
Hebraisms have Spanish suffixes: the word *tefil.lim* [phylacteries] is already plural, but in Morocco it has an additional Spanish plural ending,
tefelimes or *tefelines*, and that form is used to refer to the ceremony of
becoming a *bar mišvá* [son of the covenant]; *kahal* [synagogue] has as
its plural *kahales*.

4) Arabic influence appears both in vocabulary and in phonetics.
The complex Arabic vowel system has not influenced the dialect, which
retains the same vowels as Spanish, but Arabic has determined one of
the most characteristic traits of the dialect—the tendency to reduplicate
consonants in imitation of Arabic long consonants. Reduplication is
common in words of Arabic origin that begin with the article *al-: al-
zait* does not become *aceite* [oil] as in Spanish but *azzeite;* from *al-zahr*
the dialect does not form Spanish *azahar* [orange blossom] but rather
azzahar.

Reduplication also occurs in Spanish words, and not only in situations favorable to assimilation (as for example, *el rey* [the king], which
assimilates to *er rey*, or *contarle* [to tell him], which becomes *contalle*),
but in words where there seems to be no plausible explanation for that
reduplication: *asar* [to roast] becomes *assar, desear* [to wish] is *dessear,
puso* [he put] is *puśśo, mayor* [larger, older] becomes *mayyor*.

Although the dialect is practically extinct now, several of its characteristics
are still preserved in the speech of the Spanish-speaking Sephardim in Morocco today, some of whom have settled in the Iberian Peninsula. As a result,

one can now hear elements of Haketía in the contemporary Jewish communities in Madrid, Malaga, and Seville.

I have discussed the affective function of the preservation of these dialectal traits, the speaker's feeling of greater emotional connection to the reality to which he or she refers. Colloquial expressions such as *dar mancía* [to be pitiable] or *hacer una misvá* [to do a favor]; terms specific to Sephardic life, such as *las fadas* [naming ceremony for girls], *los tefelines* [religious adulthood]; and even phonetic traits such as preserving the intervocalic voiced *s* (/z/) (*caśa* in place of *casa* [house, home]) convey a feeling of familiarity, and their use implies some affective connection of the speaker to the context. Consequently, if one says that something is *de caśa* [homemade], it is much more emphatically so than if it were *de casa*. A person asked to do a *misvá* will feel much more obligated to help than one asked simply for a *favor*.

Language Registers

Up to this point we have considered various aspects of Judeo-Spanish, concentrating on its historical evolution, its geographic distribution, and some internal characteristics. However, not all the Sephardim of any given time and of any given place speak alike. Other variables—such as gender, age, occupation, education, and social class—influence speech, leading to many language registers. These were discerned more easily in the past (especially prior to World War I) than they are in the sparse remains of the language. Judeo-Spanish was not only more of a living language then, but it had not achieved the distinction of language levels—produced by greater cosmopolitanism, more geographic movement, the influence of other languages and of the media, all of which are true of modern life.

Four large social groups may be differentiated in terms of language register (as regards Levantine Judeo-Spanish):

1) The rabbinic and educated group, made up of the *hahamin* [Hebrew, wise men], a title given to rabbis and *melamedim* [schoolteachers]. They formed the traditional cultural element of society, and were educated in *yešivot* [Hebrew, rabbinical schools] and knowledgeable about the venerable traditional culture of Judaism: the Bible, the Talmud, the Midrash, the *dinim* or religious precepts, and all types of rabbinic literature in general. They often held positions in the community related to religious practice or education.

It is not surprising, then, that this group would use more Hebrew-Aramaic expressions than the rest of their coreligionists, which is precisely the outstanding characteristic of this speech register. It existed mainly among men, who were the ones given this sort of rabbinic education, but it was also heard among some women—wives or daughters of rabbis or teachers—who used more Hebraisms than did women of other social classes.

2) The upper or upper-middle class (whose members are occasionally referred to as *gebirim* [gentlemen]) was made up of wealthy businessmen or great bankers who often had political influence, especially in the Ottoman Empire. Their education level was quite high and not limited to the religious sphere; they often attended French or Italian schools and sent their children to Europe to study. There are few texts to document their speech, but some contributions to satirical periodicals that try to imitate their language indicate that the Hebrew-Aramaic component of their speech was less than in the rabbinic group. The number of Turkisms was greater, however, without approaching the use and abuse of them found in the middle and lower classes.

3) The lower-middle class (whose members were known as *benonim, medianeros,* or *balebatim* [home owners]), the lower class, and the *aniyim* [poor], despite their economic differences, held jobs that kept them in contact with their non-Jewish neighbors, for example, liberal professions such as medicine, small business, artisanry, banking and money-changing for the lower-middle class, and street vending, merchandise transport, manual labor, or domestic service in the case of the lower classes. They were characterized by a low level of education, generally limited to elementary religious training, if they were not completely illiterate (especially the women). Their cultural knowledge consisted largely of orally transmitted popular knowledge (sayings, refrains, stories, ballads, songs, folk medicine).

This is the group whose speech was most receptive to Turkish-Balkanic elements, as is logical given their continual contact with people who did not speak Judeo-Spanish. In addition, (a) they used pure Spanish forms, but these forms were considered inelegant by Sephardim from other social classes (for example, *semos* for *somos* [we are], *muncho* for *mucho* [much, a great deal of], *eshuegra* for *esfuegra* [mother-in-law]); (b) Hebrew-Aramaic elements are distorted or used with meanings other than the original, or both at once (for example, the biblical quote *ben porat Yosef,* literally "Joseph is a fertile sprout," pronounced as *benporayusé,* appears as an expression of admiration "may he or they prosper"); (c) the fusion of morphemes from different languages was more frequent than in other speech registers (as in the formation of affectionate diminutives of proper names: Isterulacha from Hebrew Esther + the Turkish suffix *-achi* + the Spanish morpheme *-a* to indicate feminine gender); (d) they made extensive use of set phrases, formulae, sayings, proverbs, and refrains.

4) The Westernized or *franqueados* [Frenchified] Levantine Sephardim in some ways constituted a social "class" different from preceding generations. Their culture was no longer traditionally Jewish, nor was it the orally transmitted popular culture. They studied *a la franca* [in French style] in schools where instruction was in a European language (French, Italian, German, or English); their occupations were different from those of their parents (with a marked preference for liberal professions); and they traveled to Europe. This cosmopolitanism came to Morocco later than it did to the Levant and consequently caused the progressive loss of the Ḥaketía dialect. In the Levant, however, these Westernized Jews began to speak a different Judeo-Spanish in which Hebrew-Aramaic and Turkish-Balkan elements were almost completely replaced by loan words and calques of French and Italian. The loan words even began to erode the Hispanic base of the language (so that *padres* [Spanish, parents] came to be called *ĝenitores* as in Italian or *parientes* in the style of French *parents*).

Sometimes the linguistic "class war" manifested itself in curious expressions, such as the following note (laden, as it is, with Gallicisms) that appeared in *El Ĵuguetón,* a Judeo-Spanish newspaper in Constantinople, apparently accusing the *franqueados* of using too low a language register:

En una konversasyón ke tuvimos kon una dama de Pera . . . moz dišo ke eya detesta El Ĵugetón *porke su avla ez muy vulguer i ke en el venten syeklo onde la enstruksyón i la edukasyón vinyeron al nivó, kale no solo avlar ala franka, ma tambyén bivir ala franka. No le vamoz a dizir a esta sinyora ke nwestra gazeta rindyó munčos servisyos kon su lingwa populer.* (Bunis, "Types," 64 n. 12)

[In a conversation we had with a woman from Pera . . . she told us that she detests *El Juguetón* because its language is very popular and that in the twentieth century when instruction and education have achieved such a level, it is proper not only to speak in Western style, but also to live in Western style. We are not going to tell this woman that our newspaper has provided many services in its popular language.]

5) Finally, and without getting into discussions of feminism, Sephardic women to some extent constituted a social class in regard to their language register—at least until the unstoppable wave of cosmopolitanism and Westernization reached the Sephardic world. They received little education and were often completely illiterate. Their participation in religious life was more passive than that of the men and was more limited to the home; consequently, they had less exposure to elements of religious culture (rabbinical literature, liturgical poetry). Also, the Islamic society in which they lived demanded a greater degree of seclusion and isolation from women, preventing

them from having contact with men and leading to meetings composed exclusively of women. Women, too, were the repositories of traditional oral culture. For all these reasons, women's language was different from men's language. Because they knew no Hebrew, their language had fewer Hebraic elements, or distorted those elements more. Their contact—necessary for homemaking—with salesmen, maids, laundresses, messengers, and assorted skilled laborers necessary in keeping up a house (painters, plasterers, carpenters), both Jews and non-Jews, gave their speech a more popular flavor, with many non-Jewish elements. Perhaps their attachment to the ballads, songs, and maxims, whose language is always very conservative, gave their language a more archaic character.

The Sephardim were conscious of all these linguistic differences linked to gender, education, and social class, as we can see in this humorous excerpt from the satirical paper *El Kirḥach* from Salonika:

los Jidyóz de Saloniko avlamoz de mil modoz i maneraz el Judeo español. Kada klasa del pwevlo tyene sus frazas; kada kategoria de ombres tyenen suz manera de avlar; kada Jornalista tyene suz espresyonez i kada uno i uno emplea suz byervoz i por tanto todos se dan a entender kon fasildad.

Por ešemplo, kwando kyeremos ke se alivyanen de entre mozotros syerta Jente pezgada, mozotroz lez dizimos: "Arrematasyón kon boz de kantar." Loz de la yešivá uzan a emplear: "Rux." Las mužerez dizen: "Eskova detrás de la pwerta." Loz nyervozos dizen: "Vazyando"; loz merkaderez emplean el byervo: "Espalda ke te veo."

Kwando en algún lugar non konvyene a avlar demazía loz mwestroz enkomendan: "Šetiká"; Bula Klara uza a dizir: "Mudera"; el pwevlo emplea el byervo: "Amudisyón"; loz de los klubes se dizen: "Sirmá"; Ribí Avram Agadol dize: "Yodéax lašón", o "Otro lakerdí". (Bunis, "Types," 62 n. 3)

[we Jews in Salonika speak Judeo-Spanish in a thousand different ways. Each class of people has its own phrases; every category of person has its ways of speaking; every journalist has his expressions and everybody uses his own words and nevertheless makes himself understood easily.

For example, when we want some boring[15] person to leave, we tell them, "Put an end to your singing voice." People from the yeshiva generally use "Rah" ("mercy"). Women say, "The broom is behind the door." Nervous people say, "Clear out!" Merchants use the phrase, "May I see your back."

When it is not suitable to talk too much someplace our people recommend, "Silence"; Bula Clara [a common woman's name] usually says, "Use a gag"; common people use the phrase "Shut up"; members of social clubs tell each other, "Golden thread." Rabbi Abraham Hagadol says, "He understands our language," or "Another word."]

15. *Pezgada* may also mean "pain in the neck."

CURRENT STATUS

Now it is time to ask the question, "What is the current status of Judeo-Spanish?" I have already explained how the processes of Hispanization and Gallicization in Morocco have practically eliminated Ḥaketía. Levantine Judeo-Spanish, which had already suffered a great decline with the Westernization begun in the nineteenth century, also faced other adverse circumstances. The division of the Ottoman Empire, which had been so permissive in the retention of cultural peculiarities of its minorities, and the birth of new Balkan states (Greece, Bulgaria, Rumania, Yugoslavia) also contributed to weakening Judeo-Spanish. These states required the Jews, as good citizens, to become a part of all aspects of national life (including linguistic life) and even prohibited publication in their language (as in Greece in 1936). The political fragmentation of states whose relations with each other were sometimes not cordial also created isolation among Jewish communities that previously had been in close contact.

Judezmo suffered another blow with Ataturk's reforms: linguistic normalization, campaigns to have everyone speak Turkish ("Brothers, you are Turks and Turkish should be your language" went a refrain hung at the entrance of many Jewish institutions—in Turkish, of course), and even the prohibition (in 1928) against printing in any but the recently adopted—and adapted—Roman alphabet. A good illustration of the situation is the short theatrical work *Lingua y nación israelita* [Israelite language and nation], printed in Constantinople in 1910, in which several symbolic characters—most of whom represent newspapers of the time—philosophize about which should be the unifying language of Judaism. The vacillation about which one to choose is explained in this way:

A_la [lengua] turca, somos obligados al patriotismo;	To the Turkish language we are obliged by patriotism;
a_la hebrea, somos atados al judaísmo;	by Hebrew, we are tied to Judaism;
a_la francesa, camino de luź y de cultura:	French, the road to light and culture;
todas las tres, obligo santo de natura.	all three, a holy obligation of nature.

(Romero, *Teatro* 1 : 320)

Despite the fact that the author—surely Zionist in ideology—leans toward Hebrew at the end, these four lines are not simply filler. The use of Turkish is felt to be a patriotic *obligation* (and, like any obligation, more or less imposed from outside); Hebrew is the Jewish language by definition; French is considered, also by definition, the language "of culture," which has opened the "road of light" to these Levantine Sephardim. Although the work was written in Judeo-Spanish, that language is not even considered. Doubtless the author already considered it a language with no future, limited to the emotional and family setting. If he wrote his work in Judeo-Spanish, it was likely as a concession to those social strata to whom he directed his Zionist harangue. Along the lines of this loss of prestige of their own language, we can see those Sephardim from Oran who, according to Bénichou, made every effort to mold their Haketía to contemporary Spanish when they spoke with Spaniards.

As if all this were not enough, the disaster of World War II gave the deathblow to Judeo-Spanish—directly by exterminating hundreds of thousands of Sephardim, and indirectly by causing the massive emigration to the United States, Latin America, and the state of Israel after the war. The exodus actually started at the beginning of the twentieth century. The Turkish-Balkan wars, epidemics, the economic and social crisis, and World War I had driven many Sephardic families into exile. With World War II, a large new wave of emigrants enlarged the communities in America and Palestine. In the countries of the Second Diaspora—and especially in Israel—the interesting phenomenon of language leveling occurred. The mixture of speakers of Judeo-Spanish from different places and social classes contributed to eliminating the distinctive characteristics of each area and social level, producing a standardized Judeo-Spanish, so to speak. The next step was—and is—the disappearance of the dialect in these areas of immigration. It is easy to understand that the Sephardim who went to Spanish-speaking America would soon adapt their language to the norm of their host country, and needless to say, the same is true in Spain. In Israel and the United States, the first generation continued to speak Judezmo, but social pressure, the need to become part of the new country, and mixed marriages, either to Gentiles or to Ashkenazim, made the new generation of Jews—who felt less Sephardic than American or Israeli—stop speaking the language of their parents.

There are some interesting illustrations of this, such as one by a woman interviewed in the United States by Samuel G. Armistead and Joseph H. Silverman:

> She had come [from New York] to California to visit her newly married daughter. Unfortunately, the girl had committed the indiscretion of marrying an Ashkenazi who, naturally, did not speak "Christian" and, since the daughter herself could now barely communicate with her mother, the poor woman was isolated and bored.   (Armistead–Silverman, *Tres calas,* 117)

Recent works on the language of Sephardim in the United States point out this progressive loss of Judezmo. A survey conducted in 1978 in New York and Israel showed that the grandchildren of the informants no longer spoke Judeo-Spanish, and only 52 percent of the children either spoke or understood it.[16] Another survey in Israel in 1977 of sixty Levantine Sephardim (twenty-four men and thirty-six women) between the ages of twenty-one and ninety-seven provided interesting results. Every single informant spoke other languages in addition to Judeo-Spanish (and some knew, to a greater or lesser extent, up to six or seven). The author takes pains to point out the difficulty of finding a speaker of Judeo-Spanish younger than twenty, as only two of the informants were younger than twenty-five (twenty-one and twenty-four respectively). Only nine people were younger than forty, and only fifteen were under fifty; almost half of the speakers (twenty-four of them) were seventy or older. All but eight had been born outside Israel, which indicates that the new generation of *sabras* [native Israelis] no longer speaks Judeo-Spanish but thinks of Hebrew as its mother tongue.[17]

Actually, the informants spoke Judeo-Spanish with the interviewer but addressed their children and grandchildren in Hebrew. They agreed with the interviewer that it was a shame that Judezmo was being lost, but they considered Hebrew the language their children should learn so they could feel fully a part of the country. Additionally, the informants seemed to have little pride in their own language. Some called it *jargón* [slang]; others admitted that they were ashamed to speak it outside the family or a close circle of friends; several remembered that in their native Turkey it was already looked down upon, and it was considered more elegant to speak French. One woman even told the interviewer that if she wanted to hear good Spanish spoken, she should not talk to the Levantine Jews but to the recent immigrants from Mexico or Argentina.

In an attempt to stem the tide, there are movements today working for the resurgence and revitalization—in a more or less artificial manner—of Judeo-Spanish. The extent of their success, and whether they will achieve a re-Hispanization of the Sephardim through modern Spanish, a goal others openly support, only time will tell. Unfortunately for dialectologists, indications are that Judeo-Spanish is disappearing rapidly.

16. [AN] Tracy K. Harris, "The Prognosis for Judeo-Spanish."
17. [AN] Arlene C. Malinowski, "Aspects of Contemporary Judeo-Spanish in Israel Based on Oral and Written Sources."

THE WRITING SYSTEM

I cannot end this chapter about the language of the Sephardim without first making some observations about the written language and its evolution. In the Middle Ages, the Muslims and Jews in the Iberian Peninsula were already using their respective Semitic alphabets to write the Romance language. That writing is known as *aljamiado* (from the Arabic ‘*agamîya* [foreign language], as the Muslims called the Christians’ language). The famous Mozarabic *jarchas* have come down to us, for example, in both Arabic and Hebrew characters.

After their expulsion from the peninsula, the Jews who settled in the Turkish Empire played a fundamental role in the development of printing in the East. Although the Sephardim used the Roman alphabet in the Low Countries and Italy, *aljamiado* writing (that is, the Spanish language written in Hebrew characters) remained the norm in the Middle East and North Africa. Needless to say, the use of a Semitic alphabet to represent the phonetic system of a Romance language posed a series of problems: how, for example, to represent the sound of the Castilian *ñ,* or the medieval phonemes /ŷ/ (as in *journey*) and /ž/ (as in *azure*), which do not exist in Hebrew? There was also the question of how to represent the vowel sounds, since written Hebrew (like all Semitic languages) generally includes only the consonants. Only in religious texts, where it is important that the reading be exact, is a system of punctuation, called masoretic, used to represent the vowels and in some cases the accentuation by means of a series of dots placed below, above, or inside the letters.

During the Middle Ages, *aljamiado* writing had solved these problems as best it could on an ad hoc basis, but the Sephardic printers of the eighteenth century created a true, coherent system, which was surprisingly accurate phonetically. They used a series of diacritic marks or letter combinations to represent Castilian phonemes that do not exist in Hebrew.

Thus, the Hebrew letter *beth* was used for the Judeo-Spanish occlusive [b] (as in *bueno*), but the same letter with a tick above it (called a *rafĕ*) stands for the fricative [b̶] or labiodental [v] (as in *vino* or *abrir*). The letter *zayin* with a tick over it represents the sound [ž], whereas without the tick it is [z] or voiced *s.* Likewise, Hebrew *gimel* alone is the hard [g], but with a *rafĕ* it stands for the [ŷ]. The Castilian *ñ* is represented by Hebrew *nun* plus *yod,* which coincides with the history of the sound, since it comes from Latin [n] plus semiconsonant *y* (Latin *ninia,* Castilian *niña*).

Vowels continue to be marked, as they were in the Middle Ages, by the so-called *matris lectionis:* a series of consonants used to indicate specific vowels. The *vav,* the velar semiconsonant [w], is used for both velar vowels, *o* and *u;* the palatal semiconsonant *yod* represents the front vowels *e* and *i.* The *aleph* (now silent) marks the vowel *a* or, when placed between two vowels, a hiatus. Because of this writing system, one cannot be certain if the word would be pronounced /vesina/ or /visina/ (both are possible in Judeo-Spanish); another letter combination could be read as *arena* [sand] or *harina* [flour] (since the Castilian silent *h* does not appear in *aljamiado*). This graphic ambiguity undoubtedly fostered the phonetic polymorphism so characteristic of Sephardic speech.

Many books used this graphic system, which was created in the great publishing centers of Salonika and Constantinople, in two print styles: *rashi* and square or *merubá* letters. *Rashi* print (from the initials of *R*abbi *Sh*elomo *I*saac of Troyes, whose biblical commentary is printed in that script) was the most characteristically Sephardic and was always written without vowel markings. Square or *merubá* print, so called because it was more angular, was generally reserved for headings and titles, or for religious texts printed with the masoretic vowels.

There was also a handwritten *aljamiado* style called *solitreo* or *soletreo* (surely derived from *deletreo* [spelling]), *letra de carta, letras españolas,* [writing for letters, Spanish letters] or simply *español* or *Judezmo,* the same as the language. It is in this writing (which, of course, had many varieties) that the majority of Moroccan literature appears, as there were no large publishers in Morocco as there were in the Levant.

The late cosmopolitanization of the Sephardim also affected how they wrote. Other alphabets began to be used, basically the Roman alphabet in its various forms: the Turkish style in Ataturk's new Turkey and continuing up to the present (a newspaper is still published in this style in Constantinople), influenced by French writing in other parts of the Eastern Mediterranean and in North Africa, in accordance with Spanish spelling among the Sephardim of the Spanish protectorate of Morocco. The attempt to become part of the newly formed Balkan countries also led some Sephardic publications to adopt the Cyrillic alphabet for writing Judeo-Spanish in those countries where that was the usual alphabet, just as other publications had previously written Judeo-Spanish in Greek characters.

In the 1920s, booklets were still being published in *aljamiado* in Salonika and Constantinople. Today this writing system has been completely lost, and there are many speakers of Judeo-Spanish who do not even know how to read *rashi* characters, who can make out the square letters in prayer books only with difficulty. The few people who still write in Judeo-Spanish do so in Roman characters, with continuous interference of Spanish, French, or Turkish and—in the case of the most highly educated—an attempt at phonetic transcription.

RECOMMENDED READING

For the different issues that could be considered in the study of Judeo-Spanish, see the booklet by David M. Bunis, *Problems in Judezmo Linguistics* (New York: American Sephardi Federation, 1975), revised in his article "Some Problems in Judezmo Linguistics," *Mediterranean Language Review* 1 (1983): 103–38; the articles by David L. Gold. "Dzhudezmo," *Language Sciences* 47 (Oct. 1977): 14–16, "Jewish Intralinguistics as a Field of Study," *International Journal of the Sociology of Language* 30 (1981): 31–46, "An Introduction to Judezmo," in *Los sefardíes: Cultura y literatura*, ed. Paloma Díaz-Mas (San Sebastián: Universidad del País Vasco, 1987): 61–86, and "Where Have All the Sefardic Jews Gone?" in *Los sefardíes*, 143–70; and the article by Haïm Vidal Séphiha, "Problématique du judéo-espagnol," *Bulletin de la Société de Linguistique de Paris* 69 (1974): 159–89.

On Ladino, see Séphiha's publications, especially his paper "El ladino verdadero o judeoespañol calco, lengua litúrgica," in *Actas de las Jornadas de Estudios Sefardíes de 1980* (Cáceres: Universidad de Extremadura, 1981): 15–29, and his books *Le Ladino (judéo-espagnol calque): Deutéronome, versions de Constantinople (1547) et de Ferrare (1553). Edition, étude linguistique et lexique* (Paris: Institut d'Études Hispaniques, 1973), and *Le Ladino (judéo-espagnol calque): Structure et évolution d'une langue liturgique*, 2 vols. (Paris: Association Vidas Largas, 1979).

A good summary of the Hispanic and Hebraic characteristics of Judeo-Spanish may be found in I. S. Révah, "Hispanisme et judaïsme des langues parlées et écrites par les Sefardim," in *Actas del Primer Simposio de Estudios Sefardíes* (Madrid: CSIC, 1970), 233–42. Cynthia M. Crews collects and comments on some of the most outstanding traits of Sephardic speech in "Some Linguistic Comments on Oriental and Moroccan Judeo-Spanish," *Estudios sefardíes* 2 (1979): 3–20.

On Levantine Judeo-Spanish, see the classic study by Max L. Wagner, *Caracteres generales del judeo-español de Oriente* (Madrid: Centro de Estudios Históricos, 1930). Also see Révah, "Formation et évolution des parlers judéo-espagnols des Balkans," *Iberida* 6 (Dec. 1961): 173–96, reprinted in *Hispania Judaica*, vol. 3 (Barcelona: Puvill, 1982): 61–82. Also useful is the collection of articles by Marius Sala, *Estudios sobre el judeoespañol de Bucarest* (Mexico: Universidad Autónoma, 1970), in which many observations on the Rumanian dialect can be generalized to all Levantine Judeo-Spanish.

On Haketía we cannot forget the old but very helpful series of articles by José Benoliel, "Dialecto judeo-hispano-marroquí o Hakitía," *Boletín de la Real Academia Española* 13 (1926): 209–33, 324–63, 507–38; 14 (1927): 137–68, 196–234, 357–73, 566–80; 15 (1928): 47–61, 188–223; and 22 (1952): 255–89. These articles were reprinted as a book, *Dialecto judeo-hispano-marroquí o hakitía* (Madrid: n.p., 1977), but unfortunately without correcting typographical errors and without the indices that would have made it easier to consult. Despite its brevity and tone,

Américo Castro's article, "Entre los hebreos marroquíes: La lengua española en Marruecos," *Revista Hispano-Africana* 1, no. 5 (May 1922): 145–46, is an excellent summary of the characteristics of the dialect. More modern and containing excellent interpretation is Paul Bénichou's article on the language of the Moroccan ballads he collected, "Observaciones sobre el judeoespañol de Marruecos," *Revista de Filología Hispánica* 7 (1945): 209–58, and its followup, "Notas sobre el judeo-español de Marruecos en 1950," *Nueva Revista de Filología Hispánica* 14 (1960): 307–12. For the last vestiges of Ḥaketía today, see Iacob M. Hassán, "De los restos dejados por el judeoespañol en el español de los judíos del Norte de Africa," in *Actas del XI Congreso Internacional de Lingüística y Filología Románicas* (Madrid: n.p., 1968), 2127–40.

The only work on language registers related to sociocultural class and gender is Bunis, "Types of Nonregional Variation in Early Modern Eastern Spoken Judezmo," *International Journal of the Sociology of Language* 37 (1982): 41–70.

For the current status of the language in the United States and Israel, see Arlene C. Malinowski, "Aspects of Contemporary Judeo-Spanish in Israel Based on Oral and Written Sources" (Ph.D. diss., University of Michigan, 1979), and Tracy K. Harris, "The Prognosis for Judeo-Spanish: Its Description, Present Status, Survival and Decline, with Implications for the Study of Language Death in General" (Ph.D. diss., Georgetown University, 1979). See also Malinowski, "A Report on the Status of Judeo-Spanish in Turkey," *International Journal of the Sociology of Language* 37 (1982): 7–23, and Rita Mendes Chumaceiro, "Language Maintenance and Shift among Jerusalem Sephardim," *International Journal of the Sociology of Language* 37 (1982): 28–39.

Bunis analyzes the characteristics and evolution of Sephardic writing in his booklet, *The Historical Development of Judezmo Orthography* (New York: YIVO Institute, 1974).

Further bibliography in specific areas can be found in Sala's *Le Judéo-espagnol* (Paris: Mouton, 1976), 10–75, and in Bunis, *Sephardic Studies: A Research Bibliography* (New York and London: Garland Publishing, 1981), 7–59, as well as in the "Biblioteca Sefárdica" sections of the journal *Estudios Sefardíes* (1978ff.).

FOUR

LITERATURE

JUDEO-SPANISH HISTORY, language, and culture have always had two
components: the Jewish and the Spanish. These two constants are necessarily
present as well in Sephardic literature in Judeo-Spanish,[1] which includes specifically Jewish genres (Bible translations, rabbinic literature), other identifi-
ably Hispanic genres (especially those of oral transmission), and a unique
genre that combines the Spanish and Jewish legacies (the *coplas*). Other
genres, which I call *adopted,* have made their appearance recently, reflecting
new influences on the Sephardic world; they are no longer either Hispanic
or Jewish but modern and Western. All of these genres will be discussed
below.

THE BIBLE AND RELIGIOUS LITERATURE

The most Jewish aspect of Sephardic literature, derived from strictly Hebraic
sources, is the series of works whose end is to reach the pious masses with
works originally written in Hebrew (a language the Sephardim generally do
not know), including the Bible, prayer books, treatises on morality, and collections of precepts—in short, an entire rabbinic literature very important to
Jewish life.

Since the Middle Ages, the Jews played an important role in translating
the Bible into Spanish. Medieval "Romanced" Bibles were created mainly by
groups of Jews, and as late as the fifteenth century the Master of the Order
of Calatrava commissioned Rabbi Moshe Arragel de Gualajara to produce

1. [AN] In the sixteenth century and thereafter, the Jewish exiles also produced a literature
in Hebrew, which was fundamentally religious in content. I do not deal with it here because it
is actually part of Hebrew literature. I also do not include here works written in Spanish by the
first generation of exiles, published in Italy or the Low Countries, because those works should
be considered a part of Spanish exile literature rather than Sephardic literature.

a biblical translation and commentary. The Inquisition would later look askance at these Spanish translations of the Bible, fearing that they might teach Judaizing converts the religion of their forebears. As a result, biblical translations, soon prohibited in the Iberian Peninsula, also went into exile. From the sixteenth to the eighteenth centuries, the publication of Bibles in Spanish was solely in the hands of banished Protestants and exiled Jews.

Sephardic Bibles follow medieval tradition, especially in regard to language: they use archaic vocabulary and their morphosyntax is a calque of Hebrew, the Ladino calque-language discussed in chapter 3. The oldest of these Bibles is the Constantinople Pentateuch, printed in 1547 by Eliezer Soncino. It contains the Hebrew text, a Ladino translation (in Hebrew characters), and a neo-Greek translation (also in Hebrew characters).

In 1553, Ferrara saw the publication of another famous Ladino Bible, this time in Roman characters. Two versions of the first edition were printed: one for Christians, dedicated to the Duke of Ferrara by its authors Duarte Pinel and Jerónimo de Vargas; the other for Jews, dedicated by its authors Abraham Usque and Yom Tob Attias to the powerful Sephardic woman Doña Gracia Nasi. Duarte Pinel and Jerónimo de Vargas are apparently the Christian names of the re-Judaized converts Usque and Attias. Thus the Christian version continues the medieval tradition of Romance Bible translations done by Jews for the use of Christians. The Ferrara Bible was reprinted several times in Italy and the Low Countries until the eighteenth century; it was printed again in 1946 in Buenos Aires.

In the eighteenth century Abraham Asa published his Bible (Constantinople, 1739–44), the first *aljamiada* edition of the entire biblical text. It is based largely on the earlier editions from Constantinople and Ferrara, and was subsequently reprinted in Vienna (1813–16). The nineteenth century heralded another of the best-known Judeo-Spanish Bibles, printed in Smyrna in 1838 by the Protestant missionary William Schawfler. The language in this edition is more properly Judeo-Spanish than Ladino. Several reprintings gave this Bible wide circulation in the Sephardic world despite its Christian origins.

Texts published in Ladino, however, were not limited to the Bible. Daily prayer books [*siddurim*] began to be translated very early as well as prayer books for holidays [*mahzorim*]. Both appeared in editions in Hebrew and Roman characters. There are still some Sephardic communities that print their own prayer books, although the language in them has been re-Hispanized to a large degree or is completely Spanish.

Especially popular for pious Jews have been the Passover *Haggadah* and the *Pirke Avot*. The former is the story of the Jews' exodus from Egypt, which is read during the family Passover dinner. It repeatedly praises God for having freed his people from slavery in a foreign land. The *Pirke Avot* [Sayings of the Fathers] forms a Talmudic treatise collecting the sayings of outstanding rabbis.

Books of *dinim* [ritual regulations] were also translated as well as the *musar* [ethics]. Among the former are some strange booklets for community *shohe-tim* [ritual slaughterers], generally people with little education who did not understand Hebrew. These books tell how to slaughter animals and how to treat the meat so that it will be kosher, that is, suitable for ritual consumption. Many of these booklets have Hebrew titles although their text is in Judeo-Spanish.

Naturally, the sensible Sephardic rabbis would want their coreligionists to have the ethical criteria that were supposed to rule their lives in a language they understood; therefore, the popular genre of the *musar* emerged. Some editions appeared as poetry, *coplas de castiguerio* [advisory stanzas] (a form I will discuss later), and others were prose. Some of the most important were published by the first generation of exiles, which illustrates how solidly this genre was rooted among the Jews in the Iberian Peninsula.

The masterwork of Sephardic religious literature is the *Me'am Lo'ez,* an extensive, detailed commentary on the Bible. It is an encyclopedia that includes all of the treasured knowledge accumulated over centuries by the great authorities on Judaism. It was written to bring to the people all of the knowledge of the Law and biblical exegesis, translating the Hebrew into a language all could understand—Judeo-Spanish. The title, *Me'am Lo'ez* (taken from Psalms 114 : 1), means "from a foreign place" and alludes to the *la'aź* [foreign language] in opposition to the *lašón hakodeš* [holy language] in which it originally had been written.

Ya'acob ben Meir Juli, born into a family of rabbis in Constantinople, began the *Me'am Lo'ez* with commentary on *Bereshith* [Genesis], which he published in Constantinople in 1730. His commentary on the first part of *Shemoth* [Exodus] appeared in 1733. He died at the age of forty-two in 1738, before finishing the commentary on *Shemoth*.

Other Judaic scholars continued his work: Yitzhak Magriso finished *Shemoth* and published the commentary for *Vayikrah* [Leviticus] and *Bamidbar* [Numbers], and Yitzhak Argueti compiled the material for *Devarim* [Deuteronomy]. The classic *Me'am Lo'ez,* consisting of the entire Pentateuch, was completed in 1773. First published in Constantinople, it was reprinted many times, in that city as well as in Salonika, Leghorn, Smyrna, and Jerusalem.

More than a century and a half later, other authors—Menahem Mitrani (from Salonika) and Refael Pontremoli (from Smyrna)—continued the work. They published the *Me'am Lo'ez* for *Yehoshua* [Joshua] and *Esther* respectively. Of lesser quality are the books of *Ruth, Yeshaya* [Isaiah], *Kohelet* [Ecclesiastes], and *Shir Hashirim* [Song of Songs], which are part of the so-called new *Me'am Lo'ez,* finished near the end of the nineteenth century and much less popular than the classic work.

The wide dissemination and popularity of the *Me'am Lo'ez* throughout the Sephardic world can be seen by its numerous editions and by remarks such as the following:

> Until the end of the last century, the several volumes of the *Me'am Lo'ez* were to be found in the homes of all Levantine Sephardim, from the poorest to the wealthiest. (Molho, *Lit.,* 266)

> How many times in our travels through the Jewish neighborhoods of Moroccan cities have we seen pious Israelites *meldando* [reading] the *Me'am Lo'ez* very attentively at the entrance to their homes, and even sometimes on work days, taking advantage of short pauses between their business dealings, at the entrance of their shops. (Maeso–Pascual, "Prolegómenos," *Me'am Lo'ez,* 34)

What were those Sephardim reading with such pleasure? It was, indeed, an extensive biblical commentary, but along with the biblical and strictly religious material it also included elements of *halachah* [legal and religious norms], the *Aggadah* (stories, anecdotes, legends, and pious tales), the history of Judaism, and philosophical and moral works. To compose the commentary, the authors relied on a large variety of sources: in addition to the Bible, they used the Talmud, works by Hebreo-Spanish authors such as Maimonides, Gabirol, Yehuda ha-Levi, Moshe ben Ezra, and Nahmanides; chronicles by medieval historians such as Benjamin de Tudela's *Travels* and the *Shevet Yehuda* [Rod of Judah] by Ibn Verga; some classics such as Flavio Josephus's history; kabbalist works such as the famous *Zohar* or *Book of Splendor;* and even non-Jewish collections of stories and fables such as the *Thousand and One Nights.* The result is a very extensive work that uses philosophy, mysticism, morality, history, astronomy, astrology, physics, biology, medicine, zoology, pedagogy, folklore, legislation, and the most varied materials to illustrate biblical commentary.

THE *COPLAS*

The *coplas, complas,* or *conplas,* the genre most characteristic of Sephardic literature, express the most outstanding characteristics of Judeo-Spanish culture in exile in the form of medieval Spanish verses. I collaborated with the Sephardic Language and Literature team of the Instituto de Filología (formerly the Instituto Arias Montano) of the Consejo Superior de Investigaciones Científicas in Madrid in the initial phase of their efforts to prepare a detailed catalogue of the *coplas*. Much of the knowledge gained in that project is detailed below.

The *coplas* are poems that are: (a) in stanzas; (b) frequently acrostics; (c) singable; (d) of assorted themes, usually narrative or descriptive rather than lyric); (e) of educated origin; (f) mainly transmitted in writing (although some have entered the oral tradition) and, consequently, basically men's poetry; (g) their geographic distribution includes the Levant and Morocco; and (h) they have been documented from the eighteenth through the twentieth century, with some dating from the end of the seventeenth century. Below is an analysis of each of these traits:

a) In stanzas

The poems are made up of a varying number of stanzas, from fewer than ten to more than a hundred. The most frequent patterns are:

1) Long or short lines—generally four per stanza, but sometimes more—with a Mozarabic rhyme, AAAV, where V is the end line that repeats the above or is a rhyme common to all stanzas (occasionally free verse) as, for example:

De mal hablar mos apartemos,	Let us depart from gossip
bien haćer unos a los otros miremos	and strive to do well for each other
y con este żejut veremos	and with this good deed we will see
vuelta buena en Ŝiyón.	a fortunate return to Zion.

(Tópicos, 6)

2) Monorhyme or alternating rhyme in quartets, with or without a caesura, such as:

Bušquimos por toda la civdad,	We looked through the whole city
como él non topimos;	and found none like him;
tanto grandes como chicos	adults as well as children
de corazón lo llorimos;	we cried bitterly for him;
sería por nuestros pecados	perhaps because of our sins
que al šaḍic lo pedrimos;	we lost the saint;
a esta raźón	this is what
a el Dio esclamimos.	we cried to God.

(Tópicos, 2)

3) Quatrains with an ABAB rhyme (or sometimes AXAX with the even-numbered lines in blank verse). For example:

Ajuntemos, mis hermanos,	Let us join, my brothers,
a cantar esta endecha	to sing this dirge
porque mos cortó las manos	because our hands were cut off
el Dio en esta hecha.	by God in this venture.

(*Tópicos*, 1b)

4) Monorhyme tercets, with or without caesura:

Hiċieron estos tenaím los jidiós con la	The Jews arranged these conditions
Ley santa:	with the holy Law:
Te tomaré como novia, que sos de vanda	I will take you as my bride, for you
alta;	are of high station;
te estimaré como se estima el yarḍán en	I will value you as one values a
la garganta.	necklace on one's throat.

(Romero, "Coplas," 80)

5) The Purim stanza (so called because it is used in *coplas* specifically for the holiday of Purim), containing nine lines of six or eight syllables with the rhyme scheme ABABBCCDD:

Hoy no queda más Purim	Today there is no more Purim
ni abrir las manos,	nor generosity,
no ayudan guebirim	gentlemen do not help
sus propios hermanos,	their own brothers,
para vicios vanos	for useless vices
sus ijos gastan	their children spend
a puñados y no dan	with open hands and do not give
de vente ḥaċino	one single cent
ni a sus sobrino.	even to their nephews.

(Romero, "Coplas," 78)

6) The floral stanza, so called because it is the form in which the *Debate of the Flowers* (for the holiday of Tu-b'shevat) is composed. It is a stanza of eight eight-syllable lines with the rhyme XAXAXAAB or XAXAXAXB:

Ya se ajuntan todas las flores,	All the flowers get together,
ya se ajuntan todas a_una,	they all join together,
que las crió tan donośas,	for they were created so graceful,
lindas, sin tara ninguna;	Pretty, with no defect;
diċen berajot en ellas	they say blessings over them
como diċen en la luna;	as they say over the moon;
ansí diċen cada una:	and each one says:
—No ay más linda de mí.	"There is none prettier than I."

(Romero, "Tu-bišbat," 299–300)

b) Acrostic

Generally the acrostic is formed by the first letter of the first line of each stanza (or, less often, by the first letter of each line) following the Hebrew alphabet, although sometimes it spells out the author's name or a short Hebrew prayer. Many poems combine several types of acrostics.

c) Singable

Coplas are poems to be sung, sometimes to their own melodies and sometimes to the melodies of well-known songs. Thus they often have refrains. The fact that they were sung made it easier for them to serve their didactic purpose.

   While often religious in theme, the *coplas* did not have the same function as liturgical poems or prayers. Their original purpose was to add to everyone's cultural knowledge. They were meant especially for those who knew no Hebrew (that is, the majority of the Sephardim) and who therefore had no direct access to rabbinic literature. These people could be educated through Judeo-Spanish texts, which were easily learned and memorized, and could be sung with coreligionists. The poems dealt with the history of the Jewish people from antiquity to the present; the meaning, motive, and justification for the liturgical cycle of festivities; the sensible doctrines of faith and morality; the exemplary lives of outstanding Jewish personalities; the hopes and wishes that have always guided the chosen people; the bases of the religion and the promises made by God to his people; the description of the folkways and customs peculiar to and characteristic of the Sephardic community—in short, the basis of Jewish culture. Consequently, many of the *coplas* were composed for or identified with specific Jewish holidays. Through the *coplas,* the celebrants not only felt united by song, but also gained a greater understanding of the meaning of the celebration.

d) Theme

As we have seen, the *coplas* can deal with any Jewish theme.

   1) There are paraliturgical *coplas,* sung as part of the celebration of any given festival in the liturgical cycle (generally in the home), that explain the reasons for the holiday. The Hanukkah *coplas* (from the eighteenth century) form one long poem telling of the struggle of the Maccabee brothers against the Greeks. Those for Tu-b'shevat (also from the eighteenth century) personify elements of nature (flowers and fruits) as characters who argue among themselves about their outstanding qualities. Purim *coplas* (from the eighteenth through twentieth centuries) include narrations of the story of Esther as found in the Bible and the corresponding Midrashim, along with other verses describing

folkloric celebrations of the holiday or mocking historical villains. Passover *coplas* (eighteenth through twentieth centuries), as one would expect, tell about the Jews' exodus from Egypt. *Coplas* for Shavuot (eighteenth and nineteenth centuries) describe the mystical marriage between the Torah and the people of Israel. On Tisha b'av, the *coplas* are *kinot* [dirges] recounting the destruction of the first and second temples, the captivity in Babylonia, and persecution in the diaspora. Even *Shabbat* has special *coplas* praising God.

2) Another frequent theme is didactic, moral, or admonitory in intent (eighteenth through twentieth centuries) to reflect on the futility of material goods and the banality of life, and to encourage good works. Because of their sententious tone and philosophical content, they are sung mainly during the *yomim nora'im* [days of awe or penitence] between Rosh Hashanah and Yom Kippur.

3) Derived from the didactic *coplas* are the more festive and satiric *coplas de felek* [Turkish, world, century, present day], developed at the end of the nineteenth and beginning of the twentieth centuries. They contain biting criticism of modern customs—customs that have turned conservative Sephardic life on end since the middle of the nineteenth century. These *coplas* satirize the liberty of young people, modern ideas, and revolutionary inventions such as the radio or phonograph.

4) Historical and news-bearing *coplas* (seventeenth through twentieth centuries) deal with matters affecting the life of Jewish communities. Their content ranges from the death of an important person to the founding of a city, from an armed conflict to a social function, from a coup d'etat to the salvation of a Jewish community from grave danger.

5) Hagiographic *coplas* (eighteenth and nineteenth centuries) are partly historical, although they follow a concrete biography. They tell of the lives and miracles of people considered to be Judaic saints. Among their subjects are the patriarchs Abraham and Isaac, chaste Joseph, rabbis venerated for their knowledge and piety, and even contemporary martyrs such as Sol Hachuel, the young Jewish woman who died in Fez rather than renounce her religion.

6) Zionist or *aliya* [Hebrew, ascent; the name for the pilgrimage to the Holy Land] *coplas* are also religious in theme. They praise the glories of cities such as Jerusalem or Tiberias and were commonly sung by those starting a voyage to Palestine, either as a religious pilgrimage or with the intention of dying in Jerusalem.

Even the Dönmes, the crypto-Jewish followers of Shabbetai Zvi, have a collection of *coplas*. The Shabbetaian *coplas* (seventeenth through eighteenth centuries) are esoteric and sometimes completely unintelligible. They have survived in manuscripts written by members of the sect.

Other *coplas* do not fit any of the above categories, as they deal with the most varied and unusual matters, but they always retain their Judaic reference. There are, for example, the gastronomic *Coplas del guisado de las berenjenas* [verses on how to cook eggplants], a sort of recipe collection in verse, telling various ways to prepare this characteristically Jewish vegetable. One can even find a gloss of the seasons of the year (nineteenth century) that compares each season to a phase of life, wherein every Levantine Sephardi of the time could see him- or herself.

e) Learned poetry

The *coplas* are not of popular origin as one might think. Often, especially during the eighteenth century, they were authored by rabbis who belonged to the intellectual elite. Such is the case of Hayim Yom-Tob Magula and Abraham Toledo. Magula wrote some admonitory *coplas;* Toledo wrote the outstanding hagiographic *coplas* about *Yosef haṣadik* [Hebrew, "Joseph the Just" or "Joseph the Saint"], perhaps the most important poem in Sephardic literature. The compositions of both authors show great rabbinic knowledge: they often refer to the rich and imaginative Midrash to introduce traditional Jewish motifs in their works. Use of the Midrash and other rabbinic sources is common in the Sephardic *coplas,* even in those that are anonymous. This is poetry written by learned people to educate their less knowledgeable co-religionists.

f) Transmitted in writing

As is appropriate for learned poetry, the *coplas* were transmitted mainly in written form, especially in popular booklets in *aljamía* printed and distributed throughout the Levant. In Morocco, where there was a dearth of publishers, they were circulated first in Italian editions and then in manuscripts.

Many of the *coplas*—especially those linked to specific festivities—became so popular that they entered oral literature, where they were reformulated and given several variants, as in the case of any folkloric song. Their status as traditional poetry allowed this genre, originally essentially masculine, to take on feminine values as well.

g) Geographic distribution

The *coplas* were most plentiful in Turkey and the Balkans because of the great publishing centers in Salonika, Smyrna, Constantinople, Sarajevo, and Vienna. Moroccan tradition has been preserved almost exclusively through oral

and handwritten versions, many of which reflect traditional Levantine
themes. They doubtless reached North Africa through Italian publishing centers such as Leghorn.

h) History

The historic origins of Sephardic *coplas* are obscure. There are medieval *coplas*
that would indicate a distant antecedent, the clearest example of which is the
Poema de Yoçef,[2] which, curiously enough, was written in Hebrew characters.
However, the genre does not appear in the Sephardic world until the turn of
the eighteenth century. The apparent sophistication of the supposed new
genre has made scholars wonder about the possibility of a period of abeyance
that could connect the medieval *coplas* and the Sephardic ones. The scarcity
of documents (especially during the seventeenth century) seems to contradict
that hypothesis and forces one to adhere to empirical evidence. There were a
few isolated *coplas* written in Morocco in the seventeenth century, and in the
early eighteenth century the great Sephardic cultural revival resulted in a large
number of *coplas* (known as "old" in later editions), the greatest part of which
were written by educated people who composed them under the inspiration
of rabbinic learning and in the hope of teaching in a pleasant fashion. The
genre flourished throughout the nineteenth century, when the so-called
"new" *coplas* were created and the "old" ones were reprinted many times. The
sociocultural changes of "modern times" were reflected in Sephardic *coplas* in
the late nineteenth and early twentieth centuries, when creative exhaustion
became apparent in the genre. The well-known *copla* writers of Salonika come
from this period: Sa'adi Haleví, Yosef Herrera, and, above all, the prolific
Ya'acob A. Yoná (b. Monastir 1847, d. Salonika 1922), printer and composer
of *coplas*. According to Albert Matarasso, Yoná

escribía poesías sobre muchos evenimientos que se pasaban en la judería de Salónika y vendía
sus brochuras y folletos, andando las noches por las calles de la judería. Y muchos judíos le
tenían consideración y respecto, mercaban sus brochuras a la valor de aquellos tiempos—
centavos. Las meldavan con buena gana; era el mijor pasatiempo de muchos.
(Armstead–Silverman, Yoná, p. 8 n. 10)

wrote poetry about many events that happened in the Jewish quarter of Salonika and
sold his brochures and pamphlets at night, walking through the streets of the Jewish
quarter. And many Jews admired and respected him, they bought his brochures at the
price of those times—pennies. They read them gladly; that was the favorite pastime
of many people.

Yoná published more than twenty-five of these "brochures" between 1891
and 1920 (mainly popular booklets, although there were also some single

2. An anonymous Castilian work from the mid-fourteenth century.

sheets). They were of varied content, including sayings, stories, traditional ballads, folkloric medicine, toasts for banquets and circumcisions, and so on. Among the contents were approximately fifty *coplas,* some of them reprints or revisions of older *coplas,* but a good number were original compositions. Yoná took as his subject the "many things that happened in the Jewish quarter" and used the forms (that is, stanza patterns, acrostics) of the old *coplas.* Despite their unquestioned documentary value, Yoná's *coplas,* like those of his father-in-law Sa'adi Haleví, show signs of the decline of the genre. They demonstrate lack of control of the language and of expressive devices, "traveling" formulations that spread from one *copla* to another, and padded rhymes. Even the themes become insipid and mundane (the high cost of living and the poet's economic hardships), or are of very limited interest (the fires of 1890 and 1917, the 1903 earthquake, the hailstorm of 1899, the death of a rabbi, a robbery in the port of Salonika, or a charitable party).

After Yoná, the Sephardic *coplas* were limited to an occasional short poem, mainly satirical, copying the form of well-known earlier compositions. They were published irregularly in newspapers or miscellaneous collections. These later Sephardic authors—and even some of Yoná's contemporaries—preferred to cultivate Western personal poetry.

TRADITIONAL GENRES

Of all Sephardic literature, the best-known genres are those that are traditionally orally transmitted. Many people have already heard of Sephardic proverbs, stories, and especially songs and ballads. These genres are basically Spanish, although at times one can see the influence of other peoples among whom the Sephardim have lived.

Proverb

Nearly all peoples have collections of proverbs, and all cultures embody adages, maxims, and proverbs that synthesize popular knowledge. A good part of the so-called sapiential biblical books consists of collections of philosophical and moral maxims, many of which originated in the proverbs of the ancient Hebrew people. Throughout the centuries, Jewish adages and maxims began to include the sayings of famous rabbis. The Islamic world, too, took, and continues to take, great pleasure in these maxims, which condense a great deal of knowledge into just a few words. An important contributing element is the richness of Spanish proverbs.

With such components, it is no wonder that the proverb genre would acquire special vitality among the Sephardim. They united the long tradition of Hebrew proverbs with the wealth of the Spanish tradition and enriched the whole with contributions from the Islamic world (Morocco, Turkey) and other places in which they lived (Greece, Serbo-Croatia, Rumania).

The proverb remains a fundamental element in Sephardic speech, especially among women. It was and is to be found among all social classes but is most prevalent among the lower classes. Proverbs have been written in Hebrew characters—as in the collection by Shelomo Israel Cherezli in Jerusalem (1903) or in Ya'acob Yoná's booklets—and have characterized the speech of the common folk in novels and plays (as in *Bulisa la refrandjia,* discussed in the section on theater). Proverbs still abound in daily life; there is no situation for which an appropriate proverb cannot be found. As the Sephardim themselves say, "Refranico mentiroso no hay" ["There is no untrue proverb"].

To simply list the proverbs would be interminable and tedious. There are some Sephardic proverbs that are still very much alive in Spain, such as:

Quen bien te quere te faće llorar [He who loves you makes you cry].
Quien más tiene más quiere [He who has more wants more].
Más vale un pájaro en la mano que ciento volando [A bird in the hand is worth a hundred in flight].
Más vale un malo conocido ke un bueno por conocer [Better a known evil person than an unknown good one].
Más vale ser coda al león y no cabeza al ratón [Better to be a lion's tail than a mouse's head].
Más vale solo y no mal acompañado [Better alone than in bad company].
Quien se echa con criatura s'alevanta pišado [He who sleeps with a child wakes up covered in urine].

Some of these proverbs appear in almost identical form in old Spanish collections. For example, the Sephardic "¿de qué civdas sos?" "De la de tu marido" [What city are you from? From your husband's] has its Spanish parallel in "¿Dónde eres, hombre?" "De la tierra de mi mujer" [Where are you from, sir? From my wife's area]. Likewise, "quen come gallina del rey flaca, godra la paga" [he who eats the king's thin chicken will pay for it heavily] is equivalent to the Spanish "quien come la vaca del rey, a los cien años paga los huesos" [he who eats the king's cow will be paying for the bones for a hundred years]. "El gamello ve la kambura de los otros y no la suya" [the camel sees the others' humps and not his own] is the Levantine equivalent of Spanish "el corcovado no ve su corcova, sino la ajena" [the hunchback doesn't see his own hump but the others'].

The Sephardic proverb collection also adopts maxims and proverbs from the people with whom the Spanish Jews coexisted. So, beside the Spanish "gato escaldado del agua fría fuye" [a scalded cat runs even from cold water] is this Turkish proverb: "quen se quema en la chorbá asopla en el yogur" [he who gets burned by the soup blows on his yogurt]. Sephardim in Rumania also translated proverbs from Rumanian, such as "hazte hermano con el Goerco fin a pasas el ponte" [be an ally of the devil himself until the danger is over, or until you get what you want], "el estómago no tiene ventanas" [your stomach doesn't have windows], or "el buey tiene la loenga longa y no poede hablar" [the ox has a long tongue and still cannot speak]. There are also proverbs of Greek, Bulgarian, and Serbo-Croatian origin.

Moroccan Sephardim added to their body of proverbs sayings clearly of Arabic origin. For example, to satirize someone who gives orders without having the power to do so, they use an ironic burlesque Arabic and Spanish combination that makes no sense to Spaniards: "¿Mnain jrej el mando? Men el hojera uel caño" [Who gives him the authority? The privy and the dung heap]. To mock someone who is trying to call attention to himself, they say: "¿Quién te miró, la emkohlá en la dolmá?" [Who looked at you, painted woman, in the dark?].

Some proverbs betray their Hebrew origin in their syntax, such as the rabbinic maxim, "Si no yo para mí, ¿quién para mí?" [If I am not for myself, who will be for me?], a literal calque of the Hebrew construction *im en ani li, mi li?* Some have even been preserved in the original language, such as the Levantine *yeš mamón, yeš kavod* [where there is money, there is honor].

Other proverbs seem to have come from within the Sephardic world itself, given their concrete allusion to Judeo-Spanish life. Such is "venga mašiaḥ, ma no en muestros días" [may the messiah come, but not in our time], commonly used by people who hope for an event to happen but not when it will affect them. Some of these proverbs refer to customs specific to given holidays, such as "después de Purim, platicos" [after Purim, plates of goodies], alluding to the custom of presenting others with platters of sweets on Purim. There is also "que darse mi hijo, que sea en Tesabeá" [let my son preach in the synagogue, even if it be on Tisha b'av—the day of mourning], used to express the desire for something, even under considerably less than ideal circumstances.

Lines of folkloric poetry have also become proverbs on occasion, such as "desdichada fue Carmela desde el vientre de su madre" [Carmela was unlucky from the time she was in her mother's womb], from the ballad *La mala suegra* [The evil mother-in-law], used to indicate that someone is at the depths of ill fortune. A similar Moroccan saying is "cobijó Ḥanná su manto" [Hannah hung up her cloak], a phrase of bad omen indicating that some misfortune has occurred or is about to occur. It is actually a line from the song *Nacimiento de Samuel* [Birth of Samuel]. The Levantine Sephardim also uses lines of ballads as proverbs, for example, "quien se quiere casar con moza que no espere a la vejez" [he who wants to marry a young girl should not wait until he is old], or "ruda menuda, guarda de las criaturas" [minced rue, protector of children].[3]

Popular Story

Stories that are told from generation to generation also comprise a very picturesque genre of Sephardic literature. As in the case of the proverbs, the Sephardim inherited elements from Spanish tradition and from the people among whom they lived, especially in Islamic cultures (Turkish and North African), which are so fond of stories and fables. Original stories were added to this corpus as well. These traditional stories are called *consejas*. Some Sephardim, however, distinguish between the *conseja,* any popular narrative, and the *cuento,* a fantasy with magical and wondrous elements.

Consejas and *cuentos* were used not only to entertain children; they also had an important role in adult life. For example, they served to relieve the tedium of long nighttime vigils.

> Before or after dinner, neighbors would get together and have fun, since at that time [during the time of the Turkish Empire] there were no newspapers, illustrated magazines or other pastimes. . . . If the winter nights were very long, how could they kill time? The only pastime left was telling *cuentos* and *consejas.* (Molho, *Lit.,* 117)

These stories were also told on the Sabbath and—something that is shocking today—at funerals or during calls on bereaved families, according to this report from Morocco:

> They [*cuentos*] were told, in addition to the usual occasions in other places, at funerals and "duelos," visits made by relatives and friends to the widow and bereaved family; another occasion is the "sabbá" [Sabbath] during the afternoon when stories about the Law are told in the synagogue. (Larrea, *Cuentos,* 1 : iii)

The themes of the *consejas* are those usually found in any collection of folkloric stories. There are very few stories about animals, but many deal with a trick or with a hero who gets out of a difficult situation by using his brain. Many turn on the opposition of innocent Jew/guilty non-Jew, or shrewd Jew/

---

3. Rue is used on babies, especially boys who have not yet been circumcised, to protect them from Lilith and the evil eye.

stupid non-Jew. In other words, the weak but clever hero is identified with the ethnicity of the narrator and the listeners.

There are also stories with magical and wondrous elements. In some, *"los d'embajo"* [those from below] or the *"mijores de mośotros"* [the best of us] appear, that is, evil beings from beyond the tomb whom one dare not name except by euphemisms for fear of attracting them. Some of the stories even allude to that superstition. For example, there is the story of a bride-to-be who is about to take a ritual bath when her ill-intentioned mother-in-law mentions the name of one of these devils on purpose. The devil, hearing himself called, appears, kidnaps the poor girl, and marries her.

The most specifically Sephardic of these stories are made up of two groups: (a) those that have Ŷohá (Djoha) as the main character, and (b) those peopled by rabbis and biblical characters.

a) Nasrettin (or Nasreḍin) Ḥoŷa (also known as Ŷoḥa, Ŷohá, or Djoha) is a very popular character in the whole Islamic world, where people still tell stories or jokes (in Turkish or Arabic) in which he is the main character. In Turkey he is considered a historical figure who supposedly lived in the thirteenth century in the town of Akshehir in Asia Minor. The Sephardim—both in the Levant and in Morocco—borrowed this figure from their Muslim neighbors and made him the main character in innumerable stories in which he represents the prototypical dunce. He is stupid and shrewd at the same time, easy to deceive but gifted at times, with almost infantile cunning that allows him to disarm his astonished adversaries. In Morocco, Djoha has a recent competitor in the figure of Yusico Lancri, a Jewish man who apparently really lived in Tetuan in the late nineteenth and early twentieth centuries, to whom are attributed many Djoha-type stories.

b) The second group of *consejas* combines specifically Jewish themes (for example, miracles performed by holy rabbis) with others from various story traditions. The Sephardim people these stories with biblical characters, rabbis, and other important figures in Judaism. There are stories such as the *Castigo de Ḥaim Pinto* [Punishment by Haim Pinto], which tells of a miracle performed by a rabbi of that name who castigates a Muslim official for not having shown him due respect. Another story tells of the miraculous discovery of the tomb of a rabbi from Talouet (near Marrakech), above which a Muslim cemetery had been established.

Other stories deal with biblical episodes (such as the famous judgment of Solomon), or their main characters are biblical: *Eliyahu hanaví y el pobre* [The prophet Elijah and the poor man], *El Destino y el rey Salomón* [Destiny and

King Solomon], *El pobre y David* [The poor man and King David], *Los tres consejos de Salomón* [Solomon's three pieces of advice], and so on. Many of these stories are not specifically Jewish but form part of a universal corpus. The Sephardim, however, place the characters in their own cultural environment. David thus is the prototypical king; Solomon is wisdom by definition, as are some very wise rabbis; the prophet Elijah, traditional protector of the Jews, is always an ally or the provider of a magical object.

Curiously enough, there is some taboo against telling non-Jews these stories

> that [the Jews] accept as law, that is to say, stories that come from the Holy Bible or that deal with morality or simply name characters from the Old Testament, as happens in those that attribute specific qualities or happenings to King Solomon, and all for fear of ridicule with the ensuing sacrilege and profanation that might be committed by enemies of their religion. Such a problem is very difficult to overcome, because of fear and the feeling of sin. (Larrea, *Cuentos,* 1:iii)

Ballad

As Ramón Menéndez Pidal noted at the beginning of this century, the ballad is the most characteristically Spanish popular genre; wherever Spanish is spoken, ballads are sung. From the beginning, scholars recognized the great vitality of the ballad among the Sephardim. Thus it has become one of the most studied manifestations of Sephardic literature, well known among the general public. Here are two statements that express this general feeling about Sephardic ballads very well:

> The old songs are still alive in Morocco, distilled from the old Castilian epics. They appear as early as the mid-sixteenth century in collections from Antwerp and Zaragoza, including some from the late-thirteenth-century General Chronicle, which Alfonso the Wise ordered compiled. . . . Listening to these songs creates a feeling of deep melancholy. They seem to revive the triumphs and greatness of old Spain. (Ortega, 1919, 234–35)

> *Traidas de Sefarad por los antikos avuelos espanyoles, a la ekspulsyon, estas romansas . . . guadraron la savor de las kozas antikas, i, el rekodro ke trayen al tino, arrebuelve el eskarinyo.*
>
> *Kantadas de djenerasyon en djenerasyon, avian sovrebivido al "negro olvido" . . . Los espanyoles en sus paes, i los de las ke fueron sus lechanas kolonias, kontinuaron a kantar algunas kuantas, ma el "folklore" aktual sefardi es kaje mas antiko i varyado ke el suyo. Mutchas estan pyedridas o olvidadas en los paezes de lingua espanyola, de manera ke los istoryadores i los savyos muzikologos ke las buchkavan, fueron obligados de venir a notarlas en las kokmunitas [sic] sefarditas de los Balkanes onde eran, dainda, el reflekto de la vida popular. (Torre, 132)*

[Brought from Spain by our old Spanish forebears to the diaspora, these ballads . . . retained the flavor of the past, and the memories they bring to mind cause
nostalgia.

Sung from generation to generation, they had survived terrible forgetfulness . . .
The Spaniards in their country, and those from what were their distant colonies,
continued to sing a few of them, but contemporary Sephardic "folklore" is almost
older and more varied than theirs. Many are lost or forgotten in Spanish-speaking
countries, so that historians and musicologists looking for them were obliged to come
and record them in the Sephardic communities in the Balkans, where they were still a
manifestation of everyday life.]

These two statements, so different in authorship—the first by a Spaniard
and the second by a Sephardi—and in the time they were written—1919
and 1982, respectively—provide food for thought in: (a) the reference to
two different geographic traditions (the Levant and Morocco); (b) the use
of *cantar* in the first text and *romansa* in the second to refer to the ballad;
(c) the emphasis on the oral character of this poetry; (d) the belief that the
entire corpus of Sephardic ballads comes from the Middle Ages; (e) the idea
that Sephardic tradition has preserved elements lost in the rest of the Hispanic world; and (f) the emotional impact of the ballads in everyday life.
Each of these points is discussed below.

The Levant and Morocco

The first text refers to "the old songs . . . still alive in Morocco." The second,
written by a Sephardi from Salonika, expressly mentions the "Sephardic communities in the Balkans." Like all Sephardic phenomena, the repertoire of
ballads partakes of two separate traditions that, although they possess common elements, show marked differences. Differences between the Levantine
and Moroccan ballads involve not only formal literary aspects (formulations,
vocabulary, use of specific refrains) but even more basic aspects (themes exclusive to one tradition or the other, significant variants, contamination, influence of the surrounding people's folklore). Extratextual aspects also differ
in the two areas—the ritual use of specific ballads in life-cycle ceremonies, for
example.

Nevertheless, the geographic division is not rigid. On one hand, there were
migrations and more or less continuous contacts between the Levantine and
North African communities, so that the influence of Levantine traditional
poetry in Morocco is evident (although the reverse is very rare). Even more
important, however, is the Second Diaspora, which led many Sephardim to
emigrate to America, Israel, and Western Europe. While the best versions of
ballads collected in present times may have originated in Salonika, Rhodes,

Sarajevo, Tangier, or Larache, they were not collected in the vitiated communities in the Levant or Morocco but in cities in California, in Brooklyn, in Montreal, in homes for the aged in Haifa and Tel Aviv, or in apartment developments on Spain's southern coast. Sephardic emigrants have settled in these areas, bringing with them folkloric songs. On occasion, as in Jerusalem, the foreign tradition brought by these emigrants has replaced another venerable tradition native to the area.

Romansa, Romance, and *Cantar*

The Levantine Sephardim distinguish between two genres of traditional poetry: the *cantica,* the name they give to lyric songs, especially love songs (which will be discussed in the section on songs below), and the *romansa,* a category including not only true ballads (six- or eight-syllable lines with assonantal rhyme in the even-numbered lines), but also other narrative poems that show some connection—thematic or logical—between stanzas. Consequently, in one edition from Constantinople, some admonitive *coplas* are called "*romansas* from which to take advice."

As a result, the modern scholarly definition of *romance* [ballad] and the popular Levantine Sephardic definition of *romansa* are not the same, although the Levantine Sephardim refer to ballads as *romansas.* In Morocco, any traditional song, lyric or narrative, was referred to as *cantar.*

An Exclusively Oral Genre?

The two quotations above insist that the ballads were "sung" and that "listening" to them created a deep melancholy. The ballad is doubtless an orally transmitted genre, but the efforts of the publishing industry to disseminate many ballads must not be overlooked.

First, many ballad themes came to the Sephardic diaspora from Spain in print during the sixteenth century and subsequently became part of Sephardic folklore. Later, during the publishing boom in the eighteenth and nineteenth centuries, Levantine Sephardim often printed ballads in booklets in Hebrew characters. Some very rare and exceptionally beautiful versions of these ballads are still in existence. In Morocco, where the publishing industry was less active, ballads took the form of handwritten manuscripts for family use.

Medievalism and Modernity

The two quotations claim that the origin of the Sephardic ballad was strictly medieval. They tell about "the old songs . . . [which] appear in the late-thirteenth-century General Chronicle" or the *romansas* "brought from Spain by our old Spanish forebears to the diaspora." It would appear that at the time the Sephardim were expelled from Spain, they already knew all of the ballads they now sing and preserve as a souvenir of Spain. A good number of these ballads certainly are medieval in origin, but others have become part of the repertoire much more recently.

During the sixteenth and early seventeenth centuries, Judaizing converts in Spain who retained contact with the exiles provided Levantine and Moroccan communities with ballads, as Menéndez Pidal notes, "These new arrivals, such as Juan Micas, 'well-read' Jews, certainly took with them some collections of ballads printed in Amsterdam, Zaragoza or Valencia, which were novelties and in style at that time" (Menéndez Pidal, "Catálogo," 1053).

These "new" ballads must have been about recent events, such as *La muerte del príncipe don Juan* [The death of Prince John] (sung in the Levant and Morocco), which occurred in Salamanca in 1497, or *El testamento del rey Felipe* [King Philip's will] (Morocco), which deals with the death of Philip II (1527–98). Artistic ballads were also included, erudite or satirical Golden Age compositions,[4] such as *Mira Zaide* by Lope de Vega, still heard in Morocco. Continuous contact between Morocco and the Iberian Peninsula also added to the Moroccan ballad repertoire a good number of modern and/or popular compositions such as *Mariana Pineda*,[5] *El atentado contra Alfonso XII* [The attempt to assassinate Alfonso XII], *La calumnia* [Slander], and even religious ballads such as *El robo del Sacramento* [The robbery of the Sacrament] or *Santa Catalina* [Saint Catherine]. These conditions are equally true for the countries of the Second Diaspora, where the Sephardim learned ballads that had not previously been part of their repertoire.

Hispanic and Extra-Hispanic Elements

There is much evidence that the Sephardic ballad, having existed in cultural isolation for centuries, is particularly conservative and has retained some very rare compositions that have disappeared in Spain and Latin America. The best-known example is the beautiful *Conde Arnaldos* [Count Arnaldos],

4. The Golden Age in Spain began in the late fifteenth century (c. 1492) and continued through the late seventeenth century. The date commonly given for the end of that period is 1681, the year in which the great playwright Pedro Calderón de la Barca died. Although the Spanish term for the Golden Age is *Siglo de Oro* [golden century], the period lasted for nearly two centuries.

5. A Spanish heroine (1804–31), sentenced to death for having made a flag with the slogan of the Liberals on it. She is the subject of a play by Federico García Lorca.

which is cut off in its peninsular versions, both ancient and modern, at the mysterious line where the sailor refuses to teach his magic song to the count: "I will only teach my song / to those who go with me." Moroccan versions, on the other hand, preserve subsequent episodes: the kidnapping of the count and his departure for home after a seven-year absence.

This, however, is not the only case in which the Sephardic ballad collection contains jewels forgotten in the rest of the Spanish-speaking world. The ballad of the adulterous *Doña Oliva* is found only in Morocco (contaminated by *El testamento del rey Felipe*) and in Madeira. The enigmatic *Amenaza a Roma* [Threat to Rome] has only been found in Jewish versions, with some fragments existing in Burgos (Spain).

Abrísme puerta de Roma,	Open to me the door of Rome,
las puertas me habéis de abrir.	you must open your doors to me.
Aunque no me conocéis,	Although you do not know me,
de oídos lo habíais de oyir.	you must have heard of me.

(Nahón, Romances, 8)

The sixteenth-century Carolingian ballad *La prisión del conde Vélez* [The imprisonment of Count Vélez] exists only in Sephardic versions and in one from the Canary Islands. *Raquel lastimosa* [Pitiful Rachel], regularly sung at weddings in Morocco, must have been extant in Spain, judging from the discovery of a seventeenth-century manuscript version in Argentina.

It has been impossible to find a single Spanish version for some similar cases. One such is the Levantine ballad *Galiana,* based on a French epic poem, which must have existed in Spain at one time. There is also the Moroccan *La Celestina,* based on the novel by Fernando de Rojas.[6]

Along with the survival of extremely rare works lost to the rest of the Spanish-speaking world, the Sephardic ballad repertoire also contains compositions that seem to be of Jewish origin. For example, there are ballad versions of *coplas* for specific religious celebrations. Some are based on paraliturgical dirges, such as *Los siete hijos de Haná* [Hannah's seven sons], dealing with the seven boys whom Antiochus Epiphanes ordered killed during the Maccabean era for their refusal to worship idols. Some, like the Moroccan *Mostadí,* refer to an episode in the recent history of countries in which the Sephardim have lived. Others have a specifically Jewish theme, such as the Moroccan *Cristiano celoso* [Zealous Christian]:

Señores, voy a contar	People, I am going to tell
una historia que pasó,	a story that happened,

6. A novel in dialogue form, *La Celestina* by Fernando de Rojas was first published in 1499.

de una infeliz hebrea,	about a luckless Hebrew maiden
querida de un español.	loved by a Spaniard.

(Ibid., 57)

This category also includes the Levantine *La conversa* [The convert], in which a girl

Judía, más que Judía,	Jewish, more than Jewish,
Turca se fue aboltar,	She turned Turkish [i.e., Muslim],
Por unos negros yapraquitos,	Because of some damned grape leaves,
Que non los supo bien guizar.	That she couldn't prepare properly.[7]

(Levy, Chants, 1:11)

Other ballads indicate other foreign influences. Occasional ballads are actually translations of French or Italian songs; many have refrains in Turkish, Greek, or Arabic. Most notable are some Levantine ballads that, despite their Hispanic appearance, are Judeo-Spanish translations of Greek ballads. Among that group can be found *Los siete hermanos y el pozo airón* [The seven brothers and the deep well], which begins, "Ya se van los siete hermanos, / ya se van para Aragón" [The seven brothers are leaving, / they're leaving for Aragon].

Another ballad of this type is *Sueño de la hija* [The girl's dream], which begins more like a Carolingian ballad than one from the Balkans:

La reina di Fransia	The queen of France
tres ižas tenía.	had three daughters.
La una lavrava,	One did handwork,
la otra kozía,	another sewed,
la más chika d'eyas	and the youngest of them
bastidor azía . . .	embroidered . . .

(Armistead–Silverman, En torno, 157)

Occasionally an old Spanish ballad has been contaminated by a Greek poem, such as *La vuelta del hijo maldecido* [The return of the cursed son], which is a combination of the Spanish *Conde Dirlos* [Count Dirlos] and the neo-Greek *La mala madre* [The evil mother].

The Ballad and Sephardic Life

Sephardic ballads are generally mentioned with a certain sentimentality because of their great literary and musical beauty and because of the extremely

---

7. [AN] That is, although a Jew, she converted to Islam [because of her mother's scolding] for not having been able to prepare a dish of *yaprak* (a Middle Eastern dish consisting of grape leaves stuffed with rice).

important role that the *romansas* or *cantares* have played in Sephardic life. Singing ballads has helped to fill free time, to lessen the tedium of housework or artisanry, to animate groups, to accompany games, to celebrate holidays, and especially to put children to sleep. As Baruh Uziel says:

los sefaradim no tienen que muy pocos cantes de cuna: este rolo lo hinchen las romanzas españolas de la Idad Media.

Si pasabas en las calles de Solonico o Constantinople atrás aínda trenta años meśmo, en una media día ensoleada, en una calle . . . asolada y muda, puedrías oyir alzarse a traverso una ventana abierta una voź dulce de mujer que cantaba un cante sereno y endorme- ciente: . . . una vieja romanza española. Yo me acodro de mi chiquez que teníamos većinos que moraban al peso de debajo el muestro, y cada šabat de mañana, a la alborada, toda la familia que posedaba hermośas voćes cantaban con calmo y escariño romanzas medievales, que escuchábamos con borachez y que ellos continuaban hasta espuntar el sol. (*Actas,* 324)

[the Sephardim have but few lullabies: this role is filled by Spanish ballads from the Middle Ages.

If you were passing through the streets of Salonika or Constantinople just thirty years ago, on a sunny afternoon, on a lonely and quiet street, you could hear through an open window the sweet voice of a woman singing a peaceful and sleep-inducing song: . . . an old Spanish ballad. I remember in my youth that we had neighbors who lived on the floor below us, and every Sabbath morning, at dawn, the whole family who had beautiful voices sang medieval ballads calmly and nostalgically, to which we listened intoxicated, and which they continued until sunrise.]

The ballad was always so much a part of Sephardic life that the false messiah Shabbetai Zvi dazzled his supporters by singing in his beautiful voice the erotic ballad *Melisenda sale de los baños* [Melisenda leaving the baths], to which he attributed a mystic meaning.

Ballads have been a part of Sephardic life-cycle ceremonies and religious celebrations. On the occasion of the birth and circumcision of a boy, *canticas* or *coplas* were generally sung, although there are also versions of the latter that have been made into ballads. There are many ballads for weddings, some of which are erotic. An example is *La princesa y el segador* [The princess and the harvester], in which the damsel asks a farmer to use his magnificent sickle "que l'asembre trigo, que l'acojga la cebada" [to sow wheat for her, to harvest barley], which are "en su puerpo" [in her body], "en su seno" [on her breast], or "debajo de su camisa" [under her chemise].

Another such ballad is *La galana y su caballo* [The beautiful girl and her horse], in which the beautiful protagonist represents the bride and the horse is, of course, a symbol of the groom's virility, as the ending indicates:

Lyya le azen la kama;	They prepare the bed for them,
para 'eǧar 'elyyos andaron.	to bed they went.
. . .	. . .

La fin de medyya noğe,	By midnight
'un ğugo mu'evo kitaron.	they came up with a new game.
. . .	. . .
Ganó 'el novyyo ala novyya;	The groom won the bride,
¡ke le se'a para muğos anyyos!	may it last for many years!

(*Yoná,* 25)

Ballads were also present in mourning. On those occasions, people would cry and sing a series of sad and piteous ballads, along with the traditional dirges, which will be discussed soon. There was a taboo against singing these ballads on other occasions for fear that they would attract misfortune. Some of them were historical, dealing with a death (such as *La muerte del príncipe don Juan* and *El testamento del rey Felipe,* which have already been mentioned); others dealt with unfortunate episodes of Jewish history (*Los siete hijos de Haná*). In others the figure of Güerco appeared, the phonetic descendant of Orchus, the Roman god of the inferno, the personification of death. Still others related unpleasant happenings (a kidnapping, a crime, a separation), which would move the listeners and so contribute to the catharsis by means of song and tears.

These same funereal ballads were sung on the Jewish national day of mourning, Tisha b'av, but this was not the only time when the ballad formed part of the annual liturgical cycle. Other ballads were sung on Passover, such as the *Paso del Mar Rojo* [Passage across the Red Sea]:

'En katorze de nîsān,	On the fourteenth of Nisan,
'el primer di'a del anyyo,	the first day of the year,
'el pu'evlo de Yiśrā'ēl	the people of Israel
de Ayifto salyyó kantando,	left Egypt singing,
ken kon las masas al 'ombro,	some with matzahs on their shoulders,
ken kon los 'ižos en brasos;	some with their children in their arms;
las mužeres kon 'el 'oro,	the women with the gold,
lo ke 'era lo más livyyano.	which was lightest.

(*Yoná,* 9a)

Ballads about Moses were sometimes sung during Simḥat Torah and Shavuot as well. The ballad has been a part of all aspects of Sephardic life, from the most playful to the most tragic, from the most trivial to the most important, from the happiest and most festive to the most sorrowful.

Song

Traditional songs (called *canticas* in the Levant) are perhaps the best-known genre of Sephardic literature. The nostalgic beauty of these songs, their popularity among the Sephardim themselves, and a great number of commercial recordings (of varying degrees of accuracy) have helped to publicize them now that the large collection of ballads is being forgotten.

Themes

Love is the most common theme in the Sephardic song, including much wooing of beautiful women, many demonstrations of fidelity or desire, and many lamentations of love. The typical confiding mother also appears, advising her besotted daughter; so does the ill-married woman. There are songs about soldiers going to war or lamenting being in the army; other songs have satirical or humorous themes. Still other songs appear in series, which will be discussed later, as some of them have become ritual songs for specific life-cycle or religious ceremonies. Within the varied collection of Sephardic songs there are even modern anthems of political parties or welfare or sporting groups.

Purpose

Although the majority of Sephardic songs are not identified with any fixed occasion, some have been used traditionally on specific life-cycle and religious occasions, as in the case of some ballads.

Birth and Infancy Chapter 1 mentions the night of vigil or *shemirah* when friends and family guard the new mother and her child to prevent their being harmed by evil spirits. Some ballads were sung during the vigil, but there were many more *canticas de parida* [songs for the new mother], songs that welcomed the infant to the world, and considered the suffering of the mother and the happiness of the *parido* [father]. Some dealt with the different treatment accorded to women who bore boys as compared with those who bore girls:

Las que parían los niños	Those who bore boys
comían los buenos vizios.	ate good food.
Las que parían las niñas	Those who bore girls
comían flacas sardinas.	ate skinny sardines.

(Larrea, Rituales, 72)

Another song lists the dowry of a newborn, which a good-luck rooster is in charge of obtaining:

Canta, gallo, canta	Sing, rooster, sing
que ya v'amanecer;	for it will soon be dawn;
si durmís, parida	if you sleep, new mother,

con bien despertéis.	awake to good fortune.
El gallo quiería	The rooster would like
una camišica,	a little shirt,
que bien le yakišea	which would fit well
en sus carnešicas.	on his little body.

(Attias, Romancero, 122)

The few lullabies also fit into the cycle of infancy (it was more usual to put babies to sleep with ballads). Some of these lullabies achieve great beauty within their simplicity. There are also songs that used to be sung to children when they went to school:

La Torá, la Torá	The Torah, the Torah,
mi fijico a la habrá	my little boy to school
con el pan y el quezo	with bread and cheese
y el livrico al pecho.	and a book in his arms.

(Molho, Usos, 87–88)

Weddings Especially rich is the corpus of songs for weddings. Although a few ballads are also used, the majority of relevant works are songs, in which parallelism is used almost obsessively, as in this song from Morocco:

Aunque le di la mano	Although I gave him my hand
la mano le di.	I gave him my hand.
Aunque le di la mano	Although I gave him my hand
no me arrepentí.	I was not sorry.
Aunque le di la mano,	Although I gave him my hand
la mano al caballero,	my hand to the gentleman,
anillo de oro	a ring of gold
metió en mi dedo.	he put on my finger.
Aunque le di la mano,	Although I gave him my hand
la mano al hijodalgo,	my hand to the nobleman,
anillo de oro	a ring of gold
metió en mi mano.	he put on my hand.

(Alvar, Boda, xxxiva)

Several of these songs have serial themes, such as the famous *Dice la nuestra novia* [Our bride says], sung both in the Levant and in Morocco, in which, as in other Spanish songs, the parts of the woman's body are enumerated by the use of a series of beautiful metaphors.

Among the themes for weddings songs are a great many, naturally, that praise the bride's beauty and the groom's gallantry. Others refer to the different phases of the Jewish wedding: showing the dowry, the bride's departure from her father's house, the ritual bath, the bride's hairdo, the procession to

the groom's house, and the wedding ceremony itself. Other more mischie-
vous songs allude implicitly or explicitly to the consummation of the marriage, to the sexual organs of the bride and groom, to the bride's virginity
(symbolized by flowing hair, a *camisa* or *delgada* [chemise] or an orange
blossom), and to the fertility expected in the union. As examples, here are
some lines from songs from the Levant and Morocco, respectively, in which
sexual matters appear metaphorically:

—*¿Quién buška a la novia*	"Who is looking for the bride
y viene deśarmado?	and coming unarmed?"
—*Las mis armaduras,*	"My arms
con mí vo [*sic*] *las traigo.*	I bring with me."

(Attias, Romancero, 94)

Ella se metió en la cama,	She got into bed,
en la cama me metí yo.	I got into bed.
Que ni sé por qué, ni por qué no.	*I do not know why or why not.*
Ella me entregó el tintero,	She gave me the inkwell,
la pluma le entregué yo.	I gave her the pen.

(Larrea, Rituales, 53)

Death Singing dirges during mourning was customary among the Sephardim
in both the Levant and Morocco. However, while a good number of dirges
have been collected from the latter, there is only indirect evidence of Levantine dirges. As in the case of any circumstantial poetry, dirges have a series of
motifs: praise for the kindness and beauty of the departed, the inconsolable
pain of the survivors, the emptiness in the house after the death, the painful
presence of the deceased's effects, the evil omens that preceded the demise,
or the irremediable inevitability of death. Especially poignant are those
which allude to a *malogrado* deceased, that is, one who died young, without
descendants:

Malogrado muere,	He dies before his time,
malogrado ya se moría,	before his time he died,
maique a todos duele	although it pains everyone
cuando se guardan	when they stay out of
de la luz del día.	the daylight.
Malogrado muere	He dies before his time
de hermosa frente,	with a beautiful forehead,
maique a todos duele	although it pains everyone
cuando no aljadra	when none of his
naide de su gente.	family is present.
Malogrado muere	He dies before his time
de ojos pintados,	with his eyes dimmed,

maique a todos duele,	although it pains everyone,
cuando no se casa	that he is not married
y deja un deseado.	and leaves no heir

(Alvar, *Endechas,* i)

An obsessive element is the mother, whom the dying person calls in his agony:

Mi madre, mi madre,	Mother, my mother,
no me dešís salir	do not let me leave
que si ya me dešastis	for if you let me
a žamás volvería.	I will never return.

(Martínez Ruiz, song XXIV)

The mother, on her part, despairs on seeing her child dead:

¡Quién me diera las uñas	Who would give me the claws
de un gavilane!,	of a hawk!
desde que se me ha muerto mi hijo	Since my son died
yo viviendo en pesare.	I live with grief.

(Alvar, *Endechas,* i)

Other dirges have themes appropriate to Tisha b'av, as might be expected. If dirges can be sung on the national day of mourning to increase the grief of those who listen, it is logical that the remembrance of disasters, such as the siege of Jerusalem and the destruction of the temple, would be sung on the sorrowful occasion of the death of a loved one. In one dirge, lamentation for the destruction of the temple and for massacres in the Jewish quarters in Spain are combined with the speech of a deceased young man who asks his relatives not to sell his clothes so as to not increase his mother's pain:

Aljamí honrados,	Honored wise men,
grandes de Castilla,	the great men of Castile,
los sacaban jorreados	they dragged them
por toda la villa.	through the whole town.
Lloren las señoras,	Let the women cry,
las que tienen razón,	for they have a reason,
por la casa santa	for the holy place
que era nuestro valor.	which we so esteemed.
. . .	. . .
Mataban a los chiquitos	They killed little children
los enfilaban en lanzas	they ran them through with lances
salían sus madres	their mothers came out
gritando como las cabras.	shouting like madwomen.
. . .	. . .

—*"La ropa de Pascua*
sacaila al solare,
con la pez y la resina,
mi madre, lo safumare.
. . .

    Cuando queráis vender mis ropas
no las vendáis en esta villa:
lo mercarán mis iguales,
lo sacarán en ajuar y en arjadía,

lo mirará mi madre,
se le doblará el pesare."

"My Passover clothing
take it out to the garden,
with pitch and with resin,
my mother, perfume it.
. . .

When you want to sell my clothes
do not sell them in this town:
my peers will buy them,
they will show them in dowries and as
    wedding presents,
my mother will see that,
and her grief will double."

(Alvar, Endechas, viia)

There were even dirges for children to sing on Tisha b'av, parodying those of the adults. Molho gives us one of them, in whose four lines some of the most characteristic dirge themes are condensed:

Sapindi, mapindi,
Ojos pretos como el carvón,
Sejas pretas como el tizón.
Que se malogró. Y ¡guay! ¡qué dolor!

Sapindi, mapindi,
eyes as black as coals,
brows as black as soot.
He died before his time. Oh, what grief!

(Molho, Usos, 263)

Songs and Liturgy There are few songs for liturgical festivals in the Jewish calendar, as such occasions make more frequent use of *coplas* or ballads. Nevertheless, some short children's songs for Hanukkah and Passover have been preserved. Best known is the famous Had gadya or *Cabritico* [One kid] for the latter celebration. It is a round, a translation of the Aramaic song that concludes the Passover *seder* [ritual dinner]. It lists a series of elements beginning with the kid that gives the song its title:

    Un cabrito y un cabrito
que me compró mi padre por dos ochitos,
y vino el gato y comió el cabrito
que me compró mi padre por dos ochitos.
    Un cabrito y un cabrito
que me compró mi padre por dos ochitos,
y vino el perro
y mordió al gato
    que comió al cabrito,
que me compró mi padre por dos ochitos.
. . .
    Un cabrito y un cabrito
que me compró mi padre por dos ochitos,

    One kid, one kid
that my father bought me for two coins,
and the cat came and ate the kid
that my father bought me for two coins.
    One kid, one kid
that my father bought me for two coins,
and the dog came
and bit the cat
    that ate the kid,
that my father bought me for two coins.
. . .
    One kid, one kid
that my father bought me for two coins,

y vino el Santo Bendito El	and the Holy One, Blessed be He, came
y mató al malaj amabet	and killed the angel of death
que mató al sojet	who killed the slaughterer
que degolló al buey	who slaughtered the ox
que bebió el agua	that drank the water
que apagó el fuego	that put out the fire
que quemó al palo	that burned the stick
que pegó al perro	that beat the dog
que mordió al gato	that bit the cat
que mató al cabrito	that killed the kid
que me compró mi padre por dos ochitos.	that my father bought me for two coins.

(Larrea, *Rituales,* 104)

Although similar series occur in Spanish songs, stories, and anecdotes with no more reason than the sheer joy of reciting them, the Sephardim attribute a symbolic meaning to this one, as Saporta explains:

El padre ke merka el kavretiko es el Dyo ke rigme i da la liberta a los djidyos kaptivos en Ayifto. El gato ke kome el kavretiko simboliza la Asirya ke konkuisto a Israel. El perro ke modre al gato simboliza Babilonya. El palo ke aharvo al perro es la Persya. El fuego ke kema el palo es la Matchedonya (Aleksandro el Grande). La agua ke amata el fuego: Roma. El buey ke beve la agua: los Sarazinos. El ke degoya el buey: los Kruzados (Croisés). El malah ke faze muerir al chohet: los Arapes. (Saporta, *Torre,* 151)

[The father who buys the kid is God who redeems and frees the captive Jews in Egypt. The cat that eats the kid symbolizes Assyria, which conquered Israel. The dog that bites the cat symbolizes Babylonia. The stick that beats the dog is Persia. The fire that burns the stick is Macedonia (Alexander the Great). The water that puts out the fire: Rome. The ox that drinks the water: the Sarracens. The one who slaughters the ox: the Crusades. The angel who kills the slaughterer: the Arabs.]

Origins

Are Sephardic songs descendants of Spanish songs? Do Sephardim sing fifteenth-century Spanish words and melodies?

Sephardic songs show the same traits as the language or the ballads: if, indeed, the Sephardim took Spanish traditions with them into exile, they were also influenced by the peoples among whom they lived and the circumstances of the time. Therefore, while some songs are Spanish in origin, the Sephardim learned others in exile from Muslims or Christians, and still others are Sephardic creations, born out of historical, political, or social events. An example of the first type is one of the most famous Levantine songs, *La morenica* [The dark-skinned girl], often used as a wedding song:

| *"Morena" me llaman,* | They call me "dark-skinned," |
| *Yo blanca nací,* | I was born fair, |

De pasear galana	From being out in the sun
Mi color perdí.	I lost my color.
"Morenica" a mi me llaman	"Dark-skinned girl"
Los marineros.	The sailors call me.
Si otra vez a mi me llaman,	If they call me again,
Me vo con ellos.	I'll go with them.

(Levy, *Chants,* 1:24, 21)

The Spanish origin of this song is proven by its inclusion in *Arte de la lengua castellana española* [Art of the Castilian language] (1625) by Gonzalo Correas. Lope de Vega (1562–1635) used it in his comedy *Servir a señor discreto* [In service to a discreet gentleman]. The Spanish origin of other songs can be determined by their survival in the contemporary oral repertoire of Spain, as in the case of the Levantine song about a precocious lover:

A la una nací yo	I was born at one o'clock
a las dos me baptiźaron	at two I was baptized
a las tres desposí yo	at three I was engaged
niña de mi corazón,	my darling,
a las cuatro me casaron . . .	at four they married me off . . .

(Attias, *Cancionero,* 1)

It also appears in Andalusia, with the following lyrics:

A la una nasí yo,	I was born at one o'clock,
A las dos me bautisaron.	At two I was baptized.
A las tres m' enamoré	At three I fell in love
Y a las cuatro me casaron.	And at four I was married.

(Rodríguez Marín, *Cantos* 4:354, no. 7445)

Other songs are of extrapeninsular origin, such as the previously cited *Cabritico,* which has been found in one version combined with a neo-Greek serial song. *La morenica* is sung in some places with a Greek refrain, and there are other songs with Arabic or Turkish refrains. It has even been discovered that a migratory stanza, cited below, is actually the literal translation of a Greek couplet:

Echa agua ante tu puerta;	Throw water in front of your door;
pasaré y me caeré	I'll come by and fall
porque salgan los tus parientes:	so that your parents come out:
me daré a conocer.	I'll introduce myself.

The contents of many other songs indicate that they must have been Sephardic creations. One example is the following stanza, in which a young man complains about having had to go into the Turkish army. It must have

been composed as a result of the Balkan wars, when for the first time Jews
were required to serve in the military:

¿Para qué me parió mama,	Why did you bear me, Mama,
Para qué me parió a mí?	Why did you bear me?
Me pariera y me muriera	I should have been born and died
y no servía al askerlik.	and not have served in the army.

(Levy, Chants, 1:78)

ADOPTED GENRES

The mid-nineteenth century saw new winds begin to blow over the traditional Sephardic world—Western influence. This was the time of the so-
called adopted genres, which were not previously part of Jewish literature.
Sephardim cultivated these new forms with a clear desire to imitate Western
literatures. Novels and autograph poetry were written in European fashion;
theatrical groups popped up here and there, producing their own works
along with adaptations and translations of plays from other literatures; journalism flourished.

Journalism

The first Sephardic newspaper about which information can be found is the
short-lived *Ša'ré Miźrah* [Hebrew, Gates of the East], founded in Smyrna
in 1845. Since that time, three stages have existed in Sephardic journalism:
(a) 1845 to the Young Turks' Revolution (1908); (b) 1908 to World War II
(1939–45); (c) 1945 to the present.

a) The first period was formulative, a time of hesitation, due not only to
the difficulties of establishing a new reality (journalism) in a milieu as conservative and traditional as Levantine Sephardic society, but also to the
problems of rigid Turkish censorship. Despite those obstacles, some of the
most prestigious and long-lived papers were founded during this time and
continued through the second stage: *La Buena Esperanza* [Good hope]
(Smyrna, 1871); *El Tiempo* [Time] (Istanbul, 1871); *La Época* [The epoch]
(Salonika, 1875); *El Telégrafo* (Istanbul, 1879); *El Avenir* [The future] (Salonika, 1898).

b) The Turkish revolution engendered greater political and journalistic
freedom throughout the dying Turkish Empire. This freedom of expression
aided Sephardic journalism, which reached its heights during the thirty-year
period before the outbreak of World War II. The majority of Sephardic newspapers date from this period, as do some of the most outstanding figures in
Sephardic journalism (editors, directors, columnists, sometimes all in one

person): Isaac Gabay (Constantinople), Isaac de Botton (Salonika, Xanzi), Isaac Algazi (Constantinople, Alexandria), the folklorist David Elnecave (Constantinople), David Fresco (Constantinople), Shelomo Israel Cherezli (Jerusalem—also the author of a Judeo-Spanish dictionary). Many who had made names for themselves in the first stage of Sephardic journalism continued their work throughout this time, as, for example, Abraham Galante (Constantinople, Cairo).

c) World War II dealt a deathblow to Sephardic journalism, as it did to the Jewish world as a whole. The extermination of entire communities and the dispersion of survivors was the ruination of Sephardic journalism. Today Sephardic associations and communities in Spain, Israel, and America print almost exclusively newsletters for internal circulation—in modern Spanish. Istanbul still has a weekly paper, *Şalom* [Greetings], in Judeo-Spanish, but an increasing number of articles are printed in Turkish. Tel Aviv has *La Luz de Israel* [Light of Israel] in Judeo-Spanish. Other groups attempting to revive "Judezmo," for more or less academic reasons, have begun to release their own publications. Such is the case of *Aki Yerushalayim* [Here is Jerusalem], published semiannually in Jerusalem, thanks to the efforts of Moshé Shaul and his colleagues from the Judeo-Spanish broadcasts on Radio Israel. *Vidas Largas* [Long lives] is the publication of an association of the same name, based in Paris and directed by Haïm Vidal Séphiha. There was also the bulletin, now apparently extinct, *Ké Xaver?* [What's up?] from the Adelantre! [Forward!] association in New York.[8]

This is the state to which the Sephardic press has been reduced, a press that from its birth through 1939 included over three hundred titles, covering an area from Jerusalem and Jaffa to New York (where more than ten papers were published), and including contemporary Turkey (Smyrna and Constantinople), Greece (especially Salonika, but also Xanzi and Rhodes), Bulgaria (Sofia, Ruse, Plovdiv), Rumania (Turnu-Severin), Yugoslavia (Belgrade), Austria (Vienna), and Egypt (Alexandria, Cairo). Some of these publications were so short-lived that they can barely be called periodicals, as in the case of the Judeo-Spanish supplement *Al haMišmar* [Hebrew, On guard], which published only one issue, dealing with elections in Tel Aviv in 1944. Others lasted for more than fifty years, such as the Istanbul weeklies *El Tiempo* and *El Telégrafo*.

8. A new bulletin, *Los Muestros* [Our people], made its first appearance in 1990. It is being published in Brussels under the editorship of Moïse V. Rahmani, with specific emphasis on Sephardim from Rhodes. *Los Muestros* is trilingual, with articles in Judeo-Spanish, French, and English.

The majority of these periodicals were published in *aljamiado* (Judeo-Spanish written in Hebrew characters), especially during their era of splendor, but some used other alphabets, including Cyrillic. The Roman alphabet displaced *aljamiado* as the decline continued. There were also publications in other languages: Turkish, Greek, Bulgarian, Arabic, and so on, depending on the country in which they appeared. Many were in French because of the influence of the Alliance Israélite Universelle, and there is even one Sephardic publication in—of all languages—Yiddish! An outstanding example is the official organ *Salonic* (founded in Salonika in 1869), which was printed in Judeo-Spanish, Bulgarian, Turkish, and Greek. Hebrew, the holy language by definition—read in religious services but not understood—rarely appeared in Sephardic publications, even in those cases where the newspapers had Hebrew names. *Carmí šeli* [My vineyard] from Vienna and *HaMenorá* [The lamp] from Istanbul were published in Judeo-Spanish or French.

A glance through titles is sufficient to show that these publications expressed the points of view of the most varied groups, subgroups, and clusters in the Sephardic world in the late nineteenth and early twentieth centuries. Titles such as *El Macabeo* [The Maccabee] or *La Renacencia judía* [Jewish renaissance] (both from Salonika) evoke active Zionist groups. *El Pueblo* [The people], *La Solidaridad Obradera* [Workers' solidarity] (both from Salonika), *La Voz del Pueblo* [Voice of the people] (Smyrna, Salonika) and *El Amigo del Pueblo* [Friend of the people] (Belgrade) transmitted socialist ideology. *La Vara* [The staff], from Salonika, was still more radical, a newspaper with "tendencias comunistas extremistas, manifiestas y abiertas para harbar a derecha y iztiedra sin piadad, sin hatir contra la religión y la burguasía, contra el sionismo y la colonización judía en Palestina." ["extremist communist tendencies, manifest and open to hit right and left without pity, with no consideration for religion and the bourgeoisie, against Zionism and Jewish colonization in Palestine"].

In contrast is the calm reflected in titles like *El Imparcial* [Unbiased] (Salonika), *El Liberal* [Liberal] (Jerusalem, Salonika), *La Tribuna Líbera* [Free tribune], and *La Verdad* [The truth] (both from Salonika). Others show the efforts of progressive groups to keep up with the times: *El Tiempo*, *El Telégrafo* (both from Constantinople), *El Progreso* (Xanzi), *La Época* (Salonika), *El Instructor* (Constantinople), *Avanti* [Forward], and *El Avenir* (both from Salonika). The fact that being *à la page* was intimately connected to being up to date in French culture is reflected in a number of periodicals with titles in or influenced by French: *El Guión–Le trait d'union* [The guide–The footprints of togetherness] (Smyrna, in French); *El Nuvelista* [New news]

(Smyrna, in Judeo-Spanish, but with a title derived from the French *nouvelle* [news item]); and *Le Flambeau* [The torch] (Salonika, in French). Some of the titles seem strange, such as *El Amigo de la Familia* [Friend of the family] (Constantinople); *La Buena Esperanza* [Good hope] (Smyrna); and *El Luzero de la Pasensia* [The torch of patience] (Turnu-Severin).

There are a large number of satirical publications. Some of their titles allude to their contents, such as *El Kirbach* [Turkish, Whip] (Salonika); *El Burlón* [The joker] (Salonika, Constantinople); *El Chaketón* [Turkish, Slap] (Salonika); *Charló* [i.e., Charlot—French, Charlie Chaplin] (Salonika); *El Gracioso* [The comedian], *El Jugetón* [Playful] (both from Constantinople); and *El Descarado* [Rogue] (Jerusalem), which calls itself a "jurnal anual de insolencia, de descaradez, de punchones, de burla y de maskaralik" ["annual journal of insolence, impudence, quips, satire and sarcasm"].

There are also irregular publications, such as *El Foburgo* (from French *faubourg*, "suburb") founded in Salonika after the great fire of 1917, and the previously mentioned *Al haMišMar,* which appeared in Tel Aviv before a political election. Others served special interests: *El Mundo Sefaradí* [Sephardic world] (Vienna) was specifically for the publication of folkloric materials "antes que se depiedran enteramente" ["before they are completely lost"]. *Alilat haDam* [Hebrew, The blood libel] was established in Bulgaria in 1894 to combat blood-libel accusations. *Dirito* [Right, law] (Salonika) attempted to develop harmonious coexistence and mutual understanding between Jews and Christians. *Los Misterios de la Natura* [Mysteries of nature] (Salonika) was a publication dedicated to the "ciencias ocultas: mañatismo, hipnotismo, mágica, spiritismo, estrología, telepatía, quiromancía" ["occult sciences: illusionism, hypnotism, magic, spiritism, astrology, telepathy, palmistry"]. There was an endless series of such publications: official Jewish institutions (community, head rabbinate), political groups (especially Zionists and socialists), welfare and cultural societies (hospitals, schools, centers for the distribution of clothes to the poor), informal literary and political groups, and even groups of friends had their own newsletters. These documents are now invaluable for research on the Sephardic world. They show the evolution of ideas and the adoption of new customs, political tensions, social realities, tradition and folklore, the everyday life of the Sephardic world, and the relationship between the Jews and their neighbors (Turks, Greeks, Bulgarians, and Serbo-Croatians), the history and economy of the Jewish communities, the struggle between traditional Jewish education and new educational methods defended by the progressives, the popular view of morality and religion, the frivolities of high society, and serious rabbinical recommendations.

In short, the Sephardic press is a limitless source not only for historians, sociologists, and folklorists, but also—and especially—for those interested in language and literature. The language of the press shows the evolution of Judeo-Spanish from the end of the nineteenth century to the present. Periodicals were often the vehicles for disseminating autograph poetry, plays, and novels, whether they published the works as columns or as serials.

Narrative

The little-studied Judeo-Spanish novel (*romanso*) reached its greatest moment of productivity between 1900 and 1933, with a gap from 1914 to 1920 due to World War I. As one would expect, the most active publishing centers were the large Levantine communities: Constantinople and Salonika and, to a lesser extent, Smyrna, Jerusalem, Vienna, Belgrade, and Sofia.

Serials were very common during this period, either in collectible volumes or as pamphlets included in newspapers, although complete editions were also published. Newspapers such as *El Tiempo* or *El Telégrafo* (both from Constantinople), *El Meseret* (from Turkish, *meserret*, "happiness, celebration"; from Smyrna), *El Tresoro de Yerušalayim* [The treasure of Jerusalem] (Jerusalem), *El Avenir, El Liberal, La Voz del Pueblo* (all from Salonika), *La Vara* (Cairo, New York), and *La América* (New York) all published collections of novels or included them within their papers. Newspapers also published novels as pamphlets and then sold the pamphlets bound together as separate publications.

Relatively few of these texts are original. Of the approximately three hundred titles catalogued to date, fewer than half are true Sephardic creations. Many texts are *"imitados," "adaptados," "aranjados," "resumidos," "reescritos,"* and, especially, *"tresladados"* [imitated, adapted, arranged, summarized, rewritten, translated] by Sephardic authors in Judeo-Spanish, taken from originals in other languages, such as German, Greek, Italian, Russian, Turkish, and even English. The vast majority of texts, however, are in Hebrew and French, perfectly understandable, given the influence of the Zionist movement (for Hebrew) and of the Alliance Israélite Universelle (for French).

Hebrew served mainly as a bridge between other languages and Judeo-Spanish. In that language the Sephardim first discovered Ashkenazi authors (who had written in Yiddish, Polish, and so on), classical authors such as Shakespeare and even Russians such as Tolstoy, all of whom had been translated into Hebrew. Those texts were now translated from Hebrew into Judeo-Spanish.

Sephardic "authors" were often inspired by works written in French or translated into that language. Particularly popular were the preromantics, romantics, and postromantics. Eugène Prévost's *Manon Lescaut* appeared in Jerusalem in a Judezmo translation in 1905. Other such works were Jacques-Henri Bernardin de Saint-Pierre's *Paul et Virginie* (Jerusalem, 1912), the Dumas' *Camille* (Salonika, 1922) and *Count of Montecristo* (Salonika, 1926, and New York, 1928), Victor Hugo's *Les Misérables* (New York, 1921), a work also adapted for the theater, and *The Mysteries of Paris* by Eugène Sue (Constantinople, 1891).

Among French realists and naturalists, the only author to whom the Sephardim paid much attention was Emile Zola, due to his prestige in the Jewish world because of his intervention in the Dreyfus affair.[9] His short novel *Nantas* was published in Jerusalem in 1904. French was also the language in which Sephardim discovered other European authors, especially Russians such as Tolstoy, Maxim Gorky, and Fyodor Dostoyevski.

In contrast to this proliferation of French works and the interest the Sephardim showed in the literature of other countries, the Spanish novel was almost completely unknown to them. If the Sephardim knew anything about the Spanish narrative, it was through their readings in French. This is clearly demonstrated by the publicist Itzhak Ben-Rubi in a note dealing with the familiarity with *Don Quixote*[10] among Levantine Sephardim:

> *rarissimos, por no decir inexistientes, son aqueyos que conossieron al genial Cervantes y su obra* Don Quijote *por la lectura de libros en español o en judeo-español. Libros semejantes no fueron metidos entre nuestras manos, en español, y no vieron la luz en judeo-español.*
>
> *Esto no quiere decir que las classas intelectualas como también las massas de escolarios bivieron en la ignorancia de este "capolavoro", uno de los muy raros que el genio humano producio.*
>
> *Mientres que España se ulvidava completamente de las aglomeraciones sefarditas* hablando la lingua de Cervantes, *el govierno Frances, las escuelas religiosas francesas, como también las famosas escuelas de la "Alliance Israélite Universelle", se empleavan a la difusion, la illustracion y la propaganda de la lingua francesa. Fue por sus libros que yo, come diezenas de miles de sefarditas, conocimos a Cervantes.* (Ben-Rubi, "Don Quijote," 374)

9. [AN] The Dreyfus affair, a scandal that erupted in France in 1894, had a great effect on European public opinion. Captain Dreyfus, a Jew, was accused of having stolen some secret plans and was sentenced to life at hard labor in French Guiana. Anti-Semitism apparently played a role in his being found guilty. Years later, his innocence was discovered and he was pardoned. The first person to support Dreyfus publicly, creating a furor over French anti-Semitism, was Émile Zola, who in 1898 published a scathing article, "J'accuse" [I accuse], defending the supposed Jewish spy.

10. The first part of *Don Quixote*, by Miguel de Cervantes, was published in 1605; the second part appeared ten years later.

[very rare, if not nonexistent, are those who knew the genius of Cervantes and his work *Don Quixote* through reading *books in Spanish or in Judeo-Spanish*. Such books were never given to us in Spanish, and they were not published in Judeo-Spanish.

This does not mean that the intellectuals as well as the masses of scholars lived in ignorance of this "masterpiece," one of the very few produced by human genius.

While Spain completely forgot about the Sephardic communities *who spoke the language of Cervantes,* the French government, French religious schools, as well as the famous schools of the "Alliance Israélite Universelle," labored for the dissemination, explanation and publicity of the French language. It was through their books that I, like tens of thousands of Sephardim, came to know Cervantes.]

Works in French, like those in Hebrew, were translated, adapted, or revised, often very freely and generally with no indication that they were translations or adaptations. Consequently, many revisions were printed as if they were original works. (As will be seen shortly, the same course was taken in the theater.)

Violent and sentimental themes were quite popular among the Sephardim, and there were many titles such as *Anna María o el corazón de mujer* [Anna Maria or a woman's heart] (Cairo, 1905); *Una familla de matadores* [A family of killers] (Jerusalem, 1908); *La güerfanica desmamparada* [The deserted orphan girl] (Constantinople, 1923); *La hija de dos padres* [The girl with two fathers] (Cairo, 1907); *La bebedera de sangre* [The blood-drinking woman] (Salonika, 1928); *La hermośa historia de la hija maldicha* [The beautiful story of the cursed girl] (Constantinople, 1901); *Una venganza salvaje* [Savage vengeance] (Smyrna, 1913); *¡Pasion!* [Passion!] (Salonika, 1922); and *Amor sin esperanza* [Hopeless love] (Cairo, 1900). Also very popular, to judge from the frequency with which they appeared, were detective, spy, and adventure novels, bearing titles such as *Un curiośo ladrón* [A curious thief] (Constantinople, 1922). Their characters included "Nic Carter, el más ilustre polís amator americano de muestros días, la teror del quartier quinés a Niu-York" ["Nick Carter, the best-known detective of our times, the terror of New York's Chinatown"] (Salonika, 1910); "Ĵim Ĵacson, célebre polís amator americano" ["Jim Jackson, famous American detective"] (Salonika, 1931); or "*Nat Pinkerton,* el más grande romanzo polizario del mundo" ["*Nat Pinkerton,* the world's greatest detective novel"] (Salonika, 1930–31).

Peculiar to the Sephardic world were novels with three specifically Jewish themes: memories of the Jewish past, contemporary life, and propagation of Zionist ideology. Titles included *Vengadores de sus pueblo* [Avengers of their people] (Salonika, 1922), described as a "novela inédita de la vida judía en el galut y el Eretz Yisrael" ["unpublished novel about Jewish life in the diaspora and in the land of Israel"]. Others were *Los jidiós* [The Jews] (Salonika,

1923); *El muevo jidió erante* [The new wandering Jew] (Salonika, 1922); *La sangre de la maŝá* [The blood in the matzah], dealing with the blood libel (Constantinople, 1910, and Salonika, 1926); *El convertido* [The convert] (Constantinople, 1921), which described itself as the "romanzo nacional judió" ["national Jewish novel"]; *Los misterios de los judiós* [Mysteries of the Jews] (Smyrna, 1875); and *Amor de Ŝiyón* [Love of Zion] (Salonika, 1894).

Among the latter group, especially favored were the novels with a "Spanish" theme, that is, novels dealing with Jewish life in medieval Spain, the expulsion, or the Inquisition. Such novels included *La hermoŝa Ḥulda de España* [The beautiful Hulda from Spain] (Jerusalem, 1910), about the Jewish woman who was in love with Alfonso XI of Castile; *La judía salvada del convento* [The Jewish woman saved from the convent] (Xanzi, 1924); *Don Miguel San Salvador* (Jerusalem, 1909); *El apreŝado de la Inquisición* [The prisoner of the Inquisition] (Jerusalem, 1904); and *La hermoŝa Raḥel* [Beautiful Rachel] (Jerusalem, 1904), "cuento histórico que se pasó entre una familla de los 'judiós forzados' en Portugal" ["a historical incident that happened in a family of forced converts in Portugal"].

Judeo-Spanish narrative died, along with the other literary genres, in World War II. Books were published sporadically after that, until 1953, when the second edition of Itzhak Ben-Rubi's *El sekreto del mudo* [The mute's secret] appeared. No further Judeo-Spanish novels appeared until 1982, when Enrique Saporta y Beja published *En torno de la Torre Blanka* [Regarding the White Tower] in Paris, the latest Sephardic novel in Judeo-Spanish.

Theater

Sephardic theater is usually categorized among the adopted genres, even though a sort of traditional theater associated with the festival of Purim (when it was customary to wear costumes) predated the influence of Western culture. Disguises led to pantomime, and then to rudimentary plays, based on texts relevant to the celebration of Purim, such as the *Purim-Shpil* [Purim plays] of the Central European Jews. Here is how Gina Camhy describes it:

> *La noche viniendo se empezava las manifestaciones de las mascaras. . . . Ocho dias antes, diversos groupos se ajuntavan por estudiar y reglar el programa comprendiendo piezas de theatro, cantos, declamaciones.*
>
> *Dunque después dela Seouda estos groupos con mascaras en las caras visitaban diversas casas onde jugavan ciertos pedazos del repertorio, quien travestido en Ahasveros, quien en Haman, otro en Mordehaï, otro en Esther.* (In Romero, *Teatro*, 1 : 596–97)
>
> [At nightfall began the masquerade shows. . . . A week earlier, several groups got together to pick and arrange the program, which included plays, songs, speeches.
>
> Then after the holiday meal these groups, wearing masks, visited several houses

where they performed certain excerpts of their repertoire, one dressed as Ahasueros, another as Haman, another as Mordehai, another as Esther.]

The earliest notice of such performances comes from Smyrna before 1747, but the custom is documented through the beginning of the twentieth century. In Mordehai M. Monassowitz's *Nešef Purim* [Soul of Purim], translated from Hebrew by Nisim Natán Catalán and published in Kazanlik (Bulgaria) around 1909, there appears a group of these *jugadores de Purim* [Purim players], acting out the story of Esther in a family's home. Although this custom has disappeared, Jewish communities continue to celebrate the holiday of Purim with theatrical presentations.

Aside from this traditional and almost improvisational theater, of which no texts are extant, there are school plays. It is interesting that the first performances of which there is evidence (other than the one in eighteenth-century Smyrna) were presented by "elevas de la escola HaTorá vehaḤohmá" [pupils of the HaTorá vehaḤohmá (Hebrew, the Law and wisdom) school] (Constantinople, 1877); "alumnos del Talmud Torá" [religious-school pupils] (Salonika, 1885); and "elevos de nuestra escola" [pupils in our school] (Rhodes, 1886). School plays have existed throughout the entire history of Sephardic theater.

This kind of theater, naturally enough, was markedly pedagogical in character. It could focus on: (a) religious and moral education, (b) teaching the holy language (there are innumerable short pieces in Hebrew), or (c) knowledge of Western cultures, especially French. Sometimes these objectives were combined, as in the case of the performance of four short pieces with biblical themes (religious education) in Hebrew (teaching the holy language) by pupils of the Mikveh Israel [Hebrew, hope of Israel] school in Edirne around 1870. Among the titles were *Salidura de Ayifto* [Exodus from Egypt] (Constantinople, 1873);[11] *Historia de la vendida de Yosef de sus diez hermanos* [History of the sale of Joseph by his ten brothers] (Constantinople, 1873 and 1874); *Ester* (Edirne, 1902; Xanzi, 1928; etc.); *Ya'acob y sus hijos* [Jacob and his sons] (Shumen, 1915); *Haná* (Serre, 1916), which dramatizes an episode from the book of Maccabees; and *Šošanat Ya'acob* [Hebrew, Jacob's lily] (Constantinople, 1912), dealing with the story of Esther.

There are also plays that are completely pedagogical but not biblical in theme. Examples include *Déguel haTorá* [Hebrew, standard of the law] (Sa-

11. [AN] The place and date mentioned are those of a documented performance; the designations "publ." or "ed." refer to the place and date of publication, but do not mean that a work was performed there.

lonika, 1885), which is basically a discussion in Judeo-Spanish about the importance of considering the material and spiritual needs of the poor; and *¿Qué es la Alianza?* [What is the Alliance?], a discussion in Turkish of the aims and functions of the Alliance Israélite Universelle.

The theater helped to acquaint the Sephardim with French culture, as can be seen in numerous "dialogues," "monologues," "comedies," "performances," and "pieces" *"en lingua francés"* [in the French language], as well as the frequent appearance of works by French authors in school repertoires. Particularly popular was Molière, several of whose works were more or less freely translated or adapted: *El casamiento forzado* [The forced marriage] (Rhodes, 1886); *El médico contra su veluntad* [The doctor in spite of himself] (Constantinople, 1890); and *El malato imaginario* [The imaginary invalid] (Smyrna, 1906).

The desire to emulate Western culture was a deciding factor in the extension of the theater beyond the school play into other aspects of Sephardic life. Political groups and charitable societies began to take advantage of the theater, the former for propaganda purposes and the latter for fund-raising. It is therefore common to find announcements of performances arranged by the "Soĉetá Cáritas compuesta de viejas elevas de la escola italiana, la más parte israelitas" ["Caritas Society composed of former Italian school pupils, most of them Jewish"], "la filantrópica obra de 'Oźer Dalim" ["the philanthropic work of Ozer Dalim" (Hebrew, aid to the needy)], the "Soĉietá Los Amigos de la Instrucción" [friends of education society], or "un grupo de amatores, hijos y hijas de las mejores famillas" ["a group of devotees, sons and daughters of the best families"], all to raise funds "al profito de la escola" ["in benefit of the school"], "al profito de una institución de muestra comunidad" ["in benefit of an institution in our community"], "al profito de la sociedad 'Oźer Dalim" ["in benefit of the Ozer Dalim society], or "a profito de la Soĉietá de Bienfeĉencia francesa" ["in benefit of the French Welfare Society].

Between 1915 and 1925 political groups were extremely active. Sephardic theatrical life in this century has been almost entirely amateur, made up of members of Zionist and socialist organizations. There was never any professional theater among the Sephardim. We find the "hijos y hijas elevos de los cursos de 'hebreo organizados por la Federación Ŝionista" ["male and female students of the Hebrew classes organized by the Zionist Federation"], actors who are members of the "Societá ŝionista Max Nordau" [Max Nordau Zionist Society], the "artistas amatores de la soĉetá Tedoro Herẑl" ["artists who are members of the Theodore Herzl society"], "jóvenes actores de la soĉietá ŝionista Lebanón" ["young actors from the Lebanon Zionist society"], the "Societá ŝionista Šibat Ŝión" [the Shivat Tzion (Hebrew, return to Zion) Zionist Society], the "sociedad Makabí" [Maccabee society]. These are just a few of the Zionist groups to present plays in Salonika during that decade. The troubling, sometimes conflictive, Socialist Federation of Salonika was especially important because of the quantity and quality of its performances. This group staged some of the most interesting works while constantly opposing Zionist ideology from the stage.

The kinds of groups, or their ideologies, determined the content of the works presented. Elena Romero has established a thematic classification of Sephardic theater in which she distinguishes three types: (a) specifically Sephardic theater, by which she means "works born of the communities . . . produced in Judeo-Spanish and/or by Sephardic authors, and which reflect the *realities* of the *community's world* or the *historical surroundings* in which it lived" (Romero, *Teatro,* 1 : 32); (b) theater with generally Jewish themes; and (c) theater with non-Jewish themes.

a) A great variety of themes can be found within the specifically Sephardic theater, from everyday family and community problems to the history of countries where the Sephardim have lived (Turkey, the Balkans). There is also the so-called "new comedy," which reflects modern changes in life-style and outlook. Examples of the first group are *Despośorios de Alḥerto* [Alberto's engagement party], *La boda de Alḥerto* [Albert's wedding], and *Mi yernećico* [My dear son-in-law], all three of which were published in Jerusalem in 1903 and portray customs connected to courtship and marriage. *Los males de la colada* [Washday evils] (publ. Salonika, 1900) describes the travail of a housewife in doing the laundry; it was written to publicize the opening of a laundry at that time in Salonika. *Ocho días antes de Pésaḥ* [A week before Passover] (publ. Constantinople, 1909) deals with the ritual housecleaning before Passover.

Laura Papo wrote a series of plays about the life of Bosnian Jews: *Esterka* [Dear Esther] (Sarajevo, 1930 and 1931); *Había de ser* [It had to be] (Sarajevo, 1930); *Ojos míos* [My eyes] (Sarajevo, 1931); *La pacencia vale mucho* [Patience is worth a lot] (Belgrade, 1934); *Sḥuegra ni de baro buena* [Not even the statue of a mother-in-law is good] (Sarajevo, 1933; Belgrade, 1934); and *Tiempos pasados* [Times past] (Sarajevo, ca. 1932). Two other plays by Papo—*Vendetta* (publ. Ruse, 1894) and *Lo que hićieron todos* [What everybody did] (publ. Constantinople, 1909)—are difficult to understand since they allude to community quarrels about which nothing is known today. Another, *Belachi* (publ. Salonika, 1930), pokes fun at a Zionist candidate in an election of delegates.

Alemdar Pačhá (Constantinople, 1912), about the Turkish grand vizier of that name, is an example of plays that reflect the milieu of the peoples among whom the Sephardim lived. *La batalla de Plevna* [The battle of Plevna] (Constantinople, 1914) reflects an episode in the Turko-Russian War of 1877–78. *La fuite d'Abdul Hamid* [The flight of Abdul Hamid] (in French) deals with the sultan whom the Young Turks deposed.

Representative of the "new comedy" are many short works similar to one-act farces, such as those in the series published by the Constantinople newspaper *El Juguetón* between 1927 and 1929. *Espośorio del felek* [Destiny's betrothal] deals with an unfortunate modern marriage. *Mi mujer quere campaña* [My wife wants the country] illustrates a marital fight over where to spend summer vacation. *Cale vivir a la moda* [One must live in style] features two friends discussing the advantage of living in tune with modern times. *Misiú Jac el parišiano quere espośar* [M. Jacques the Parisian wants to get married] shows the amorous circumlocutions of a young man "a la franca" [in French style]. Other titles include *El marido moderno* [The modern husband], *No me v'a caśar* [He won't marry me], *No quero espośar* [I don't want to get married], and *La vida moderna* [Modern life].

b) Another category consists of works of general Jewish interest. Many of these works have biblical themes, and a large number have to do with the story of chaste Joseph. Some of those titles are: *Yosef haŝadic* [Joseph the saint] (Edirne, ca. 1870); *Yosef vendido por sus hermanos* [Joseph sold by his brothers] (ed. Constantinople, 1910: *Yosef topado por sus hermanos* [Joseph found by his brothers] (ed. Constantinople, 1915–16); and *Ya'acob y sus hijos* [Jacob and his sons] (Shumen, 1915). Another popular theme is the story of Queen Esther; these works were generally presented on Purim. Among this group are plays varying from translations of Racine's *Esther* (ed. Constantinople, 1882, and performed several times) to plays in Hebrew such as *Mordehay hayehudí* [Mordehai the Jew] and *Hamán harašá* [Haman the wicked] (Serre, 1933) to versions of the biblical story written in Judeo-Spanish by Sephardim.

Two other very common themes should be mentioned within this group of works of general Jewish interest. One deals with the Jews in classical times, especially during the era of the Maccabees, represented by works such as *Antiojos* [Antiochus], *Haná y sus siete hijos* [Hannah and her seven sons] (Salonika, 1914), *Haná* (Serre, 1916), *Los Macabeos* [The Maccabees] (ed. Constantinople, 1920), *Los Hašmonaím* (Constantinople, 1913).[12] The other theme involves the Jews and Spain, concentrating—as do the novels with a similar theme—on matters such as the history of the Jews in the Middle Ages, the expulsion, converts, and the Inquisition. This group is represented by the following titles: *Don Abravanel y Formośa o Desteramiento de los Jidiós de España* [Abravanel and Formosa or the exile of the Jews from Spain] (Ruse, 1897) and *Don Isḥac Abravanel o el ministro judió* [Isaac Abravanel or the Jewish minister] (Constantinople, 1920), both about this Jewish administrator for the Catholic monarchs; *Los maranos* [The Marranos] (publ. Salonika, 1934), a melodrama about the converts and the Inquisition; *Los maranos en España* [The Marranos in Spain] (Beirut, 1907); and *Don Yosef de Castilla* [Joseph of Castile] (Shumen, after 1925).

Also of general Jewish interest are several plays presented in the Levant about the Dreyfus affair, and others that deal with anti-Semitism. Among these are *El triumfo de la justicia* [The triumph of justice] (ed. Salonika, 1921), which presents a case similar to that of Dreyfus but in czarist Russia, and *La sangre de la maśá* [The blood in the matzah], an adaptation of the novel of the same name, dealing with blood-libel accusations.

c) The third category of Sephardic theater is made up of plays with universal themes, either by Sephardic authors or translated into Judeo-Spanish and presented by and for Sephardim. Most popular were French classical and contemporary plays. Molière's works were often performed in schools, but interest in this author extended well beyond schoolchildren. There are three known Judeo-Spanish editions just of *The Miser*, with the titles *El Escasso* (Constantinople, 1882), *Historia de Ḥ Binyamín* (Salonika, 1884), and *Ḥan Benyamín* (Salonika, 1909), and no fewer than seven documented performances, some done by Sephardim in Turkish, Bulgarian, and French.

Also staged was *El abogado Patelén* (Constantinople, 1890; Smyrna, 1910), an adaptation of the fifteenth-century farce *Maistre Pierre Pathelin* [Master Pierre Pathelin]. Scenes from *Les Plaideurs* [The litigants] by Racine were staged in Smyrna (1906) under the title *Le pledör*. Contemporary authors were also quite popular. "*Tereśa Raquén, potente dram de Emil Źola*" ["*Theresa Raquen,* powerful drama by Émile Zola"] opened in Salonika in 1932. In the same city in 1913, a version of Mirabeau's play *Les affaires sont les affaires* [Business is business] was presented under the title *Los hechos son los hechos.* Salonika's socialist theater group staged Pagnol's *Topaź.* There were

---

12. An influential Jewish family in Maccabean times.

also theatrical adaptations of French novels, such as Victor Hugo's *Los miserables* (Salonika, 1928) and *Cyrano de Bergerac* (Salonika, 1907).

Italian works became part of Sephardic theater in their original language or in French translations, for example, Carlo Goldoni's *La escoêesa* [The Scotswoman] (publ. Constantinople, 1883) and *Lo Scàmpolo* [The remnant] by Dario Niccodemi (Salonika, after 1916). English plays included *El soldado de čhocolata* [The chocolate soldier] (Salonika, 1932) and a translation of George Bernard Shaw's comedy *Arms and the Man*. Russian plays, too, appeared on the Sephardic stage: Dostoyevski's *Les frères Karamazoff,* apparently in Judeo-Spanish despite the French title (Salonika, 1929), and *Resurrección,* "renomada pieza del escribano ruso Tolstoi" ["renowned work by the Russian writer Tolstoy"], which, staged repeatedly in its adaptation as a play (1915–16) by the Socialist Federation of Salonika, created such controversy that conservatives classified it as immoral.

As was true of the novel, many of the works in Sephardic theater were translations and adaptations from other languages, often published or presented with no indication of that fact. As with the novel, too, Sephardic playwrights manifest a complete ignorance of Spanish literature despite their great interest in the literature of other Western countries. Spain appeared in the Sephardic theater only as a setting for plays about the expulsion, the Inquisition, or the Marranos. There is not one single work by a Spanish author in the more than six hundred titles that make up the repertoire of the Sephardic theater.

Alongside the many translations and adaptations, there were also many original plays by Sephardic authors. Among these playwrights were Alexander Ben-Guiat (Smyrna, ca. 1869–1924), Laura Papo, who wrote under the pseudonym Bojoreta (Sarajevo, 1891–1941), Abraham A. Cappón (Bucharest, 1853–Sarajevo, 1931), and Sabetay Y. Djaén (Pleven, ca. 1886–Tucumán, 1935). Very few Sephardim write plays today. An exception is the veteran journalist Shelomo Reuven, who published his folkloric *Bulisa la refrandjia* in numbers 9 and 11 of the journal *Aki Yerushalayim* (1981).

Autograph Poetry

The Westernization of culture and customs changed the understanding (and creation) of poetry. The "new poetry" of the late nineteenth and twentieth centuries is characterized by greater consciousness of authorship, abandonment of traditional metrical forms, Westernization of the language, and the appearance of new themes unusual in the old *coplas*.

Regarding the question of authorship, it should be noted that the authors of the old *coplas* occasionally left traces of their authorship in their works. Abraham Toledo occasionally used acrostics that spelled out his name; Ya'acob Yoná often did. Yehuda Cal'í "signed" his *Coplas de los frutos* [Verses on fruits] with a stanza in which he declared, "mi nombre es Yeudá / mi alcuña es Cal'í" ["my name is Yehuda / my family name is Cal'í"].

Most *coplas,* however, circulated anonymously. Even in the case of verses that originally were "signed," memory of the author disappeared as the verses became a part of Sephardic tradition. Autograph poets had a more Western concept of authorship, very distant from the belief that poetry was ownerless, which made the Archpriest of Hita[13] (and surely many *copla* writers would have agreed) say:

Qualquier omne quel oya,	Anyone who hears it,
si bien trobar sopiere	if he can write well
más á y añadir e emendar,	may add and change it,
si quisiere;	if he likes;
ande de mano en mano	let it go from hand to hand
e quienquier quel pidiere:	to whoever wants it:
como pella las dueñas,	like the ball the damsels use,
tómelo quien podiere.	take it whoever catches it.

The impoverishment of metric form has already been mentioned. The new authors tended to abandon the stanza forms most strongly identified with traditional *coplas* (Purim stanzas, Arabic stanzas) and instead used patterns more like those of Western poetry: couplets, eleven-syllable quatrains, occasional eight-syllable quatrains, and even free verse that seemed more like rhyming prose or—when also blank verse—simply like bits of prose. The language also reflected the influence of modernization—the replacement of traditional Judeo-Spanish words with the Gallicisms that were so common in the Sephardic speech of the time. Theme, too, varied with respect to traditional folkloric poetry, largely as a reflection of new realities in the Sephardic world. Modern poetry extends from Zionist anthems to short poems criticizing the follies of modern times, including poems of social content. Rather than writing admonitive *coplas,* poets like Šelomó Šalem recast in Judeo-Spanish verse the edifying fables of Jean de La Fontaine. Poets also attempted to write intimate lyric poetry, previously unheard of in Sephardic poetry, with more or less success, in love and nature poems.

13. Juan Ruiz, the Archpriest of Hita (c. 1283–c. 1350) was the author of the *Libro de buen amor* [Book of good love], a masterpiece of medieval clerical poetry.

It is not easy to determine where traditional *coplas* end and new autograph poetry begins. The so-called last *copla* writers often combined traits inherited from traditional poetry with others more characteristic of autograph poetry (acknowledged consciousness of authorship, themes not found in the *coplas,* as in a poem by Yoná dealing with the seasons of the year).

More clearly in the tradition of the new poetry are the "Sephardic publicists," who were at their most productive from the beginning of this century to World War II. They were a group of leaders enchanted with Western culture, generally educated in Alliance schools, almost none of whom wrote poetry exclusively. In the main, they were men of letters who devoted their efforts to the various adopted genres. Nearly all of them were connected to journalism in one way or another, either as founders and backers of periodicals or as writers.

Šelomó Šalem, for example, wrote for *La Época* in Salonika, although he also published his poems independently in an anthology entitled *La Gavilla/ La Gerbe* [The sheaf] (Salonika, 1900). More popular were Gershom Saḍic and Moshé Cazés who, under the names Saḍic and Gaśóś, published poems in assorted newspapers as well as a series of pamphlets called *Cantes populares* [Popular songs] (Salonika, 1924–33). Among the newspaper founders touched by the muses were Abraham A. Cappón, who established *La Alborada* [The dawn] in Sarajevo, playwright and author of a two-volume book, *Poeśías* (Vienna, 1922), and Yosef Romano, editor of *Ṣalom* and *La Voź del Pueblo* in Smyrna and writer for *El Avenir* and *El Punchón* in Salonika. With such figures, it is no surprise that the newspapers became a regular vehicle for the dissemination of poetry, just as they were for novels and plays.

Sephardic autograph poetry, like the other literary genres, received its deathblow from World War II. Today only a few speakers of Judeo-Spanish dispersed throughout the world still express their feelings in Judeo-Spanish verse. Among them are two outstanding women: the poet of Constantinople, Esther Morguez Algrante, author of books of poetry such as *9 Eylül* [The ninth of Elul] and an occasional columnist for the weekly *Ṣalom,* who cultivates poetry very similar to that of Cappón or Šalem. In a poetic tradition closer to contemporary taste there is Clarisse Nicoidsky, descendant of Yugoslavian Sephardim (but born in Lyon in 1938), author of seven French novels—in one of which, *Couvre-feux* (Paris, 1981) she evokes the Sephardic world of her childhood—and of poems in Judeo-Spanish, such as those collected in the book *Lus ojus, las manus, la boca* [Your eyes, your hands, your mouth] (Paris, 1978). Here is a sample:

Kontami la kunseja   Tell me the story
ki si kamina in tus ojus   that shows in your eyes
kuandu lus avris   when you open them
la manyana   in the morning
kuandu il sol   when the sun
entra su aguja de luz   sends its needle of light
in tus suenyus.   into your dreams.

RECOMMENDED READING

For a clear and succinct summary of literature in Judeo-Spanish, see Iacob M. Hassán, "Hacia una visión panorámica de la literatura sefardí," in *Actas de las Jornadas de Estudios Sefardíes de 1980* (Cáceres: Universidad de Extremadura, 1981), 51–68, and Hassán, "Visión panorámica de la literatura sefardí," *Hispania Judaica,* vol. 2 (Barcelona: Puvill Libros, 1982), 25–44. See also Elena Romero, "Generalidades acerca de la literatura judeoespañola," in *Los sefardíes: Cultura y literatura,* ed. Paloma Díaz-Mas (San Sebastián: Universidad del País Vasco, 1987), 87–102. The only manual or anthology presently available is Michael Molho, *Literatura sefardita de Oriente* (Madrid and Barcelona: CSIC, 1960). Samples of various genres of Sephardic literature, with English translations by David Herman, can be found in Moshe Lazar, *The Sephardic Tradition: Ladino and Spanish-Jewish Literature* (New York: Norton, [1972]).

Dealing specifically with marriage customs in Morocco, see Sarah Leibovici, "Nuestras bodas sefarditas. Algunos ritos y costumbres," *Revista de Dialectología y Tradiciones Populares* 41 (1986): 163–88. An impassioned exposition of Sephardic language and literature may be found in Haïm Séphiha, *Le judéo-espagnol* (Paris: Entente, 1986).

Some volumes of the classic *Me'am Lo'ez* are available in transliteration by David Gonzalo Maeso and Pascual Pascual Recuero, "Prolegómenos," *Me'am Lo'ez: El gran comentario bíblico sefardí* (Madrid: Gredos, 1964). See the careful selection of texts by Cynthia M. Crews, "Extracts from the *Meam Loez* (Genesis) with a Translation and Glossary," in *Proceedings of the Leeds Philosophical and Literary Society: Literary and Historical Section,* vol. 9 (Leeds: Leeds Philosophical and Literary Society, 1960), 13–106. Also forthcoming is a penetrating textual analysis by Luis Landau, "La Antología del *Me'am Lo'ez* y sus fuentes," *Estudios Sefardíes* 5 (forthcoming). On the translation of a midrash into Judeo-Spanish, see Elena Romero, "Una versión judeoespañola del midrás *Yeṣirat havalad,*" *Sefarad* 42 (1987): 383–406.

On the *coplas,* see Romero, "Las coplas sefardíes: Categorías y estado de la cuestión," in *Actas de las Jornadas de Estudios Sefardíes,* 69–98; the notes include an extensive bibliography. Also, dealing with specific aspects such as theme and meter, see Hassán, "Un género castizo sefardí: las coplas," in *Los sefardíes: Cultura y literatura,* 103–24. Specific types of *coplas* have appeared in the following easily obtained studies and monographs (some with edited texts): Romero, "Complas de Tu-bišbat," *Poesía* [I Reunión de Málaga de 1974] (Málaga: Diputación, 1976), 277–311; Romero, "La última jornada del hombre en una copla sefardí de moral," *Estudios Sefardíes* 3/*Sefarad* 41 (1980): 403–13; Hassán and Romero, "Poesía luctuosa judeoespañola:

Quinot paralitúrgicas," in *Proceedings of the Sixth World Congress of Jewish Studies* (Jerusalem: n.p., 1980), 7–16; Hassán and Romero, "Quinot paralitúrgicas: Edición y variantes," *Estudios Sefardíes* 1 (1978): 3–57; Romero and Leonor Carracedo, "Poesía judeoespañola admonitiva," *Sefarad* 37 (1977): 429–51; and Carracedo, "Coplas sefardíes del tiempo de Juan Chabás," *Dianium* (1987): 213–57. On the hagiographic Joseph *coplas*, see Hassán, "Las *Coplas de Yosef haŝadic,*" *Módulo Tres* 2 (Mar.–Apr. 1973): 8–10; Hassán, "Una versión ¿completa? de las *Coplas de Yoçef* publicadas fragmentariamente por González de Llubera," in *Actas del I Encuentro de las Tres Culturas* (Toledo: Ayuntamiento, 1983), 283–88; and Hassán, "Coplas sefardíes de *Las hazañas de José:* Ediciones ciertas e inciertas," *Sefarad* 46 (1986): 235–52. María Martín Heredia discusses Hanukkah *coplas* in "Las Coplas de Hanuká," in *Actas de las Jornadas de Estudios Sefardíes de 1980,* 69–98, and "Hanuká: Luminarias y coplas (A propósito de Cansinos y de una festividad judía)," *Dianium* (1987): 259–70. Not specifically on the *coplas* but containing some points connected to that genre is Romero's study of a song, "La canción sefardí *El merecimiento de los patriarcas* y su vida tradicional," *Sefarad* 68, (1988): 357–71.

As an introduction to the proverb, see Isaac Jack Lévy, *Prolegomena to the Study of the Refranero Sefardí* (New York: Las Americas, 1969). Indispensable is the careful work by Carracedo and Romero, "Refranes publicados por Ya'acob A. Yoná (edición concordada) y bibliografía del refranero sefardí," *Sefarad* 41 (1981): 389–560. On the negative treatment of women in maxims and proverbs, Carracedo, "Misoginia en textos proverbiales sefardíes," *Revista de Dialectología y Tradiciones Populares* 43 (1988): 87–93.

For an idea of the traditional story, see the Moroccan collection by Arcadio de Larrea Palacín, *Cuentos populares de los judíos del norte de Marruecos,* 2 vols. (Tetuan: Editora Marroquí, 1952–53), although the texts have been edited. On the translation of a Hebrew story into Judeo-Spanish, see Romero, "*Maimónides el mago:* Versión sefardí de un cuento tradicional judío," *Revista de Dialectología y Tradiciones Populares* 43 (1988): 507–12.

There are numerous studies of the Sephardic ballad, the basis of which is Ramón Menéndez Pidal's classic "Catálogo del romancero judío-español," *Cultura Española* 4 (1906): 1045–77 and 5 (1907): 161–99, reprinted in Menéndez Pidal, *Los Romances de América y otros estudios* (Madrid: Espasa-Calpe, 1958), 114–79. A continuation of that work is Samuel G. Armistead et al., *El Romancero judeo-español en el Archivo Menéndez Pidal (Catálogo-índice de romances y canciones),* 3 vols. (Madrid: Cátedra–Seminario Menéndez Pidal, 1978), an indispensable bibliographical and reference source for those interested in this topic. It is impossible to cite here all of the classic and/or recently published editions of texts and studies. Consequently, here are just two extraordinarily useful and interesting works. Distinguished by its thoroughness and approachability for novices in the field is Paul Bénichou, *Romancero judeo-español de Marruecos* (Madrid: Castalia, 1968), and the collection of articles by S. G. Armistead and J. H. Silverman, *En torno al Romancero sefardí (Hispanismo y balcanismo de la tradición judeo-española)* (Madrid: Seminario Menéndez Pidal, 1982), the only monographic work dedicated to the question of Hispanic and extra-Hispanic elements in the Judeo-Spanish tradition.

On wedding songs, see Manuel Alvar, *Cantos de boda judeo-españoles* (Madrid:

CSIC, 1971); on dirges, see Alvar, *Endechas judeo-españolas,* rev. and enl. ed. (Madrid: CSIC, 1969). Also on wedding songs, see Oro Anahory-Librowicz and Judith R. Cohen, "Modalidades expresivas de los cantos de boda judeo-españoles," *Revista de Dialectología y Tradiciones Populares* 41 (1986): 189–209. For an overview of problems and possible approaches to the study of the traditional Sephardic song, see Paloma Díaz-Mas, "El cancionero popular sefardí," in *Los sefardíes: Cultura y literatura,* 191–222.

A good summary of Sephardic journalism appears in Hassán, "El estudio del periodismo sefardí," *Sefarad* 26 (1966): 229–35, a review of the book (in Hebrew) by M. D. Gaon, *A Bibliography of the Judeo-Spanish (Ladino) Press* (Jerusalem: Ben Zvi Institute, 1965). On the novel, see David F. Altabé, "The Romanso, 1900–1933: A Bibliographical Survey," *Sephardic Scholar* 3 (1977–78): 96–106, and María Dolores Sánchez García-Arcicollar, "El género narrativo en la literatura judeoespañola," in *Actas de las Jornadas de Estudios Sefardíes 1980,* 107–13. The great monograph on theater is by Romero, *El teatro de los sefardíes orientales,* 3 vols. (Madrid: CSIC, 1979), which includes detailed reviews of previous works in the field. The much-needed complement to this work is Romero's *Repertorio de noticias sobre el mundo teatral de los sefardíes orientales* (Madrid: CSIC, 1983). Specifically on Sephardic adaptations of Molière's works, see Romero, "*L'avare* de Molière en el teatro de los sefarditas del Oriente," in *The Sephardi and Oriental Jewish Heritage,* ed. Issachar Ben-Ami (Jerusalem: Magnes Press–Hebrew University, 1982), 269–76. A recent summary of Sephardic theater is Romero's "Aspectos literarios y sociológicos del teatro de los sefardíes de los Balcanes," in *Los sefardíes: Cultura y literatura,* 171–90. On contemporary autograph poetry, there is some data in Moshé Shaul, "La poezia djudeo-espanyola kontemporanea," *Aki Yerushalayim* 10, no. 36–37 (Jan.–June 1988): 28–30. Sephardic poetry that reacts to the Holocaust may be found in Lévy, *And the World Stood Silent: Sephardic Poetry of the Holocaust* (Urbana: University of Illinois Press, 1989).

FIVE

THE SEPHARDIM
AND SPAIN

WHAT DO THE Sephardim think of Spain? What ideas do Spaniards have about the Sephardim? Do the Sephardim really feel like "Spaniards without a homeland"? Has this alleged homeland done anything for these alleged Spaniards?

It is difficult to consider these questions without falling prey to some of the commonplace beliefs that have developed over the years. In this chapter I will attempt to give a historical overview of the development of relations between these two groups, avoiding the sentimentalism, mawkishness, and patriotism that so often have accompanied similar discussions.

SPAIN'S REACTION TO THE SEPHARDIM

From the time the Sephardim were expelled until the nineteenth century, Spain knew very little about the exiled Sephardim. During the sixteenth and seventeenth centuries, there was sporadic contact between the Sephardim and the Spaniards, non-Jews as well as crypto-Jews. Some illustrious Jews came to Spain representing their respective governments, such as Samuel Palache, Moroccan ambassador to the Low Countries. Spanish travelers, too, such as Gonzalo de Illescas and Captain Domingo de Toral (freed from the Turks by a Jew from Aleppo), included in their memoirs accounts of how the Levantine Sephardim lived. Sephardic characters also appear in the *Viaje de Turquía* [Turkish trip].

During the eighteenth century, Spaniards knew nothing about the existence of those distant people, because during three centuries of progressive lack of communication they had forgotten about the Jews. The Jews, in turn, had lost all contact with Spanish life. If any word of that "exotic" group came to the Iberian Peninsula, it went unnoticed by the eighteenth-century world whose interests were so different from those of the Sephardic world.

The War in Africa

Spain rediscovered the Sephardim in the mid-nineteenth century. Spain's African campaign and the taking of Tetuan in 1860 put Spaniards in direct contact with the Jewish communities in Morocco, where a group that Spaniards had ignored until that time had preserved both the language and the memory of Spain. The impression that the Moroccan Sephardim made on the Spaniards can be seen in the works of the chroniclers of the campaign, the most important of whom was Pedro Antonio de Alarcón.[1] The chroniclers show a mixture of curiosity and wariness toward these individuals, most of whom lived in absolute poverty. Sometimes this wariness turned into contempt or outright anti-Semitism when the material poverty of the *mellah* was identified with the moral poverty of its inhabitants.

> Their appearance, their attitude, as well as that studied pride in speaking Spanish repelled me greatly. . . . I compared them with the elderly Moor whom we had met earlier and I immediately recognized the profound difference between one race and another. How dignified the man from Agar was! How miserably abject the Israelites were!   (Alarcón in Vilar, *Tetuán*, 70)

> The most base human passions, avarice and distrust, distinguish these unfortunate slaves. . . . They have a special ugliness found in no other race; even though their features themselves are not unusual, their physiognomy, a reflection of their spirit, has a certain ignoble and brutal appearance. . . . It is necessary to have seen this degraded people to realize the effect that a long-lived system of oppression and tyranny can have. Intelligence has long been extinguished in these unfortunate beings, who are no more than people of base instincts and coarse appetites.   (Alermón in ibid., 70–71)

On other occasions, curiosity turned to admiration of the beauty and modesty of upper-class Jewish women, such as the famous Tamo Pariente, praised for her charm, pleasant manner, and intelligence.

The writings of people who went into Tetuan with the Spanish troops provide interesting documentation about how the Moroccan Sephardim lived in the mid-nineteenth century. At the time, those works also brought attention to this peculiar people with their own customs and ways of speaking Spanish. When, almost fifty years later, Benito Pérez Galdós[2] recreated

---

1. A Spanish novelist (1833–91) whose *Diario de un testigo de la guerra de Africa* [Diary of a witness to the war in Africa] (1860) speaks of his experiences there.
2. Galdós (1843–1920) was perhaps Spain's best-known realist novelist.

that moment in his historical novel *Aita Tettauen,* he could not resist including some more or less stereotypical Sephardic characters.

Pulido's Campaign

Isolated bits of information about the Sephardim in the Balkans reached Spain toward the end of the nineteenth century. A great change, however, occurred at the beginning of the twentieth century when Dr. Angel Pulido Fernández discovered the Levantine Sephardim. Here is how his son, Angel Pulido Martín, describes the episode:

> My parents and my sister Elena came to Vienna to visit me during the summer of 1903. Once there, they decided to accompany me on a trip to Eastern Europe: Budapest, Belgrade, Bucharest, Constantinople, etc. It was on that trip, and on the deck of a ship from Budapest to Serbia, that the pro-Sephardi campaign began. My sister was then twelve years old; in her walks on deck, in a place where she had not expected to hear her language, she met an elderly couple who spoke a Spanish that sounded strange to her, and she came to tell us about it. I guessed that they were probably Sephardim and went there. In fact, they were speaking fifteenth-century Spanish. I went back to my father and told him, "If you want to see what I wrote about in my letter to *El Siglo* [referring to a letter written earlier that year to *El Siglo Médico* (The medical world) with information about the Levantine Sephardim], come and talk to these people." My father did, and he was so astonished and happy to hear them that his life changed direction right there. (*Actas,* 74)

The elderly Sephardic couple whom the Pulido family had met were Enrique Bejarano and his wife. Bejarano, head of the Sephardic community's school in Bucharest, was a great admirer of the Spain that his ancestors had left and he had never seen. He was apparently overjoyed to meet a Spanish family. His enthusiasm turned Angel Pulido into a publicist for the Sephardic world. The doctor himself explains:

> [Bejarano's] broad knowledge attracted me. . . ; and more than that I was impressed by the outburst of love for Spain that he expressed with a great deal of emotion and in very delicate and tender phrases, as if it were a matter of religious and secular belief. (Pulido, 3)

Bejarano's love for Spain convinced Pulido that all Sephardim felt similarly linked to Spain, that they considered it their homeland, and that, despite their expulsion and the persecution they had faced there, they had retained an almost religious veneration for the land of their ancestors. Continued use of the Spanish language almost five centuries after their exile was concrete proof of this veneration. Consequently, all Spain (and especially its government) should reciprocate such generous and selfless loyalty by strengthening contacts with the Sephardim, giving them various kinds of aid, and, especially, granting them the Spanish citizenship they so desired.

Returning from his trip, Angel Pulido published several articles in Spanish newspapers, which he later collected in his first book, *Los Israelitas Españoles y el Idioma Castellano* [Spanish Israelites and the Spanish language] (Madrid, 1904), and which were disseminated throughout Spain, Morocco, and the Eastern Mediterranean. Pulido's enthusiastic and almost messianic character, along with his role in the government (he was a senator), helped his book become well known in Spain. Its impact on the world of the Spanish Jews was enormous, and it introduced Pulido to Levantine and Moroccan communities and leaders, with whom he maintained close contact, both in person and by letter.

In 1905 he published his second book, *Españoles sin Patria y La Raza Sefardí* [Spaniards without a country and the Sephardic race], in which, among other things, he published part of his voluminous year-long correspondence with Sephardim and Spanish leaders whom he had interested in the topic. Pulido was an untiring publicist for the "Sephardic cause" until his death. "Españoles sin patria" became a set phrase to define those Jews for whom the senator sought Spanish citizenship, Spain's attention and help at all levels, and the friendship and affection of all Spaniards. Through innumerable articles, speeches, trips, and personal contacts, Pulido affected Spanish public opinion, as his son points out:

> In Madrid my father, involved in many activities (political, professional and social), devoted most of his time to the Hispano-Sephardic campaign. In Spain he found enthusiastic colleagues: Cansinos Assens,[3] Unamuno,[4] Mújica,[5] Menéndez Pidal,[6] Maura,[7] the Count of Romanones[8]. . . . Outside Spain, in nearby Tangier, which became his second residence, he obtained the inestimable cooperation of the brilliant author Rahma Toledano, of Pinhas Assayac and of the entire Moroccan Sephardic colony. (*Actas*, 75)

3. Rafael Cansinos-Assens (1883–1964) was a literary critic and translator.

4. Miguel de Unamuno (1864–1936) was a writer, rector of the University of Salamanca, and a leading Spanish intellectual.

5. The translator has been unable to identify Mújica.

6. Ramón Menéndez Pidal (1869–1968) was the founder of Spanish philology. Among his books are *Los orígenes del español* [The origins of Spanish] and *El romancero español* [Spanish ballads].

7. Antonio Maura (1853–1925) was head of Spain's Conservative Party and headed the government several times.

8. Alvaro de Figueroa y Torres, Count of Romanones (1863–1950) was a writer and politician. He presided over the Spanish government for several terms.

His enthusiasm reached many intellectuals who wrote about the Sephardim and tried, both emotionally and patriotically, to understand them. The writer Rafael Cansinos-Assens was an extreme example: he not only began to write about Jewish themes but also, believing himself descended from converts, apparently became Jewish.

Pulido's ideas were accepted, repeated, and echoed by writers and politicians. Gabriel Alomar wrote the following in his prologue to a book by José Estrugo (who will be discussed later):

> In Palma de Mallorca I had an interesting and significant visit from a "Sephardic" Israelite, Spanish in origin and a citizen of the United States. He brought a card of introduction from our illustrious friend Rafael Cansinos Assens. He had come to Spain as his homeland. . . . This Spaniard (who has more right than he to that nationality?) was José Estrugo. . . . For the first time I saw a Spaniard who proclaimed his exile ancestry with dignity and noble pride.   (Estrugo, *Retorno*, 7, 10, 15)

In the prologue to the third edition (1929) of Manuel Ortega's book *Los hebreos en Marruecos* [The Hebrews in Morocco], which will be discussed later, Pedro Sainz Rodríguez wrote the following:

> A collective state of conscience is finally developing that makes us feel cultural and linguistic unity with these "Spaniards without a homeland," as they have been called . . . they have come to represent romantically a new kind of messianism, the melancholy remembrance of a lost homeland, contact with which can again offer them the tolerance of contemporary civilization.   (Ortega 1929, v–vi)

The Campaign during the Moroccan Protectorate

A few years after Pulido's campaign started, the Spanish protectorate was established in Morocco and the Spaniards were able to strengthen their contacts with the North African Sephardic communities. Some reactions to Jewish presence in the protectorate were like those of 1860—mistrust, contempt, or outright anti-Semitism. An example is the book *España en Africa y el peligro judío* [Spain in Africa and the Jewish danger], published in Santiago de Compostela in 1918 by Africano Fernández (actually a pseudonym for a Spanish Franciscan), which is full of expressions like the following:

> Unfortunate people who wander all roads and moisten them with your tears! If my heart once roared, indignant on contemplating your infamy, today [the day of Tisha b'av] when I see you cry I take pity on you and lament your immense misfortunes. . . . Reader, if you abhor the Jew because you have dealt with him in secular life, look for him today and you will take pity on him, you will venerate him . . . and, if it is not possible to love him, at least who is not moved by a people that is grieved and prays?   (Fernández, *España en Africa*, 301–2)

Pesah is also generally called *Passover of the cake,* because for bread they substitute cakes made of flour mixed with egg and sugar. . . .
This is the bread which they so often made with the blood of Christians.   (Ibid., 300)

Others, however, influenced by Pulido's campaign, wrote about the Sephardim with loving and zealous enthusiasm. The clearest example is Manuel Ortega, author of the previously mentioned book *Los hebreos en Marruecos,* published in 1919 and very well received by the public, as successive editions attest. It was reprinted in the same year, reedited in 1929, and reprinted yet again in 1934. The book is full of expressions very like those of Pulido, such as affirmations of the deep Sephardic love of Spain:

The Sephardim of the Maghreb love Spain, as their brothers in Asia, Europe and America love her, with a pure love uncontaminated by any base interest. . . . Pinhas Assayag [Pulido's friend], one of the most educated Hebrews in Tangier in present times, expresses the Hispanicism of the Moroccan Israelites in enthusiastic terms. . . . Here we are Spaniards in all aspects . . . in our tastes, impressions, exaltations and feelings. We are Spaniards by vocation, by temperament and by sympathy; Spanish blood circulates in our veins; we think in Spanish and we feel in Spanish; some of our prayers are in Spanish. . . . Spain is our homeland, the blessed territory where the remains of our ancestors rest, and it is natural for us to feel affection and veneration for her.   (Ortega 1919, 221–22)

This love, according to Ortega, lasts until death:

Even in the hour of death love for their lost homeland shines through, for the so-called Castilian cemetery in Tetuan is shown to strangers with pride by the Sephardim. The Castilian cemetery! . . . On African soil one finds this bit of earth baptized with the legendary name of Castile, declaring the love of some Spaniards for Spain, a love that has not grown cold because of persecution or contempt, because it is a love stronger than the will of men: it is the love of a child for its mother.   (Ibid., 230)

This attitude extends to the Spanish Jews in the Levant as well: "They have been living among the Turks for centuries, although without abjuring at all their Spanish homeland, its language, its customs or its loves. The Spaniards of Turkey never wanted to be Turks. Forever Spanish!" (Ibid., 341).

Based on the fact that the Sephardim are and feel themselves to be Spanish, Ortega, like Pulido, repeatedly deplores the lack of official attention the Sephardim receive from their supposed homeland, especially on the cultural level:

Spain has done little, considering the duties that its position in the Jewish world imposes on it, to develop its influence on the Moroccan Sephardim through education.   (Ibid., 269)

We lost Algeria forever. Will we also lose our influence over the Moroccan Sephardim, blood of our blood?   (Ibid., 276)

For Ortega, the Sephardic question is a "great national problem," as one can see from the following commentary on the few practical results of the Second African Congress held in Zaragoza in 1908:

> Nothing was done then. The governments dedicated to the lowly needs of despicable politics have paid very little attention to great national problems. Senator Emilio Díaz Moreu, in a speech before the High Chamber on July 12, 1908, again put to the floor this patriotic question. It would be plausible to speak of maintaining schools in Morocco to protect our language, he said . . . but I have experienced the sorrow of going to the Isle of Rhodes . . . and I was invited . . . to the opening of a Spanish school supported by Spanish Jews, and I saw with great pain that they were left to their own recourses, with Spain not bothering to support our language or anything else. We did the same in Morocco; we napped while France, England and Germany worked.   (Ibid., 270–71)

The comparison to France's labor in the Sephardic world was inevitable. Well-intentioned patriots like Pulido, Ortega, and many others knew that the schools of the Alliance Israélite Universelle were the access route for Spanish Jews to Western culture at that time, and had been so for fifty years.

> The occupation of Teutan [by Spain in 1860] partially rescued them from the servitude in which they were vegetating, but the great work of the schools of the "Alliance Israélite Universelle" is what most influenced the intellectual progress of Maghrebine Hebrews in modern times.   (Ibid., 265)

It was urgent, then, to counter the French effect by creating Spanish schools for the Sephardim. That is what Wenceslao Orbea proposed explicitly in the 1908 African Congress:

> It is necessary to counter the influence of the French schools, which the "Alliance Universelle" maintains so determinedly, and the Spanish government ought to create scholastic groups in Tangier, Tetuan, Larache, Rabat, Mogador, Safi, Casablanca and wherever it may be necessary. Thus we would increase our influence, attracting Moors and Hebrews who today go astray because of the education they receive in foreign schools.   (In ibid., 270)

Ortega himself proposed a detailed plan of studies for the Moroccan Jews, including Jewish religious education as well as secular courses. He enumerated not only the subjects to be taught, but even vacation periods (to coincide with Jewish holidays), how faculty would be attracted (he proposed going to "the talented graduates of Alliance schools"), and other details. As might be expected, none of this was carried out officially and the zealous patriot forever suffered about the unfavorable comparison of his country with France: "Spain continued contemplating with arms crossed how other nations, especially France, harvested in our field, slowly gaining control over the intelligence and the hearts of the Moroccan Hebrews" (Ibid., 271).

The same pain had afflicted Pulido years before:

> What is to be done in this matter of Spanish among the Spanish Israelites? Abandon it as impossible? Declare ourselves powerless and conquered? There would certainly be laughter from France, who went in search of everything where she had nothing, over the fact that we, who had so much, did nothing because of faintheartedness or lack of interest! (Pulido, 610)

Seeing that the Spanish government was not willing to invest money and effort in creating schools for the Moroccan Jews, Ortega thought that he had found the ideal solution in a generous offer from the Alliance: it would move into more inhospitable areas and leave the work already done in the hands of Spain. This is what Ortega proposed in all ingenuousness:

> We understand that since the Alliance Israélite is universal, and there are colonies of Hebrews in other world areas that do not enjoy the benefits of education, it would not be difficult for Spain to take charge of the schools in Spanish Morocco, maintaining them and providing them with teaching materials. Thus the Alliance could develop its welfare in other countries, moving its components, certain that the needs of the Moroccan Hebrews would be well attended and guaranteed. This should be a legitimate aim of Spain; nobody will be able to argue against such a just demand. (Ortega 1919, 267–68)

Practical Results

Although Pulido's campaign and its successors were markedly political, they bore little fruit, for it was, after all, a case of a few very enthusiastic people who never managed to exert much influence over those in power. The most important result of these actions is generally considered to be Primo de Rivera's law of December 20, 1924. When Turkey and the Balkans did away with consular protection, this law awarded Spanish citizenship to "former Spaniards or their descendants and, in general, members of families of Spanish origin," if they sought it before December 31, 1930. While the law did not specifically mention the Sephardim, they were its greatest beneficiaries.

The campaign achieved no spectacular cultural results either. The Spanish government did not compete with the French in creating schools for the Jews, as the defenders of the Sephardic cause had demanded. Some private Alfonso XIII schools were opened in Morocco to educate Sephardic children; the first was established in Alcazarquivir. In 1919, 230 boys were enrolled, more than 150 of whom were Sephardim, and 150 girls, almost all Jewish.

The schools in Tangier, which had government assistance, opened in 1913 and soon were educating six hundred boys and five hundred girls, a good number of whom were Jewish. There was a smaller school in Arcila, half of whose pupils were Jewish. The establishment of chairs of Spanish language and literature in Levantine universities, such as that of Bucharest, provided some Sephardim with access to Spanish culture.

Growing interest in Jewish matters resulted in the University of Madrid creating a chair of rabbinic language and literature. The eminent Hebraist of Sephardic origin, Abraham Shalom Yahuda, was named to that chair. Perhaps the greatest success of the campaign, however, was making the Spaniards— and especially a good number of intellectuals—conscious of the existence of this previously unknown group.

Except for the philological work I will discuss in the next section, this consciousness was manifested more in symbolic gestures than in practical results, for example, the group of leaders who interceded with the French and Italian governments during World War I to convince them to receive Sephardim seeking refuge. A positive reaction in France brought a thank-you letter signed, of course, by Angel Pulido and Rafael Cansinos-Assens, but also by others who would never even have considered the Sephardic problem had it not been for the senator's campaign: the scientist Santiago Ramón y Cajal, the writer Benito Pérez Galdós, the journalist Miguel Moya, the politicians Alejandro Lerroux, Gumersindo de Azcárate, Melquíades Alvarez, and Manuel Azaña, the musician Master Bretón, and the intellectual Francisco Giner de los Ríos.

By today's standards, Pulido's campaign seems like a strange, romantic effort—both to Spaniards and to Sephardim—full of passionate declarations, exalted patriotic proclamations, and fantastic projects for cultural and political brotherhood. Despite its anachronistic character when it appeared, the campaign was doubtless a revelation in its time. For the first time the Sephardim became a matter of public consciousness in Spain. Some of the ideas of the campaign are still alive today.

On the other hand, the campaign unleashed violent opposing reactions, especially on the part of Jews who refused at this late date to be "adopted" by the mother country that had expelled them centuries earlier. This matter will be discussed later.

Philology

The most positive work realized by Spain regarding the Sephardim has certainly been done, quietly and efficiently, by philologists who began to collect linguistic documentation, ballads, and traditional songs in Judeo-Spanish. Those efforts preserved a great deal of oral literature that otherwise would have been lost. Many popular melodies and interesting data about the language have also been saved.

Although the philologists had already discovered the Sephardim at the end of the nineteenth century, Pulido's campaign was a substantial factor in Spanish scholars' increasing interest in the Judeo-Spanish language and literature. Many people contributed to this body of work. In 1922 Américo Castro visited the Jewish communities in Tetuan, Arcila, Larache, and Xauen, collecting very interesting linguistic and literary documentation. Ernesto Giménez Caballero and Tomás García Figueras did likewise. However, it was Ramón Menéndez Pidal who did the most to encourage oral interviews with Spanish Jews, aided by numerous correspondents and collaborators, some of whom definitely deserve the title they have been given: "champions of the Judeo-Spanish ballad."[9]

Between 1896 and 1956, Menéndez Pidal collected almost twenty-five hundred Judeo-Spanish texts, many with annotations of their melodies. Between 1896 and 1904, he had already collected a dozen texts from Salonika, Rosiori (Rumania), and Oran. In 1904, the year when Pulido's first book was published, he met the illustrious Sephardic writer from Tangier, José Benoliel. Between 1904 and 1913, Benoliel sent him more than 150 ballads and traditional songs from Tangier and Lisbon. Angel Pulido contributed a couple of texts he had collected in Vienna, and many others—Sephardim and non-Sephardim, Spaniards and foreigners, scholars and interested laypeople—added their contributions to the collection. Eugenio Silvela, Max Leopold Wagner, Emma Adatto, María Sánchez Arbós, Baruh Uziel, Diego Catalán, and Moshé Attias are but some of those who saved part of Judeo-Spanish literature from oblivion by giving it to Menéndez Pidal.

Among all of these people, Manuel Manrique de Lara stands out. He was a person of many abilities who put his military discipline, artistic sensitivity (he was a painter and composer), and musicological knowledge to the service of ballad collecting. As the resulting of an almost accidental meeting with Menéndez Pidal when accompanying him to an interview in Navas del Marqués (in Avila) in 1905, Manrique became interested in retrieving traditional poetry from the mouths of the people. Years later he had the opportunity to act on his desires.

9. [AN] José Benoliel and Manuel Manrique de Lara are given this title in the dedication of *Cat.-Ind.*; see 1:7–39 for information about Menéndez Pidal's collection.

In 1911, with a grant from the Centro de Estudios Históricos, Manrique undertook an extraordinary expedition to the Eastern Mediterranean, where he visited each
of the major communities: Sarajevo, Belgrade, Sofia, Salonika, Istanbul, Izmir,
Rhodes, Beirut, Damascus and Jerusalem. In 1915 and 1916, he carried out equally
massive investigations in Morocco, visiting Tangier, Tetuan, Larache, and Alcazarquivir. He collected, sometimes under rigorous, uncomfortable, and even dangerous conditions, many hundreds of versions—almost two thousand in all. Not only did
Manrique gather ballads from oral tradition, but he also copied manuscript texts from
the eighteenth and nineteenth centuries and transcribed popular ballad chapbooks
printed in Hebrew characters.   (*Cat.-Ind.* 52)

On occasion his travels through communities took on the aspect of a true
odyssey, as when he arrived at Constantinople in 1911 in the midst of a
cholera epidemic. Here is how he described it in a letter to Menéndez Pidal:

I had the bad luck of coming to Constantinople and Salonika when the ravages of
cholera were at their worst. In Constantinople, on one of my excursions to the Balat
quarter, one of the largest Jewish districts, I even found various corpses of cholera
victims abandoned in the streets. I arrived in Salonika when the entire population was
terrified by the outbreak of the epidemic, which started the week before and had
already attained a rate of fifty cases per day. There was this same number during the
final days of my residence there. . . . Cholera and war are making my travels enormously difficult. From Salonika, I was unable to go directly to Smyrna, because there
was no direct passage and I had to go back to Constantinople, enduring three days
on shipboard and one in quarantine. From here I can go more easily. In any event, I
am very far behind on my itinerary.   (Ibid.)

The texts collected by Manrique de Lara are preserved today, along with
those of the rest of Menéndez Pidal's collaborators, in the Archivo Menéndez
Pidal in Madrid. It is the world's largest collection of traditional Sephardic
poetry.

During the Second Republic

Pulido's campaign still resonated in public opinion during the Second Republic (1931–36). A legal consequence was the decree of April 29, 1931,
which specified the "residence norms for naturalization." One of its articles,
although not directed specifically at Sephardim, helped Moroccan Jews to
obtain Spanish citizenship: "The period of residence established in Article 2
[ten years] will be reduced to two years in the cases of citizens of Spanish
American republics, Portugal and Brazil, or natives of the Spanish Protectorate in Morocco" (In *Actas,* 591).

During Franco's Regime

After the Civil War (1936–39), a political regime was established that sympathized ideologically with German Nazism and Italian fascism. The State also proclaimed itself to be Catholic. Under these conditions, it would be logical that Franco's Spain would not show much interest in or sympathy for Jews of Spanish origin. Nevertheless, as has been repeated often both nationally and internationally, Franco's regime saved the lives of a good number of Jews during World War II and the Nazi persecution by allowing them to begin their flight from Europe through Spain or by taking them under the protection of its consulates.

Direct responsibility for this humanitarian gesture has been attributed to General Franco himself, giving rise to a variety of conjectures. Why had a fascist soldier intervened in favor of the Jews at such a delicate time? Why confront the Nazi regime over a matter of such little benefit to Spain? Some have tried to attribute it to Franco's hypothetical Jewish origin.[10]

It is true that during those anguishing years from 1940 to 1944 a number of Jews found in Spain the life raft that would save them from extermination. However, it is no less true that the number of Jews saved was smaller than is generally assumed, nor was the Spanish attitude as decidedly and openly pro-Jewish as it was made to seem. In the first place, one must distinguish between those Jews who took refuge in Spain and those who were expressly protected by the Spanish government. The former came to Spain from France after that country surrendered to the Germans on May 10, 1940. Tens of thousands of people—among whom, naturally enough, were some Jews, both French and German—fled south across the Pyrenees Mountains.

At first the Spanish authorities were permissive and issued transit visas to all who applied, thus an undetermined number of Jews were able to leave for other countries, since they were not permitted to stay in Spain. Little by little, however, restrictions were imposed, in order to not anger the Vichy government. A limit was put on the number of people allowed to cross the border daily, and they were required to present a French exit visa.

The legal migration of Jews stopped in August 1942, when French authorities annulled all exit visas for Jews. Illegal emigration increased, and refugees crossed the Pyrenees (sometimes during terrible weather) with the aid of humanitarian border guards or smugglers who charged a high price for their services. Here is how a Belgian refugee tells of his trip:

10. [AN] Franco is, in fact, a common family name among Sephardim. That does not mean, however, that all who carry that name are of Jewish descent.

When the Germans conquered the south of France, I sold all my property, took my wife and child, and paid two hundred thousand francs to smugglers who were supposed to get us to Portugal. But the smugglers left us in the Pyrenees mountains, where I was stuck with my wife and child among the mountains and valleys. We wandered around until the Spanish caught us, took everything we still had, and placed my wife in a prison, me in Miranda de Ebro, and my child in an orphanage. (In Avni, 112)

The above quote mentions the concentration camp in Miranda de Ebro, an unpleasant memory for the refugees who found themselves trapped in Spain at that time because they could not get into Portugal or because they had missed a ship to another country. In the camp in Miranda, which had been created at the end of the Civil War for the losers, Jewish and non-Jewish refugees coexisted with political prisoners. Conditions were very harsh.

The food was mostly hunger rations scarcely sufficient to sustain life; prisoners were housed in windowless huts, where their scanty clothing and thin blankets gave no protection from the biting cold; medical care was poor; and the isolation and separation from family was exacerbated by daily fear of the future. Apparently, however, in Miranda de Ebro there was no indiscriminate torture of imprisoned refugees, and this applied also to Jewish refugees. . . . The length of imprisonment in Miranda de Ebro was not defined in advance, however, and some refugees imprisoned in 1940 were still there by 1943.

The harsh conditions of imprisonment, which perhaps can be explained by the general shortages and hunger in Spain, were even more difficult for the displaced Jewish refugees because of the prohibition against activities of foreign welfare organizations. Since late 1940, Jewish and non-Jewish welfare organizations sought permission to operate in Spain, but to no avail. (Ibid., 77)

Despite all the restrictions and difficulties, refugees kept coming to Spain. Some seventy-five hundred Jews are estimated to have escaped extermination by going through the Iberian Peninsula between the summer of 1942 and the fall of 1944.

The slightly over thirty-two hundred Sephardim who had the active protection of Spanish consulates because of their Hispanic origin were in a very different situation. Consular protection was offered especially in France and the Balkans, often for services rendered. That was the case of 150 Jews in Bulgaria and 107 in Rumania who received Spanish visas and help in fleeing because they had supported the Franco regime and maintained contact with its representatives during the Civil War.

If several hundred Sephardim were able to take advantage of protection by Spanish consulates, it was because of the efforts, occasionally bold and even rash, of a few Spanish diplomats and politicians, such as Bernardo Rolland, consul in Paris; Eduardo Gasset, consul in Salonika until April 1943; his successor, Sebastián Romero Radigales; Miguel Angel Muguiro, the Spanish minister in Budapest; and Julio Palencia y Tubau, Spanish minister in Sofia. Palencia sided so actively with the persecuted Jews that he put his diplomatic role at risk, as Haim Avni explains:

> His openly pro-Jewish stance earned Palencia the epithet "the well-known friend of the Jews" in German correspondence. Indeed, the Spanish minister and his wife openly expressed their shock at the persecution of Jews. When Leon Arie, a Sephardic Jew, was sentenced to death for allegedly raising the price of the perfume he sold by a few pennies, Palencia and his wife appealed to various people of influence to prevent his execution. Their efforts were in vain, however; the man was put to death. The Palencias later surprised their diplomatic colleagues by requesting permission from a Bulgarian court to adopt Arie's son and daughter. On June 5, 1943, the official Bulgarian newspaper published the court's decision confirming the adoption of Klodi and Renée, Arie's 21- and 26-year-old son and daughter, by the 58-year-old Spanish minister and his wife, Zoé Dragumiz de Palencia.
>
> The Germans and the Jew-haters in Bulgaria were furious. Palencia was declared persona non grata and was recalled to Madrid. (Ibid., 166)

The resolute posture of these honorable politicians contrasts notably with the ambiguities and vacillations of the government in Madrid. For example, to evacuate 365 Sephardim from Salonika between 1943 and 1944, Romero Radigales not only had to struggle against the stubbornness of the Nazi commanders but also against the continuous and sudden changes of opinion in Spain's Ministry of External Affairs, which one day demanded the repatriation of those Jews who were Spanish citizens and the next day refused them entry to Spain.

Where the Jews could not find a champion to defend them personally, they were left to their own devices. A good example of this is the journey of a letter several leaders of a Sephardic association in Paris sent to General Franco on March 13, 1941, seeking permission to settle in Spain. It is not known if the letter ever reached its destination or if it was lost in the maze of offices, secretariats, and subsecretariats. In any case, it was returned after some time with the following note: "The General Security Office has decided not to grant the request."

The saving of Jews by Spain during World War II, then, was due, depending on the individual case, to the efforts of individuals or to administrative permissiveness rather than to a clear and resolute official stand. Franco's regime was characterized by an ambiguous vacillating posture with regard to Jews.

On the positive side, in 1948, when the series of agreements with Egypt and Greece that had permitted Spain to protect Sephardim expired, a legal decree allowed 144 Greek Sephardic families and almost three hundred Egyptian Jews to be granted Spanish citizenship. Nearly twenty years later, following the Six Day War, 110 Egyptian Sephardim were able to seek refuge in Israel because of their Spanish passports.

There were some important cultural events during the forty-year dictatorship as well. In 1940, the Instituto Arias Montano was founded. Originally defining itself as devoted to "Hebraic studies" (and later "Hebrew, Sephardic and Near Eastern studies"), it was part of the autonomous Consejo Superior de Investigaciones Científicas (CSIC). The Instituto Arias Montano is currently part of the Instituto de Filología, still within the CSIC. Also important were the World Sephardic Bibliographic Exposition in 1959 at the National Library in Madrid and the creation of the Institute for Sephardic Studies (subsequently absorbed into the Instituto Arias Montano) in 1960; in 1964 the First Symposium on Sephardic Studies was organized by the CSIC and the Sephardic Museum was founded in Toledo.

However, at the same time that Levantine Sephardim were being granted Spanish citizenship and institutions for Sephardic studies were being established, Spain's Jewish communities faced serious obstacles. Immediately after the Civil War, the few Jews who lived in the country were in a state of legal limbo that put them almost outside the law.[11]

> There was no room in the new Catholic State for an organized Jewish community, openly conducting its prayers, circumcising its sons, and providing a Jewish education to its children. Synagogues in Madrid and Barcelona were closed, the community disintegrated, and religious worship was forced underground. The sense of terror that pervaded the post-Civil War period prompted many Jews to convert. (Ibid., 68–69)

This aura of illegality lasted for most of Franco's regime, even after the great exodus of Moroccan Sephardim in 1956. Spain had no difficulty in taking in these emigrés from its old protectorate. If they found it easy to settle in Spain, however, organizing their communities was by no means simple. The Franco regime's fear of any activity that might lead to associations and public meetings prohibited the legal constitution of Jewish communities. Some communities, such as the one in Madrid, presented elaborate proposals yearly to the Ministry of Governance within the framework of the existing law of associations; time and again, the documents were returned with permission denied.

11. [AN] For more information about the history of the new Jewish communities in Spain, see chapter 6, "Sephardim in Spain."

The State was still officially Catholic. The law of religious freedom was not promulgated until 1967, and even then its approval was preceded by angry debate in the Cortes.[12] Two hundred fifty-one amendments were proposed to the law, and even its defenders, such as then Minister of Justice Antonio María de Oriol y Urquijo, argued as follows: "Let the regulation of a civil right of religious freedom not be confused with warped interpretations that seek, overtly or covertly, cowardly or stupidly, to weaken or destroy our Catholic unity."[13] The following year, 1968, the modern synagogue in Madrid was dedicated in a new building.

The Present

Spain's new government has inaugurated a series of official changes generally favorable to Hispano-Sephardic relations. Greater liberty under the current democratic regime makes it possible for Spanish Jews (most of whom are Sephardic) to hold religious services with no obstacles and to participate in Jewish associations. The law of June 30, 1982 allows Sephardim to obtain Spanish citizenship after two years of residence in the country (rather than ten years, which is the usual case). This law considers them citizens of other areas culturally tied to Spain, such as Hispanic America, the Philippines, Equatorial Guiana, and Andorra. The establishment of diplomatic relations with Israel (which did not take place until 1986) has certainly aided Spain's contact with Israeli Sephardim, who are very curious about anything related to Spain.

Many Spaniards are interested, or at least curious, about Sephardim. This is shown by the appearance of Sephardic matters in the media (articles and newspaper reports, television and radio programs), the increasing frequency with which talks about Jews or recitals of Sephardic music are announced, and the increasing number of recordings of Sephardic songs released. Attention to Sephardic themes increases as 1992 approaches. During that year, among other activities, there will be a commemoration of the Jews' expulsion from Spain by the Catholic monarchs five centuries ago.

Any news or cultural activity related to the Sephardim awakens interest and creates reactions, sometimes contradictory but always lively. When the newspaper *El País* published an article in its Sunday supplement about the Israeli Sephardim in 1983, it was still receiving letters from readers com-

12. The Spanish Parliament.
13. [AN] In Samuel Toledano's speech at Miranda de Ebro on May 30, 1981. I have a typed copy generously supplied by the author. A revision of the text will be found in *Estudios Mirandeses* 1 (1982): 153–65.

menting on the information two months later. One of those letters suggested that Spain make some type of official reparation to the Sephardim, but it confused the question of the Sephardim with that of relations with Israel:

> I even think that it would be appropriate to give the director of *Kol Israel, the Voice of Israel in Judeo-Spanish,* the chance to broadcast a statement recognizing the gratitude of Sepharad to all of the Sephardim for retaining over 500 years the Spanish that their ancestors spoke, recognizing as well the historical error that was committed in March 1492 with the expulsion edict. Finally, I think that the government should bear in mind these words of Salomón Seruya, "Para que se desarrolle una fructífera cooperación cultural en torno al sefardismo es indispensable que Espanya establezca relaciones diplomáticas con Israel" ["for the development of fruitful cultural cooperation with the Sephardic world, it is absolutely necessary for Spain to establish diplomatic relations with Israel"].[14]

Another letter, responding to the one just cited, although against establishing relations with Israel, speaks of reparations and seeks automatic Spanish citizenship for all Sephardim:

> The letter seems right on the mark in asking for reparations for the unjustified expulsion of the Jews from Spain and for support for a community that for nearly 500 years has been living proof of the enormous injustice and outrage committed by the intransigent and sectarian Catholic monarchy. The preservation of living Spanish as the language of the Sephardim speaks in their favor, and they deserve immediate reparation for that deed, as well as Spanish passports. The State should also apologize publicly, as well as the Church, as has been done in other cases. But please explain what that has to do with recognizing Israel. What does it have to do with recognition of the most Nazi and racist state in the world?[15]

These are just some samples, perhaps anecdotal but not therefore insignificant, of the interest in Sephardim in present-day Spain. Along with this general curiosity, however, there is also a great deal of generalized misinformation, which is not surprising since Spaniards have had very little opportunity to coexist with Jews or even to know them for the last five centuries.

Illustrative anecdotes are innumerable. It is not necessary to cite extreme cases, such as the woman who, in the 1920s, lifted the skirt of a Jewish girl to see if she had a tail.[16] As recently as 1976, I mentioned to a colleague at the university that a Jewish friend of mine worked in a government agency. He replied, "How strange that he would work for the State since he is a *foreigner.*" He could not conceive of someone being both Jewish and Spanish. No less knowledgeable was the person who, after listening to a program

14. [AN] *El País,* 14 Aug. 1983, Sunday supp., 6, col. a.
15. [AN] *El País,* 25 Sept. 1983, Sunday supp., 6, cols. c–d.
16. [AN] Samuel Toledano told the story in his speech mentioned in note 13.

on Hebrew culture on Spain's Radio Nacional, called the station to participate in the discussion with the question, "Are the Jews Catholic?" Further
complicating matters is the confusion of terms, a problem that has implications not only for Judaism but for everything that is not Christian. Of course,
that is understandable in a country that has been completely Catholic for
centuries.

Just as many Spaniards—including university faculty and students—do
not know the real meaning of the word *Shi'ite* (despite its almost continual
presence in international news), or the difference between Muslim and Arab,
neither do they understand the meaning of terms such as *Sephardi, Ashkenazi,
Yom Kippur,* and *Ladino.* Even the most prestigious media speak of the "*Israelite* army" and "*Israelite* politics" (rather than the correct *Israeli*) when
giving news about Israel.

Sometimes the difference between Jewish and/or Sephardic and terms dealing with the Islamic world is not clear. This fact became apparent during the
defense of a graduate thesis on Sephardic literature in the College of Philology at a Spanish university in 1977. One of the members of the committee
offered excuses for not being able to evaluate the thesis stringently enough
because he did not have "enough knowledge about *Arabic* language and
literature."

In light of such misinformation, it is not surprising that stale and tenden-
tious commonplaces are widespread. The majority of Spaniards who find the
topic of Sephardim somewhat interesting have a very incomplete knowledge
of it. They know almost nothing of the history and sociocultural characteristics of the Sephardim, and they still identify Judeo-Spanish with fifteenth-
century Spanish, as if a language could avoid evolution over five hundred
years. Even people in university settings believe that Judeo-Spanish literature
is limited to the beautiful and melancholy *romanzas* and *canticas;* they know
nothing about *aljamiada* literature or the modern adopted genres.

When the subject of relations between the Sephardim and Spain comes up,
some of the most hackneyed, jingoistic, and sentimentalist remarks are heard,
the same ones refuted at the beginning of the century by Pulido's opponents:
the Sephardim are Spaniards without a country; they long for Spain and hold
a deep love for the country, proven by their conscious and deliberate retention of Judeo-Spanish as a remembrance of their lost homeland and by their
preservation, for five centuries, of the keys to the houses that their ancestors
abandoned in Toledo when they were expelled from Spain. These ideas are
clearly shown in a very short story I myself published (mea culpa) in 1973,
when I had not yet begun to work in Sephardic studies:

If it is relatively easy through the course of history to find the lives of men who wrote just one poem, it is more difficult to find an entire family who dedicated all of its energies, for generations, to just one work.

This is the case of a Jewish family whose firstborn were always named José Maimón.

Expelled from Spain in the fifteenth century, they left Toledo with the keys to their old home. After some years of wandering, they settled in Salonika and opened a small fabric store.

Generation after generation, all the José Maimóns dedicated their efforts to maintaining respect for Spain in the family, retaining the Spanish language and the old keys to the house in Toledo.

The Maimón family perished during World War II.[17]

SEPHARDIC REACTION TO SPAIN

What is and has been the Sephardic attitude toward Spain? Do Sephardim willingly accept being called "Spaniards without a homeland," the expression coined by Dr. Pulido, which many people still use?

The polemical senator started a two-pronged movement. On the one hand, the Spaniards learned about the existence of the forgotten Sephardim, and intellectuals began to take an interest in them. On the other hand, there were also Sephardim who, thanks to Pulido, found out that the country called Spain was a current reality and not just a historical vestige filed away in their memories from the time of the expulsion.

The substantial correspondence that Pulido carried on with many Sephardim and the dissemination of his books in the Levant aroused some Sephardi interest in Spain. Jewish newspapers in the Eastern Mediterranean printed arguments for and against Pulido and even Spain itself and, as a by-product, for and against the use of Judeo-Spanish as a language linking the Sephardim to their "mother country."

Pulido's books were received with enthusiasm and a veneration bordering on mawkishness by many Sephardim in the Levant and Morocco. José Elmaleh, a Jew from Gibraltar, wrote Pulido that his first book had moved him to tears: "I am very young—barely twenty-five years old—and I can tell you that my impression on reading *Los Israelitas Españoles* was such that I could not help but shed some tears" (Pulido, 185).

For others, such as the young Moritz Levy, a philosophy student in Vienna, the senator's publications were a true shock:

17. [AN] In my book *Biografías de genios, traidores, sabios y suicidas, según antiguos documentos* [Biographies of geniuses, traitors, wise men and suicide victims, according to old documents] (Madrid: Editora Nacional, 1973), 102–3.

*Me es imposible por expresar las impresiones que—como judio—mi corazon siente en
leendo su libro, como también sus artícolos yenos de amor y amistad por nuestra nación judia.
Una moción niervosa se empatrona de mi cuerpo, mis penserios se revueltan y en vano busco
por calmarme.* (Ibid., 121)

[It is impossible for me to express the impressions which—as a Jew—my heart
feels on reading your book, as well as your articles filled with love and friendship for
our Jewish people. A nervous movement takes hold of my body, my thoughts whirl
and I seek in vain to calm myself.]

The dominant impression among others was of zealous admiration, as in
the case of Yosef Romano, editor of the newspaper *El Meseret* in Smyrna: "en
leendo vuestro estudio en 'España' yo creí leir o sientir las palabras de un
apóstolo, de un Paulo moderno" ["when I read your study in 'España' I
thought I was reading or hearing the words of an apostle, of a modern Paul"]
(Ibid., 185).

Some accepted the idea that Spain was truly the country of the Sephardim.
Isaac Pisa, from Smyrna, justified it in a letter to Pulido, referring to the
glorious Spanish past of Hebraic culture:

*La España es nuestra patria, la tierra donde estan nuestros padres. Alli duermen nuestras
glorias y alli nuestros monumentos; alli se escribieron las páginas mas gloriosas de nuestra
historia.* (Ibid., 187)

[Spain is our homeland, the land where our ancestors are. There sleep our glories
and there are our monuments. There were written the most glorious pages of our
history.]

Isaac Alcheh y Saporta, also Sephardic, spoke on December 2, 1916 in the
Ateneo in Madrid[18] and affirmed: "Spaniards we were, Spaniards we are and
Spaniards we will be" (In Estrugo, *Retorno*, 25).

Curiosity about Spain, contacts by mail with Spaniards, and even the con-
viction of their own Hispanism drove some Sephardim to travel—almost as
pilgrims—to that country, as unknown to them as it was idealized by them.
One who most fervently expressed his desires was Enrique Bejarano, the
Jew from Bucharest through whom Pulido had discovered the "Spanish
Israelites":

*Si Vd. leía en mi corazón, cuánto se arde del deseo de besar un día las piedras de aquella
patria y fregar mis ojos con el polvo de aquella tierra donde duermen los huesos de mis
abuelos. . . . Ah ¡si tenia alas! ¡Si era yo paloma! . . . Si, Señor mío, yo seria el mas infeliz
hombre si muriese sin ver el suelo de mis antepasados!* (Pulido, 180–81)

18. The Ateneo científico, literario y artístico [scientific, literary and artistic Atheneum] was
founded in Madrid between 1820 and 1823 by the Economic Society of Madrid. It has been
one of the most important associations in Spain's progress.

[If you could read how my heart burns with the desire one day to kiss the stones of that homeland and rub my eyes in the dust of that land where the bones of my ancestors sleep. . . . Oh, if I had wings! If I were a dove! . . . Yes, my dear sir, I would be the most unhappy of men were I to die without seeing the land of my ancestors!]

Those who made the pilgrimage to that "land of their ancestors" scrutinized it all, trying to discover the common features of those peoples who had lived separated and isolated from each other for five hundred years. They compared Madrid, Barcelona, or Alicante to the Jewish quarter in their native Smyrna, Bucharest, or Salonika. They emphasized the similarity of Spanish and Sephardic family names, of physical characteristics and of thought processes, of foods and of customs. They even found flamenco music like synagogue chants or like Levantine ballads and songs. Here is how José Estrugo described his impressions on arriving in Spain:

From my infancy Spain filled my imagination like a fairy tale. . . . In October 1922 I first arrived in Spain. . . . I was rejoining an ancient country from which my ancestors had been expelled so cruelly! It seemed to me that I was going to find intact the beautiful dwellings . . . whose rusted keys I had occasionally seen in the Jewish quarters. . . . For the first time in my life I felt truly at home, like a native. Here I was not, I could not be an intruder! For the first time I felt completely at home, much more so than in the Jewish quarter where I had been born! I am not ashamed to confess that I bent down, in an outburst of indescribable emotion, and kissed the ground on which I was standing. . . . I coincided with the observations of other Sephardic travelers and thought I saw everywhere faces of friends and relatives, the same women, the same children, the same classes, the same mindset and, above all, it was a stabbing joy to hear my language spoken for the first time in a Christian country and by Christians—that language which in the Levant is called "Jewish." The names were very much like ours. The foods, the music . . . in short, everything. Even the stones seemed to have messages for me. (Estrugo, *Retorno,* 35–37)

This living contact with the "homeland" and its inhabitants confirmed the feeling of Hispanism, just as M. J. Bensasson expressed it:

I was proud to think that I was as Spanish as all those who comprised the life of Madrid. . . . My Spanish blood seemed to feel the influence of that milieu, the pleasant temperature of the environment, the refreshing homeland air, the happy noise of all those beings through whom ran the same blood. . . . Madrid, Spain, Spaniards, I love you, I adore you because I am Spanish. (Bensasson, 215)

Not all Sephardim, however, were as enthusiastic about Pulido's ideas. They did not all proclaim their emotional ties to Spain, nor did they take on their "Spanishness" equally fervently. The Zionist leader Max Nordau noted the following:

The fact that several Jews have had the good fortune of meeting Dr. Pulido during his trip and have told him how happy they were to hear Spanish spoken by a Spaniard should not cause one to think that all Spanish Israelites are equally interested in returning to and learning about Spain. The excitement of the moment and the awakening of feelings have surely caused them to speak without thinking.   (In Pulido, 181)

Of course, there were and are Hispanophiles and Hispanists among the Sephardim. In Pulido's time, these were the people who, given their interest in Spain and things Hispanic, kept up correspondence with Pulido and other Spaniards, who came to Spain and made emotion-charged trips to areas important in Jewish history, and who then published or spoke about their impressions, proclaiming their love for Spain.

Nevertheless, for many Sephardic Jews, Spain was and is the country that expelled and persecuted them, where their ancestors were tortured or burned for continuing to practice their religion. If these people have been heard less often, it has not been only for political reasons but because, logically, those who thought and still think that way have had virtually no contact with Spain, nor have they wished to establish such contact.

Pulido himself once came up against the opposition of people who, considering Spain to be the country of the Inquisition and exile, refused to have any contact with him, not even by letter or the exchange of publications.

A distinguished [Sephardi] from a city in Hungary, asked by an illustrious Budapest attorney to establish correspondence with us, resists doing so. From his letter it seems that they (the Israelites) can be proud of their ancestors, of whom they speak gladly; that there is interest in Spain, but no thoughts of going where their ancestors were treated horribly. They are not interested in seeing modern Spanish books and journals.   (Ibid., 186)

This was not an unusual case, as Gad Francos, a Jew from Smyrna, pointed out to Pulido:

Bejarano is an exception among the Israelites who (to be honest and not hypocritical), I can assure you, have no feelings of sympathy for your country. They use Spanish for no other reason than that they know only that language and have not learned any other.   (Ibid., 111)

Preservation of the Spanish language has always been the argument used most often by those who attempted to show that the Sephardim have retained undying love for Spain. Gad Francos is not the only Sephardic opponent of that idea. Even when Sephardim fought for the preservation and development of Judeo-Spanish, many made it very clear that they were not doing so out of love for Spain, but because they felt the language to be their own. For example, here is a memo from the Esperanza [Hope] Society in Vienna, dated 1900:

Dunque no por amor de Espana, absolutamente no; sino por amor de nosotros mismos, por amor de nuestra existencia y por amor del judaismo debemos SOSTENER LA LENGUA ESPANOL que nuestros padres hablaban y que nosotros aprendemos desde la más tierna edad como nuestra lengua madre!! (In ibid., 157–58)

[Therefore not out of love for Spain, absolutely not; but out of love for ourselves, love of our existence and love of Judaism we should RETAIN THE SPANISH LAN-GUAGE that our forebears spoke and that we learn from our infancy as our mother tongue!!]

There were others who considered abandoning Judeo-Spanish once and for all in favor of another language that, for one reason or another, would satisfy Sephardic needs more fully. In chapter 3 I quoted from the play *Lingua y nación israelita*. To that one could add what Elias Arditti, a Sephardi from Smyrna, said in an article that appeared in the Trieste newspaper *Il Corriere Israelitico* in 1904. Among other things, he stated, "We have studied and loved the language of exile quite a bit. Enough. Let us learn the language of independence [Hebrew], at least as a good omen if not in preparation" (In ibid., 114).

Pulido's campaign also drew violent responses and harsh attacks in the Sephardic press of the time, an examination of which could be quite surprising. Here, as an example, is an extract from the newspaper *El Avenir*:

Nosotros no somos "un pueblo español diseminado por el mundo". Nosotros somos judios y como tales no debemos dexarnos aquistar por ninguna nacion, cuanto que tenemos en igual estima todos los pueblos sin diferencia de raza y de religion. . . .

Nosos [sic] somos y queremos restar antes de todo judios, y esto demanda de nosotros una conocencia de mas en mas profunda de nuestra lengua, el hebreo, nuestra historia y nuestra literatura. Nosos somos súditos [sic] otomanos y debemos laborar por los enteresses generales del pais que nos abriga y nos acorda tantos favores. Nosotros somos hombres y por esto somos obligados de ambesar por nuestros hijos y por nuestros estudios el frances, el italiano, el aleman y quien sabe cuantas otras lenguas. Despues de esto no queda tiempo ni lugar para el español. (In ibid., 113)

[We are not "a Spanish people scattered throughout the world." We are Jews and as such we should not allow ourselves to be acquired by any nation, since we esteem all peoples equally without differentiating race and religion. . . .

We are and wish to remain Jews above all, and this requires of us an ever-increasing knowledge of our language, Hebrew, our history and our literature. We are Ottoman subjects and we should work for the general interests of the country that shelters us and grants us so many favors. We are people and therefore we are obliged for the sake of our children and our studies to learn French, Italian, German and who knows how many other languages. After that, there is neither time nor place left for Spanish.]

If Pulido noted that "one sometimes finds in some [Sephardic] Hispanophobes a fund of bitterness toward Spain because of past abuses" (ibid., 143),
it was not only "Hispanophobes" who have been conscious of the dark side
that Spain presented to them. The very Moritz Levy who became so emotional on reading Pulido wrote the following:

En mi memoria suben recuerdos de la historia de nuestros abuelos en España. Gloria,
riqueza, sencias y adelantamiento, decadencia, miseria, desterramiento; delantre mis ojos
torna suben los horribles images de los tribunales de la inquisición. . . . "Ma que hicieron
nuestros abuelos para que fuesen perseguidos en tal manera?" "Es posible que no se hallo un
corazon humano que interviniese por ellos?" (Ibid., 122)

[To my mind come recollections of the history of our ancestors in Spain. Glory,
wealth, science and progress, decadence, poverty, exile. To my eyes come the horrible
images of the courts of the inquisition. . . . "But what did our ancestors do to be so
persecuted?" "Is it possible that there was no human heart to intervene on their
behalf?"]

As recently as 1981 a Canadian scholar of Sephardic origin was surprised
to learn that groups of Moroccan Jews had settled in Spain:

One question arises immediately. Why would Moroccan Jews go to settle in a
country that, until a few years ago (1968), still had not abrogated the shameful expulsion edict of 1492? In the present context, it is not difficult to understand why.
Faced with the imminent threat of physical persecution in Morocco, the Jews are
forced to emigrate. For those who are not wealthy and those who feel a certain tie to
the southern way of life, Andalusia is the immediate solution and perhaps a bridge to
new lands. Also, Spain is still a second homeland for many Sephardim, somewhat
unpleasant, but with fits of generosity. Nevertheless, there is no doubt that the majority of Sephardim who emigrate to Spain feel a bit uneasy about renewing a tragic
past and perhaps they think that it is the lesser of two evils. (Librowicz, 11)

These observations take for granted that religious intolerance is still alive
in Spain, as it was at the time of the expulsion, as if the five centuries had
passed unnoticed and the Spaniards' worries and feelings were not now very
different, far removed from the "Jewish problem" and concerns with the purity of lineage. To the Sephardim, however, most of whom have never been
in Spain, it is not at all clear that Spain has changed. As a result, thoughts of
the expulsion and the Inquisition equal or outweigh Sephardic curiosity
about Spain. This is especially true in the case of the Levantine Jews, whose
isolation from Spain has been greater.

The so-called "adopted" literary genres which began to appear in Judeo-
Spanish in the nineteenth century, serve as a good example of this phenomenon. An outstanding aspect of that literature, especially the novel and the
theater, is the complete absence of translations or adaptations of Spanish

works. Yet at the same time there appeared numerous translations or original works in Judeo-Spanish dealing with themes such as the Marranos, inquisitorial persecution, and the leaders among those expelled. This indicates that Spanish culture was completely unknown, and there was a typical view of inquisitorial Spain in novels such as *La judía salvada del convento* [The Jewish woman saved from the convent], *Don Miguel San Salvador* (about a convert), and *La Hermośa Raḥel* (dealing with the Portuguese *cristãos novos*). Among plays were *Don Yosef de Castilla, Don Abravanel y Formośa o Desteramiento de los jidiós de España* [Abravanel and Formosa or exile of the Jews from Spain], and *Los maranos*. In the last work, the main character is a convert who has become an inquisitor. He gives the following speech:

Ma habiendo sido persecutido hasta la muerte	But having been persecuted to death
yo dobí, por fuyir a la triste suerte,	to flee my sad lot I was supposed
inclinarme al escuro fanatiśmo	to incline toward dark fanaticism
y aḥrazar el cristianismo.	and embrace Christianity.
Mas, ¿cuántas lágrimas yo no vertí	But how many tears have I shed
desde el día que me convertí?	since the day I converted?
Hoy de Torquemada, el que mancha la historia	Today for Torquemada, he who stains the history
de toda la España y de su gloria	of all Spain and of its glory
¡yo!, el falso Migüel, so su brazo derecho.	I, false Miguel, am his right hand.

(Maranos, 26)

At another point in the play the persecuted Jewish woman Elena (who ends up discovering that she is the mother of the inquisitor Miguel) exclaims:

¡Ah, maldicha Inquiśición! ¡Maldicha Inquiśición!	Oh cursed Inquisition! Cursed Inquisition!
Las víctimas de nuestra nación	The victims among our people
non se contan, no se asuman más;	are uncountable, are no longer counted
y Israel ğime de dolor, ¡helás!	And Israel groans in pain, alas!

(Ibid., 20)

These were some of the works that the Levantine Spanish Jews wrote, watched, or read. No less indicative is a composition, supposedly in praise of Spain, by the Yugoslavian poet Abraham Cappón:

A ti, España bienquerida,	You, beloved Spain,
nosotros "madre" te llamamos,	we call "mother,"
y, mientras toda nuestra vida,	and, during all our lives,
tu dulce lingua no dejamos.	we do not abandon your sweet language.

Aunque tú nos desterraste	Although you exiled us
como madrastra de tu seno,	from your breast like a stepmother,
no estancamos de amarte	we do not tire of loving you
como santísimo terreno	as the blessed earth
en que dejaron nuestros padres	in which our parents left
a sus parientes enterrados	their relatives buried
y las cenizas de millares	and the ashes of thousands
de tormentados y quemados.	who were tortured and burned.
Por ti nosotros conservamos	For you we preserve
amor filial, país glorioso,	filial love, glorious country,
por consiguiente te mandamos	and so we send you
nuestro saludo caluroso.	our warm greeting.

(*Actas,* 261)

Is it not curious that almost the only thing that Cappón has to say about that "beloved mother," for whom he feels "filial love" and to whom he sends such a "warm" greeting, is that she has behaved like a stepmother who exiled his grandparents, and he worships her soil because the ashes of those whom the Inquisition burned after having tortured them are scattered in it? The poem expresses Sephardic ambivalence toward Spain very well, a feeling that is still prevalent. The previously mentioned article in *El País* (see note 14) collected similar opinions from Sephardim in Israel:

If in the marketplace in Jaffa some passersby, on discovering the presence of Spaniards, proclaim that "no ay nada mijor que la Espanya" ["there is nothing better than Spain"], others immediately answer that "la Espanya fue negra porké mos echó afuera" ["Spain was evil because she threw us out"]! The majority of the Sephardim interviewed do not know Spain, although they show a great deal of curiosity, mixed with a good dose of ignorance, about the country that expelled them almost five centuries ago. They ask, for example, . . . if Spain is anti-Semitic, as if that intolerant spirit that led to their expulsion still existed five hundred years later. . . . When, by chance. . . , they visit the Iberian Peninsula on vacation, they take rolls of photographs, which they proudly show in the Jewish quarters of several Spanish cities, they have their pictures taken with haughty expressions in front of the Santa María la Blanca synagogue in Toledo, and they even ask the Chuetas in Palma de Mallorca if they still feel Jewish.

The text needs no commentary, because it expresses perfectly the ambivalent feelings the Sephardim have toward Spain. On one hand, they emotionally evoke the glorious history of Judaism in Spain; on the other, they recall with pain the expulsion and persecution.

RECOMMENDED READING

On relations between Spain and the Sephardim (especially during the Franco regime), see Haim Avni, *Spain, the Jews, and Franco,* trans. Emanuel Shimoni (Philadelphia: Jewish Publication Society of America, 1982). There is a more recent book by Antonio Marquina and Gloria Inés Ospina, *España y los judíos en el siglo XX* (Madrid: Espasa-Calpe, 1987). Dealing specifically with Franco's aid to Jews during World War II, and including material from the author's personal interviews with Franco, is C. U. Lipschitz, *Franco, Spain, the Jews, and the Holocaust* (New York: Ktav Publishing House, 1984). Some matters dealing with the Sephardim in the Balkans are collected in Antonio Marquina Barrio, "La acción exterior de España y los judíos sefarditas en los Balcanes," in *Encuentros en Sefarad, Actas del Congreso Internacional "Los judíos en la historia de Espana"* (Ciudad Real: Instituto de Estudios Manchegos, 1987), 417–40.

Information on the Spaniards' first contact with Sephardim during the African campaign can be found in the booklet by Juan Bautista Vilar Ramírez, *La judería de Tetuán (1489–1860) y otros ensayos* (Murcia: Universidad de Murcia, 1969). On the early news of the Levantine Sephardim, see the contribution of Manuel Alvar, "Un descubrimiento del judeo-español," *Studies in Honor of M. J. Benardete*, ed. Izaak A. Langnas and Barton Sholod (New York: Las Americas, 1965), 363–66.

On Pulido's campaign, Angel Pulido Fernández's own two books are informative: *Los Israelitas Españoles y el Idioma Castellano* (Madrid: Librería de Fernando Fé, 1904), and *Españoles sin Patria y la Raza Sefardí* (Madrid: Estab. Tip. de E. Teodoro, 1905). On Pulido's effect during the Moroccan protectorate, a good source is Manuel L. Ortega, *Los hebreos en Marruecos* (Madrid: Editoral Hispano-Africana, 1919; reed. 1929, rept. 1934). A rebuke of the supposed Hispanism of the Sephardim and its modern political use will be found in Iacob M. Hassán, "La Diáspora sefardí," *España–Israel: Horizonte de un reencuentro* (Toledo: Junta de Comunidades de Castilla–La Mancha, 1988), 25–34. Other discussions collected in this volume about the establishment of diplomatic relations between Israel and Spain, and about Spain's attitude toward Jews, are substantial. On some Spaniards' attitudes toward Judaism and Jews, I have written "Los españoles ante lo judío: Sobre un prejuicio de simpatía," *Raíces: Revista judía de cultura* 5 (Mar. 1989): 13–16. Other less sympathetic prejudices are reflected in another article in the same issue of *Raíces:* Simón Hassán Benasayag, "El desconocido, ese judío," 18.

S I X

THE SEPHARDIM TODAY

In preceding chapters I have discussed the history, language, and culture of the Sephardim in the past. These questions remain: What is happening to the Sephardim in the present? Where do they live? How many of them are there? Do they still have their own cultural identity, or have they assimilated to the surrounding cultures? Who deals with Sephardic studies? This chapter will analyze the current situation of the Sephardim, discuss the state of their communities in Spain and elsewhere, and list the various Spanish and international organizations that treat Judeo-Spanish language and culture.

Current Worldwide Status

Analyzing the situation of the Sephardim today is difficult due to the lack of reliable and up-to-date information. There are no systematic statistics for several reasons. On one hand, most governments have never felt the need to gather statistics on national minorities. On the other hand, in countries that have had a large number of Sephardic immigrants (such as the United States and Israel), the ideal has been for the immigrants to assimilate and become a part of national life; thus the tendency is not to emphasize differences among citizens of different backgrounds but to minimize them. Israel, for example, does not care how many of its citizens are Sephardic and how many are not; it wants them all to feel like Israelis.

In other instances it is the Jewish communities themselves who, because of previous experiences, are reticent about any effort to record the number of Jews in a country. A good example is the way the Israelite Community of Madrid reacted to an attempt to include the religious tax on the tax return forms in Spain. The Community criticized the measure as unconstitutional, and one of its leaders said:

We know that these returns are cross-checked and that lists are compiled from them. Doubtless these lists are made up with the best intentions. But the history of the Jewish people has shown us the danger of such lists. For centuries Germany was a cultural model for Europe . . . and, nevertheless, one fine day it had a regime that nobody expected and that kind of list brought many Jews to extermination camps.[1]

Consequently, the figures on Sephardim, and on Jews in general, that exist throughout the world are based on estimates and not on the systematic collection of data. There is also the problem of the definition of "Sephardic." The most "official" data on Jewish population generally comes from Israel or from institutions such as the Jewish Agency or the World Sephardi Federation, which use the term "Sephardi" in the broad sense of "non-Ashkenazi," so that the figures on Sephardim include Jews from Iraq, Iran, Yemen, Libya, and so on. In addition, the estimates—approximate and subjective—are not even current; most date from ten or even twenty years ago, and the situation has certainly changed since then.

For all these reasons it is almost impossible to tell how many Sephardim there are today and how they are distributed. At most one can determine in what countries groups of Sephardim are known to live, how many Sephardim there are in relation to the total population and to the total number of Jews in the country, if the Sephardic population has increased or decreased during this century, and why. In general, the majority of Sephardim are in countries of the Second Diaspora—the United States, Israel, and, to a lesser extent, Latin America. Of traditional Sephardic areas, Turkey may be the only country in which the community has any vitality.

The number of people who currently speak Judeo-Spanish is also unknown. Estimates range between 150,000 and 300,000. The margin of error is broad, as is the range of estimates within individual countries. Certainly, the countries with the most Judeo-Spanish speakers are those that have the largest Sephardic communities: Israel, the United States, and Turkey, in that order.

In the Levant

Turkey

Of that area in which Sephardic culture flourished, the only country that still has sizable communities is Turkey. Travelers can see their presence by going through the Great Bazaar in Istanbul, where many small business people still speak their characteristic Judeo-Spanish. In 1979 there were some 23,000 or

1. [AN] *El País,* 27 Aug. 1983, 13.

24,000 Jews among a total population of 45,000,000. The majority are Sephardim, except for a small Ashkenazic community of 1,000 in Istanbul and
some small groups of Syrians in a southeastern area that became part of Turkey in 1939.

The largest Sephardic community is in Istanbul, with some 20,000 members. This community and that of Izmir, which has over 2,000 members, are
the only ones with synagogues. Much smaller communities are found in
Ankara (225), Antalya (164), and Bursa (192); the communities in Adana,
Edirne, Iskenderun, Gelibolu, Tekirdag, and Çanakkale are virtually insignificant since the members can be counted in tens. There are a total of fourteen
such communities, aside from places where isolated Jews live.

Judeo-Spanish is known even among the relatively young, but it is being
replaced by Turkish. Judeo-Spanish is also spoken by some Turks and Armenians, who learned it through business dealings with their Jewish compatriots. Also, the weekly *Şalom,* published in Istanbul, is the outstanding
Sephardic publication and, although one sees more and more articles in Turkish, it is one of the few Judeo-Spanish publications in the world today.

Greece

The situation is more somber in Greece, where the Nazis deported and mas-
sacred entire communities. The few survivors emigrated to Israel, America,
or, less often, to other European countries, such as France. The most outstanding case was the large community in Salonika, which fell from over
56,000 members in 1940 to fewer than 1,300 in 1959. It is estimated that
more than 46,000 Jews from Salonika (that is, 80 percent of the community)
were deported during World War II, most of whom perished in the extermination camps.

The case of other communities was equally bloody, for example, the Isle of
Rhodes, where 2,000 of its 2,200 Jews were deported. The small community
in Serre (600 members) was reduced to three people in 1947. Xanzi is in a
similar situation; of its 600 members, only six were left after the war.

The only Greek city whose Sephardic population grew was Athens—from
over 3,500 to 4,930 people, despite the great number of deportations
(1,690). This growth, however, occurred because many Jews from other
areas of the country fled to the capital at the end of the war while awaiting
the opportunity to emigrate elsewhere (2,000 Jews came to Athens from
Salonika alone). Consequently, by 1959 the Jewish population of Athens had
fallen again to slightly over 2,500, a thousand fewer than when German persecution began.

Overall, the Jewish population in Greece fell from almost 80,000 in 1940 to just over 10,000 at the end of World War II. More than 60,000 people were deported, and in the fifteen years following the war there was so much emigration that by the end of the 1950s only some 5,000 Sephardim still lived in Greece.

There is no current data, but it can be assumed that the Jewish population of Greece has continued to decrease. The only sizable community is in Athens, which consisted of some 2,500 Sephardim in the mid-1960s. At that same time, the community in Salonika, which had been so large before the war, was down to 1,300 people, and in 1978 the remaining 1,100 were in the process of losing their cultural identity primarily because of mixed marriages and the assimilation of young people to Greek culture. The third largest Greek community was in Larisa, consisting of fewer than 500 people, among whom Judeo-Spanish had almost completely disappeared. Perhaps the most recent statement on Greece's Sephardim was given by Mordehay Avishay, who visited Salonika and Serre in 1977, with the following disheartening results:

During my visit to Salonika, the first thing I did was to visit the Jewish Club. . . . There are a few Jewish adults, men and women, most of whom are still active, who play cards, chat, drink in the small bar and watch television. . . . Of the dozens of synagogues—perhaps a hundred—that used to exist in the city, there remains only one beautiful temple, built in our time by the Jews from Monastir. . . . Its iron doors are closed, open only on holidays. . . . I went to Serre, a city of some 40,000 or 50,000 inhabitants. . . . There I discovered that there is only one Jew whom everybody knew . . . he had married a Greek Christian and they had two daughters. . . . Is there no reminder in the city of its past Jewish life? Nothing remains: neither a synagogue nor a school. Everything was destroyed. The only thing left is the cemetery. . . . Throughout Thrace, in Drama, Kavala, Kesanti, Komotimi, as far as Alexandropolis on the Turkish border, you will only meet isolated Jews. That is what remains of Salonika and its "daughters." (Avishay, "Supervivientes," 81–84)

Yugoslavia

At the end of World War I, the area that is contemporary Yugoslavia contained no fewer than 100 Jewish communities with 70,000 members, many of whom were Sephardim. The Jewish population varied, but it never dipped below 70,000. On the eve of World War II, Yugoslavia's 71,000 Jews included 29,000 Sephardim.

As in Greece, the German (and also Italian, Hungarian and Bulgarian) invasion led to the extermination of some 55,000 Sephardic and Ashkenazi Jews. At the end of the war, more than half of the survivors left the country (mainly for Israel and the United States), and in the early 1950s there were only 7,000 Jews left, half of whom were Sephardim.

At the end of the 1960s, Yugoslavia had thirty-eight Jewish communities, some of which were very small. The largest were in Belgrade (1,500), Zagreb (1,300), and Sarajevo (slightly over 1,000). The largest communities today are in Sarajevo and Belgrade, with approximately 1,000 members each. The World Sephardi Federation has a branch in Yugoslavia that promotes cultural activities, maintains a museum and a library, and publishes the monthly *Jevrejski Pregled* and the annual *Jevrejski Almanah* in Serbo-Croatian.

Bulgaria

Martin Gilbert gives contradictory figures on Bulgarian Jews in his *Jewish History Atlas*.[2] According to his data, of 48,000 people at the beginning of World War II, 40,000 were exterminated and 37,000 emigrated to Israel between 1948 and 1965 [sic!]. Séphiha gives the following figures: in the 1920s, there were 45,000 Jews in Bulgaria, a minority of whom were Sephardim. That number increased to about 50,000 at the end of World War II.[3] Yet because many of the Jews had lost all of their property and spent the war years in forced labor camps, there was such a large wave of emigration to Palestine (which became Israel a few years later) that by the end of the 1940s fewer than 10,000 Jews still lived in Bulgaria.

Presently, there are some 2,500 Sephardim in Sofia. The second largest community is in Plovdiv, which had 1,000 members in the late 1970s. The Jewish minority in Bulgaria receives unusual attention from the government. There is an official cultural and educational society, which publishes *Godisnik* (in Bulgarian) and *Annual* (in English).

Rumania

A few years ago, the Spanish newspaper *El País* published a brief note giving the most current, and apparently most accurate, information on Rumanian Sephardim. According to that note, the Jews in Rumania, like those in Bulgaria, were not exterminated but interned in forced labor camps. When the state of Israel was created in1948, 360,000 of them (85 percent of Rumania's Jewish population) emigrated there. In 1983, 30,000 Jews were left in Rumania, one percent of whom were Sephardic, almost all of them in Bucharest.

---

2. [AN] Martin Gilbert, *Jewish History Atlas* (London: Weidenfeld & Nicholson, 1969), maps 96 and 106; hereafter designated *Atlas*.

3. [AN] In *L'agonie des judéo-espagnols* (Paris: Entente, 1977), 54–55, 83–84; hereafter designated *Agonie*.

More than half were over sixty years old. Their traditions as well as the use of Judeo-Spanish were disappearing, as they themselves said, according to *El País:* "mixed marriages and the small size of our community have been contributing factors, resulting in our original language being infested with Rumanian words."[4]

In North Africa

If the estimates of the number of Sephardim in the Eastern Mediterranean are confusing and contradictory, those dealing with North African Sephardim are even more so.

Egypt

The majority of the Egyptian Sephardic community was made up of Turkish Jews who had immigrated at the beginning of the century. In 1949, 126 Jews from Cairo and 146 from Alexandria and Port Said took on Spanish citizenship (under the agreements between Spain and Egypt). In 1968, after the Six Day War, another 110 Sephardim were able to leave because their visas indicated that they were Spanish citizens. After these emigrants left, most of whom went to Israel, little remained of the now-sparse Egyptian Jewish communities.

Morocco

Estimates of the Jewish population in general and Sephardic population in particular vary greatly, depending upon the source. According to Gilbert, the entire Jewish population of Morocco decreased from 285,000 in 1948 to 20,000 in 1974.[5] Avni calculates the Sephardic population in the Spanish protectorate at some 19,000 at the beginning of the century, falling to under 13,000 in 1935 and to slightly over 11,500 in 1941.[6] The journal *Sephardi World* reports a total Jewish population of 18,000 in 1982. Only some of those are Sephardim; the rest are Arab-speaking Jews and a few Ashkenazim.[7]

Jewish population decreased drastically in the 1950s, immediately after Morocco's independence and subsequent Arabization, which motivated a large wave of emigration to Israel, France, the United States, Canada, and Hispanic America. Séphiha states that the Tetuan community, which had

4. [AN] *El País,* 12 Apr. 1983, 6, box in cols. *b–d.*
5. [AN] *Atlas,* map 78.
6. [AN] Haim Avni, *Spain, The Jews, and Franco* (Philadelphia: Jewish Publication Society of America, 1982), 29, 69.
7. [AN] *Sephardi World* (Oct.–Nov.–Dec. 1982): 48–49.

been the largest one in Morocco, fell from 7,630 members in 1949 to slightly over 1,000 by 1968.[8] Today that community numbers some 500 people.

Renard estimated an impossible total of 15,000 speakers of Judeo-Spanish in Morocco in 1966.[9] Given the re-Hispanization of Moroccan Sephardim since the mid-nineteenth century, however, it is more probable that the majority of those 15,000 actually spoke Spanish (in its Andalusian dialect), although they might have preserved some peculiarities of Judeo-Spanish.

The most recent reports on Morocco's Sephardic communities come from scholars who have been seeking traces of oral literature there. The communities in Tetuan and Tangier—however impoverished and feeble in comparison to their glorious past—still exist, although one would be more likely to find Sephardim from both cities in Israel, the United States, or Spain than in their birthplace. There is also a large community in Casablanca, established later, mostly by Sephardim from Tetuan. Sephardim in Alcazarquivir and Larache were interviewed in the 1960s, but the current status of those communities is unknown. During that decade, a few Sephardim lived in Arcila, but in 1962 there was only one Jew in Xauen, and he spent part of the year in Tetuan.

The communities in Ceuta and Melilla will be discussed along with the Jewish communities in Spain. Those in Gibraltar, although British by passport and geographically in the Iberian Peninsula, more properly belong to the Moroccan Sephardic world by history and culture.

Algeria

Many of the Jews from Algeria have recently emigrated to Israel, France, Canada, or Latin America. Those who remained are completely assimilated to the national culture and speak French. There is virtually nothing left of the community in Oran, established by Jews from Tetuan, which still spoke Haketía fifty years ago.

In the New Lands

United States

The United States was one of the most popular targets of secondary immigration. According to Marc Angel, more than 25,000 who declared them-

---

8. [AN] *Agonie,* 80–81.

9. [AN] According to Tracy K. Harris, "The Prognosis for Judeo-Spanish: Its Description, Present Status, Survival and Decline, with Implications for the Study of Language Death in General" (Ph.D. diss., Georgetown University, 1979), 352.

selves Levantine Sephardim came into the United States between 1899 and
1925.[10] The actual figure was doubtless higher, as many would have entered
the country simply as Balkan citizens without revealing that they were Jewish.
Séphiha gives the figure of 70,000 immigrants between 1908 and 1925.[11]
Even the most recent estimates are old; in 1964 there were some 120,000
Sephardim in the United States; Angel calculated at least 100,000 in 1973.

   Whatever the exact number, the greatest concentration of Sephardim is in
New York City—some 40,000. There are large communities in Los Angeles,
Seattle, Atlanta, Montgomery, and Cincinnati, and some smaller communities (some of the smallest of which are either disappearing or have been established recently). The United States has about fifty Sephardic communities
in all.

   The number of Judeo-Spanish speakers is much smaller and constantly decreasing—from some 45,000 just in New York in 1930 to 15,000 in the
entire United States in 1966. Angel's 1972 survey in revealed that 73.6 percent of third- and fourth-generation Sephardim in the United States knew no
Judeo-Spanish at all. Cultural peculiarities disappear as progressive Ameri-
canization takes place. Contributing factors are not only the pressure of the
dominant culture and the lack of specifically Sephardic educational centers
(although the Ashkenazim have established schools), but also frequent mixed
marriages, either with Christians or with non-Sephardic Jews. Professor
Samuel G. Armistead tells the following revealing anecdote:

   Sephardic youth is exposed to an Anglo-American social milieu that is
   powerfully assimilationist and, regarding Jewish religious and cultural patterns, to norms imposed by the Ashkenazim. The young Sephardim, like all
   minorities in the United States, have naturally become totally Americanized.
   New generations are as completely ignorant of their mother tongue as they
   are unmindful of their ancestors' cultural legacy. It is rare to find an individual
   sensitive to the old vanishing values, who bothers to cultivate the use of *Judezmo* with elders in the family. Much more typical is the case of a Sephardic
   girl, a student in one of my classes. When told that she should know the
   meaning of this or that word in Spanish, she would answer, "Yes, I know.
   But I never talk to my father in *his* language." Fatal possessive, "his language!" That is, it is not mine! This case shows clearly the cultural erosion
   among Sephardic youth.   (*Actas,* 282)

   10. [AN] Marc D. Angel, *The Sephardim of the United States: An Exploratory Study* (New
York: Union of Sephardic Congregations, 1974), 87. All data dealing with Sephardim in the
United States come from this source, unless otherwise indicated.
   11. [AN] *Agonie,* 65.

Canada

Although there were hardly any Sephardim in Canada before World War II, some 15,000 have entered since, mostly from North Africa as a result of Moroccan and Algerian independence. Most of the immigrants settled in Toronto and Montreal. In 1967 the latter city had almost 9,000 Sephardic and Oriental Jews, 7,000 of whom were Moroccan. The remaining 2,000 were from Greece, Tunisia, Iraq, Iran, Algeria, Egypt, and so on.

Present estimates indicate some 10,000 Moroccan Jews living in Canada. The majority are French- or Arabic-speaking originally, although there are also some Spanish speakers from the old Spanish protectorate in Morocco. A 1976 survey, conducted to collect traditional stories, is quite significant regarding Judeo-Spanish. Forty-three Moroccan Jews of both sexes were interviewed and more than 340 stories were collected. Some two hundred of those stories had been told in Judeo-Arabic, over one hundred in French, and only thirty in Judeo-Spanish.[12] Despite the fact that they are a minority in the process of assimilation, Canadian Sephardim have shown some interesting initiatives, such as the creation (in 1980) of the musical group Gerineldo, for research into and performance of Sephardic folkloric material.

Latin America

Like the United States, Latin America is a major focus of secondary Sephardic immigration. According to *Sephardi World* there were some 200,000 Sephardim (in the broad sense of "non-Ashkenazi") in Latin America in 1982.[13] In 1952, Mair José Benardete calculated 100,000 Jews of Spanish origin.[14] They are, nevertheless, a minority among more than one million Latin American Jews (according to some estimates), most of whom are Ashkenazi.

Those countries that have large communities also have branches of the World Sephardi Federation and Jewish societies. Venezuela is an example, where there are more than 10,000 Sephardim (and some 15,000 Ashkenazim). The Israelite Association of Venezuela, which publishes *Maguen/ Escudo* [Shield], was founded in 1930, with its headquarters in Caracas. In

12. [AN] See André E. Elbaz, "Moslem Influences in the Folktales of Canadian Sephardim," *Sephardic Scholar* 4 (1979–82): 54–64, esp. 54.

13. [AN] *Sephardi World* (Oct.–Nov.–Dec. 1982): 52.

14. [AN] That is the year of publication of his book, *Hispanic Culture and Character of the Sephardic Jews*. A second edition was edited by Marc D. Angel (New York: Sepher-Hermon Press, 1982), 186.

1980 that organization founded a Center for Sephardic Studies, also in the capital.

There are many more Jews in Argentina. Some 80 percent of the total Jewish population—350,000 people—live in Buenos Aires. The majority of them, however, are Ashkenazim from Russia or Poland. Sephardim make up a mere 8 percent of that figure—slightly more than 30,000 in the entire country—more from the Levant than from North Africa. Buenos Aires is the headquarters of the Center for Research and Dissemination of Sephardic Culture (CIDiCSef), which publishes the journal *Sefárdica*. There are also Sephardic settlements in smaller cities, such as Rosario, Santa Fe, Cordova, and Tucuman. The latter was home to a Sephardic community of slightly over one hundred people in 1978, most of whom were second- or third-generation Argentinians, although some thirty immigrants, nearly all from Turkey, were also part of that community.

Uruguay, too, has a somewhat sizable Jewish community, again with Sephardim in the minority. In the early 1970s some 7,500 Sephardim, mostly from Smyrna, lived in Montevideo.

Another important Sephardic community is in Mexico. The journal *Voz Sefardí* was published there, and in 1981 the ABC Radio Network began to broadcast a program for Jewish listeners. The network has an exchange for the Judeo-Spanish broadcasts of Kol Israel, the official Israeli radio network. Countries such as Colombia, Chile, Peru, Cuba, Paraguay, and Brazil also have Sephardic settlements. Of course, the language of Latin American Jews is modern Spanish (Portuguese for those in Brazil), and Judezmo is no longer heard, except for some specific characteristics in the speech of the elderly.

Israel

The tendency in Israel is, or has been, to identify as Sephardic everything that is not Ashkenazi. Consequently, the data on true Sephardim are not accurate. Estimates vary between 300,000 and 600,000 Sephardim among a total population of four million.

The lower figure seems more accurate. Between 1948 and 1970 some 110,000 Jews came to Israel from the Balkans and Turkey; during approximately the same period there were 120,000 immigrants from Morocco, of whom some 30,000 were Sephardic. Adding those Sephardim who came from other places, and those from the communities in old Palestine (Jerusalem, Safed, Tiberias), yields an approximate total of 300,000. They are scattered throughout the country, although the greatest concentrations are, logically, in the large cities: Tel Aviv–Jaffa, Haifa, Jerusalem, Beersheba, Dimona, and Ashkelon (the latter two communities consist mostly of Moroccan Sephardim).

As in other countries, only a small percentage of these Sephardim continue to use Judeo-Spanish. There are great differences among estimates of Judezmophones, ranging from the most pessimistic (or realistic?) of slightly over 50,000 to an optimistic 300,000. Different sources give a series of numbers: 80,000, 100,000, 120,000, 200,000, and so on. The higher estimates doubtless include many people who have only a passive knowledge of the language or who hardly ever speak it. In some cases, the count of Judeo-Spanish speakers probably included the more than 60,000 Latin American Jews who live in Israel and whose language is not Judeo-Spanish but modern Spanish. These Jews are mostly Ashkenazi.

The circulation of the Judeo-Spanish weekly *La Luz de Israel* [The light of Israel] provides a better idea of the number of speakers of Judeo-Spanish. The newspaper, published in Tel Aviv, has a circulation of 7,000, of which 6,500 are sold in Israel. Its editors estimate, perhaps optimistically, that nearly ten people read every copy, so that it may reach over 60,000 readers. That figure, too, is optimistic.

The official radio network, Kol Israel, broadcasts in Judeo-Spanish for fifteen minutes a day, and the program has between 80,000 and 100,000 listeners in Israel, Turkey, and the Balkans. The network also publishes the journal *Aki Yerushalayim,* which has a circulation of 1,200, although that figure is worldwide and not limited to Sephardim; it includes people and institutions who are interested in Sephardic studies. Whatever the number of people in Israel who know Judeo-Spanish, the number of those who use it regularly as a means of communication is constantly decreasing. This was clearly shown in an article that appeared in *El País:*

> After having tenaciously resisted the erosion of time, Judeo-Spanish is a language in the process of disappearing. In Israel itself . . . the progressive acquisition of an Israeli national identity operates to the detriment of original Sephardic culture. If the grandparents still use Judeo-Spanish at home, their children no longer do so, although they still understand it. The grandchildren speak only Hebrew and English, the second being the language they learn in school.[15]

What is true of the language is equally true of the culture as a whole. Customs become uniform and traditions are replaced by standard Israeli lifestyle. Marriages between Jews of different origins contribute to the dilution

---

15. [AN] *El País,* 3 July 1983, Sunday supp., 14–19 and 22, 14 col. *d.*

of the cultural peculiarities of each group. The children of those unions feel themselves to be Israeli and not members of their parents' ethnocultural background.

In Contemporary Europe

Sephardim came to the various European countries under different circumstances and at different times, although nearly always for the same reasons: to escape persecution or to seek better living conditions when things became difficult in their homelands. The current situation in Europe will be examined here; Spain will be discussed later.

Portugal

There is practically no information about the Sephardim in Portugal. According to Gilbert, there were 3,000 Jews in Portugal during World War II.[16] A good number of them must have been Sephardim from Morocco, who had begun to enter the country at the end of the nineteenth century, as did the illustrious writer José Benoliel, who left Tangier to settle in Lisbon in the early twentieth century. The journal *Sephardi World* reports the figure of only 350 Jews in 1982, most of whom lived in Lisbon.[17]

France

Jewish population in France has increased considerably since World War II. The 300,000 who lived there at the beginning of the war have become, despite the 60,000 who were deported, some 600,000 currently. The basic cause of this growth was the arrival of immigrants after the war and the independence of the countries in North Africa. Only a small number of these Jews, however, are Sephardim.

After the war only 20,000 Jews of Hispanic origin lived in France, most of whom had come from the Balkans at the beginning of the century, but that figure also includes the sparse remnants of communities that had settled in the south (Bayonne, Biarritz, Bordeaux) after their expulsion from Spain. In 1977 there were some 10,000 speakers of Judezmo. As is happening elsewhere, their language and cultural peculiarities are disappearing, especially among the youth. Being a minority within a large Ashkenazi and non-Sephardic North African Jewish population also works against their maintaining their own identity.

Nevertheless, signs of Sephardic culture have appeared in France. The Se-

16. [AN] *Atlas,* map 93.
17. [AN] *Sephardi World* (Apr.–May 1982): 28–29.

phardic Federation began publishing the journal *Le Judaïsme Sephardi* [Sephardic Judaism] in Paris in 1932, and there has recently been a movement for the revitalization of Judeo-Spanish, which I will discuss later.

Great Britain

The World Sephardi Federation had its headquarters in London for many years, but the Sephardim are a very small minority among English Jews. In 1977 Britain's Jewish population was estimated at some 400,000, of whom only 13,000 were Sephardic; only 1,000 to 2,000 had preserved any traces of their culture or spoke Judezmo. A larger number follow Sephardic liturgy, which other Jews, such as those from Iraq, also practice.

The Low Countries

The Low Countries provided a safe haven for Jews when they were expelled from Spain. Spanish and Portuguese Jewish communities have existed there for centuries. Although they lost their vernacular over time (the Spaniards sooner than the Portuguese), they nevertheless preserved Sephardic liturgy and remained aware of their origins. At the beginning of this century, those ancient communities received a small influx of Levantine Sephardim who settled in Antwerp, Brussels, and Amsterdam.

Before World War II some 3,000 Sephardim lived in Belgium and 2,000 in Holland, most of whom were deported after the German invasion. At the end of the war, according to Séphiha, there were 500 left in Belgium and 700 in Holland.[18] The few who still live in these countries have lost the Judeo-Spanish language and their assimilation to Belgian or Dutch culture is practically complete.

Austria

The Sephardic community in Vienna (established at the end of the eighteenth century) preserved its identity vigorously and had an important role in publishing throughout the nineteenth century, despite its status as a minority within an Ashkenazi environment. It is estimated that at the beginning of World War II there were 160,000 Ashkenazim and only 15,000 Sephardim in the country. All were deported or exterminated during the war.

Italy

The Sephardim in Italy, like those in the Low Countries, lost Judeo-Spanish centuries ago, although they preserved Sephardic rites and the consciousness

18. [AN] *Agonie,* 58.

of being descendants of those expelled from Spain. Séphiha gives the total figure of 38,000 Jews in Italy in 1950, of whom just 10,000 were Sephardic.[19] They still retain their religious rites (for example, in the magnificent synagogue in Florence). Some long-established communities are in a state of decline, as is the once-important community of Leghorn, which now includes just a few hundred Jews.

Albania

When Albania was created by the Treaty of London in 1912, there were some Sephardim in that territory who had always lived in the area, which was formerly a part of the Ottoman Empire. According to Séphiha, 500 Jews lived in the country in 1950, all Sephardim.[20] It is uncertain whether the community still exists and, if so, to what extent its members retain their cultural identity and the Judeo-Spanish language.

In Other World Areas

As the result of several migrations and persecution, relatively large groups of Sephardim have settled in unexpected areas. A small community that had established itself in what was previously the Belgian Congo emigrated almost entirely to Belgium when the Congo became independent. There also are, or were, Sephardim in Rhodesia, China, and India. As a result of the Second Diaspora, they are found in South Africa and Australia as well. Little is known about the current situation of these communities, but it is likely that they preserve very little of their traditional culture.

Sephardim in Spain

The previous chapter showed the ambivalent relations between the Sephardim and Spain. The Spanish Jews' nostalgic mythification of the Sepharad in which their culture had flowered was mixed with bitter recall of expulsion and inquisitorial persecution. In Spain, *individual* reactions to the so-called "Spaniards without a homeland" were accompanied by an almost complete lack of *official* attention. Therefore, despite the longing for Sepharad, the pro-Sephardic campaigns—comprised more of words than deeds—and the sparse and scattered official gestures in favor of the Jews of Hispanic origin, few Sephardim have settled in Spain.

The first Jewish communities to form in Spain, several centuries after the expulsion, date from the mid-nineteenth century. They consisted mostly of

19. [AN] Ibid., 71.
20. [AN] Ibid.

Moroccan Sephardim who had immigrated as a result of the war in Africa along with a few French Jews who had come to Spain. The majority settled in southern coastal cities such as Cadiz. It was really more a case of groups of Jews residing in various areas than of organized communities. The 1877 census showed slightly over 400 Jews, scattered through twenty-one cities and towns. The largest settlements hardly numbered more than two or three dozen people, without synagogues, community activities, or even a minimum of religious services.

The first true Sephardic community was established in Seville. Although small, it had some community organization by the last quarter of the nineteenth century.

A traveler who visited Seville briefly in 1889 related that the Jewish families living there numbered a few dozen, that they had a ritual slaughterer and circumciser, and that they maintained regular prayers in a private home. . . . in 1904 . . . the community amounted to about twenty families who had come originally from various towns in Morocco and especially from Tétouan. All the Jews of Seville lived in the same modest suburb, earning a livelihood from shoemaking, the jewelry trade, and the manufacture and sale of sweetmeats. They were headed by a rabbi, appointed from within the community. . . . In 1904 the tiny community enthusiastically joined in the welcome that the city of Seville extended to King Alfonso XIII. . . . A Seville newspaper, in describing the event, mentioned the names of seventy men and women of the Jewish community who had participated; the total number of Jews in Seville was probably not much more than that. (Avni, 41)

Spain's Jewish population increased at the outbreak of World War I, when some Turkish Sephardim and Russian and Austro-Hungarian Ashkenazim, caught in France by the war, took refuge in Spain. The Madrid community was formed in 1917 (with just fifty-seven members) and the Barcelona community appeared soon after. Jewish and Zionist societies began to develop, but Jewish life in Spain declined again at the end of the war when many of the refugees left the country. During Primo de Rivera's dictatorship (1925–29) and the early years of the Republic, there was hardly any Jewish activity, except for the arrival of a small group of Sephardim from Salonika in 1932.

Hitler's rise to power in 1933 marks the growth of Spain's Jewish population, mainly by exiled Polish and German Ashkenazim who joined the Sephardim already living there. When the Civil War broke out in 1936, there were some 6,000 Jews in Spain. The beginning of the war, not surprisingly, caused the most well-to-do to flee; many who stayed in Republican territory supported that group and had to flee later. Those who stayed in Nationalist areas had a difficult time. (General Queipo de Llano went so far as to broadcast from Seville [the site of the first new Jewish community], "Our fight is not a Spanish civil war, but a war between Western civilization and world Judaism.") As a result, when the war was over, Spain's Jewish communities had nearly disappeared.

During the 1940s, Nazi persecution of the Jews caused a new wave of emigration, during which Spain was a route of passage. It became a kind of huge pier where those who had been able to save themselves from massacre and cross the border waited—often in wretched conditions—for the ship that would take them to a land where they could take refuge.

Very few Jews stayed in Spain, which lacked administrative facilities. In the battered post-Civil War economy, there was little room in Spain for another group of unemployed people without personal resources. In addition, although the efforts of Spanish officials could save them from Hitler's grasp, the Spanish government sympathized with German Nazism and Italian fascism and often spoke of an international Jewish-Masonic conspiracy. All of these factors made the political atmosphere abhorrent to the refugees.

Although only a few Jews stayed in Spain, they (mainly Ashkenazim) were the beginning of the communities that still exist today. In the 1940s and early 1950s, they were joined by a handful of young Moroccan Sephardim who had been educated in Ceuta or in the Spanish protectorate and had little hope of attending a university there. They came to Spain as students, intending to be there only temporarily; however, the majority found employment and remained in Spain.

Morocco's independence in the mid-1950s, and the subsequent Arabization of Moroccan life, created a change. It was no longer a case of young people sent to Spain by their families to study but of whole families leaving North Africa for Spain. These immigrants formed the bulk of the current Jewish communities in Spain: Madrid and Barcelona (4,000 to 5,000 members each), Malaga (1,500), Marbella, Seville, Valencia, Alicante, Palma de Mallorca, Santa Cruz de Tenerife, and Las Palmas (all with under 200 members). There are also communities in Ceuta and Melilla with some 800 members each. All told, some 14,000 Jews live in Spain today.

Not all of Spain's Jews are Sephardic, however. The lack of statistics prohibits one from citing an exact number, but estimates are that 75 percent of Spain's Jews are Sephardim from Morocco; at least, that has been the situation until now. Recent immigration from Latin America may have changed the makeup of these communities.

There are a number of Jews among the many Latin American immigrants to Spain, especially those who fled the dictatorships in Argentina and Chile in the 1970s and early 1980s. Although many are completely secularized and do not identify with their coreligionists, others participate actively in community life. All of them, of course, speak Spanish, but not all of them are Sephardic. In fact, the majority are descendants of Ashkenazim who emigrated to the New World between the mid-nineteenth century and the end of World War II. The presence of this Hispanic-American group will certainly change the composition, organization, and life-style of several Jewish communities.

How do the Sephardim in Spain live and think? Are they integrated into national life or do they form a separate group? Is Spain their "homeland," or is it a route of passage? Because of the lack of data specifically on Sephardim, what pertains to Sephardim may be said to hold for Spain's Jewish communities in general, in which, at the moment, they are the overwhelming majority.

Nearly all the Jews who now live in Spain settled there more or less temporarily when they left Morocco, and they found life relatively easy. There was no language barrier, which they would have faced in other countries, and their arrival coincided with an economic expansion (the so-called "Spanish miracle" of the 1960s), so that it was easy to earn a living. As years passed, children were born and raised in Spain, and settlement became permanent.

Few Jews are leaving Spain. Those who do so are driven primarily by economic considerations (the loss of jobs, for example). They generally go to Latin America where there are large Jewish communities and no language problem. At the same time, there has been a considerable influx of Latin American Jews to Spain, as mentioned above, although they are not from the countries to which the Spanish Jews emigrate. While Spanish emigrants head largely for Mexico and Venezuela, the immigrants tend to come from Argentina and Chile, often for political reasons.

There is not a very strong movement for emigration to Israel. Israel has the sympathy, of course, of Spanish Jews, who repeatedly deplored the lack of diplomatic relations between the two countries prior to 1986. Yet life in Israel is hard, and those who are employed and have homes in Spain do not generally make *aliyah* (that is, settle in Israel). The majority of Jews who left Morocco in the 1950s headed specifically for Israel, where cities like Dimona were created by those immigrants. It is not logical to think that those who chose to go to Spain, against the current, would leave now, nearly thirty years later.

It is common, nevertheless, for Spanish Jews to travel to Israel periodically to see that land to which they feel so tied emotionally and to visit family members who live there. Many young people also spend a few years in Israel for specialized university studies; along the way, they get to know the country well and learn Hebrew. They usually have no intention of emigrating there, but occasionally an individual will find employment, or something unforeseen—like a wedding—crops up and the individual will settle there.

The majority of Jews in Spain intend to remain there and make every effort to become Spanish citizens if they are not already. Although most of the young people were born in Spain, the majority of Jews are from other countries and must go through various bureaucratic procedures to be nationalized. The process was certainly made easier by the law of June 30, 1982, which permits Sephardim to become Spanish citizens after only two years of residence in the country (rather than the normal ten years), the same as people from Equatorial Guinea, Andorra, and the Philippines.

Spain's Jewish population is generally young and upper-middle class. Many are academics or other professionals. Some, however, are hired laborers and small business people. The relatively high percentage of medical professionals is notable, and becomes even more so when one realizes that Jews have been in the medical profession since the Middle Ages.

Spanish Jews are completely adapted to Spanish life and very cosmopolitan. They travel frequently and, although Spanish is their mother tongue, almost all of them speak more than one language. The strong cultural influence of France in Morocco makes French a frequent second language (with some cases of true bilingualism), and the third most common language is English. Many, especially the younger generation, know some Hebrew; others learned Arabic in their native Morocco.

Their life is no different from that of any Spaniard at the same socioeconomic level. The more religious among them try to adjust their lives in a non-Jewish setting to the observance of dietary laws and the sabbath (for example, by seeking employment that leaves them free on Saturdays). Attendance at religious services on Saturday mornings, or more often on Friday nights, is motivated both by religious practice and by the desire to interact socially with coreligionists in the synagogue or other quarters of the Jewish community. Some small communities that do not have their own quarters hold services and social events in rented facilities (such as a hotel reception room). Belonging to a Jewish community requires seeking membership and paying annual dues. These dues, along with individual donations, are the principal income of the communities, which offer a series of services in exchange:

a) Religious activities: daily services as well as for holidays and other ceremonies (weddings, circumcisions, Bar Mitzvah ceremonies, funerals). They provide kosher meat and wine (especially on certain holidays) and matzah for Passover.

b) Cultural activities: speakers, movies, concerts, seminars, and study groups dealing with matters of Jewish interest.

c) Educational and youth activities: The community in Madrid runs a primary school whose schedule includes time dedicated to Jewish cultural and religious matters and the Hebrew language. Between 30 and 40 percent of its students are not Jewish. There are other activities for the youth, such as camping trips and excursions. The community in Barcelona also has a school.

d) Welfare activities: Help for the needy is a basic precept of Judaism. When needed, the community offers material help, but it especially offers social assistance, that is, guidance and counseling to its members and transients who seek those services. For example, assistance was recently given to fleeing Iranian Jews who arrived in Spain confused and without money.

e) Social activities: Promoting social relations among members is not the least of the services that the Jewish communities provide. Some of the social activities (dances, trips, women's groups) have an added fund-raising component.

There are other groups in Spain, aside from the Jewish communities, in which Jews participate as Jews. Perhaps the oldest is the Judeo-Christian Friendship Association, founded in Madrid in 1962 at the initiative of a Catholic group. Its aim was to develop mutual understanding between Jews and Christians, and it had a basically religious orientation. It was the seed of the Center for Judeo-Christian Studies, founded in 1969 and headquartered in a convent for the Sisters of Our Lady of Zion. The Center arranges talks, symposia, and short courses on biblical and Judaic studies and on Judeo-Christian relations; it also publishes the journal *El Olivo* [The olive tree] and arranges tours of the Holy Land. It has also sponsored paraliturgical ceremonies to include both religions.

Barcelona has the Catalonia-Israel Cultural Relations Association, the first of a series of similar associations in the various regions of Spain. In 1982 its equivalent was established in Madrid, the Spain-Israel Friendship Association, which explained its aims in the first issue of its bulletin as:

the mutual understanding of the peoples [in Spain and Israel], the development of cultural relations of all kinds and the identification of mutual affinities. [The Friendship Association] . . . will continue to seek the establishment of diplomatic relations with Israel. . . . Culture, greater knowledge of the two peoples, and the development of economic and commercial exchanges are also objectives we will seek simultaneously. (*Amistad* I, 1–2)

Raíces: Revista judía de cultura [Roots: A Jewish cultural journal], the only informative journal on Jewish culture in Spain, made its appearance in April 1986.

To what extent do the Sephardim in Spain retain their cultural identity? Are they conscious of their origin and ancestry? Do they distinguish themselves as Sephardim from their non-Sephardic coreligionists?

Linguistically, there is almost nothing left of their old dialect, save for occasional expressions in Ḥaketía used in colloquial situations and with affective connotations. Some of the oral literature has been preserved, as shown by the publication of a collection of ballads recorded in Malaga.[21] There is almost no Sephardi over the age of forty who does not remember some *cantar* (as they are called in Morocco), be that the roguish and erotic *Paipero,* a Passover song such as the well-known *Cabritico,* a wedding song, or a ballad. Maxims and popular sayings are also still very much alive.

Of course, the Sephardim abandoned the customs and folkways of Morocco when they joined the mainstream of Spanish life. Some trace of those lost folkways will surface, entwined with the modern customs, only for an occasional special event. For example, some Sephardic women will have Western-style weddings, and wear white dresses. A day or two earlier, however, they may gather their friends for a traditional farewell to the single life. On those occasions, the bride wears an ornamental Berber-style dress inherited from her grandmother or lent to her by the community, and the women sing traditional songs.

Foods are also a part of the cultural inheritance that the Sephardim have preserved in part, due to the importance attributed to a *se'uda* or festive meal at Jewish celebrations. Sephardic housewives generally prepare traditional dishes for the most solemn holidays and—with greater or lesser frequency, depending on the time available—others characteristic of Moroccan Jewish meals, such as *adafina.*

The younger generation, born in Spain, is forgetting these traditions that their elders still recall. Dialectal expressions have practically disappeared from their speech. They have not experienced the old customs and have rarely had the opportunity to listen to the old songs that the previous generation remembers.

The Sephardic character of Spain's Jewish communities is most apparent in liturgy. More than 90 percent of religious services follow the Sephardic

21. [AN] Oro Anahory-Librowicz, *Florilegio de romances sefardíes de la diáspora (Una colección malagueña)* (Madrid: Cátedra–Seminario Menéndez Pidal, 1980).

rite. Some communities occasionally introduce Ashkenazi elements into the services. The larger communities hold two separate services (one Sephardic and the other Ashkenazi), especially on the major holidays.

Community leaders tend to eliminate as much as possible the differences between Sephardim and Ashkenazim, in religious services and in other community activities. Perhaps the rivalry between the two groups in Israel has led to this attitude. Samuel Toledano, a leader of the Israelite Community of Madrid and of pure Sephardic background (as his last name indicates), expresses a significant opinion on this matter:

> It is necessary to overcome the division between Sephardi and Ashkenazi, preserving, of course, with love and affection the traditions of our ancestors. But any division within Judaism today is counterproductive. One must retain the culture and traditions, but one must also avoid antagonism, rivalry or division. . . . Do not mistake me. I am very proud of the past, of my ancestors and of the tradition I represent. But there it must remain, as a tradition . . . my desire is for a single liturgy . . . the rite is part of the tradition, but I would be willing to sacrifice part of the traditional liturgy to avoid any separation.[22]

Such statements give the impression that the Sephardim in Spain do not insist on preserving at all costs those features that distinguish them from their coreligionists. They revere their glorious past in Spain and make emotional visits to the places where their ancestors lived out a Golden Age (Cordova, Toledo, Seville), but they realize that they cannot retain the way of life their parents had in Tetuan or Tangier now that they live in Madrid, Barcelona, or Alicante. Their view of their own language, which they see as belonging to the past, indicates the same realism. While they sympathize with the efforts to restore Judeo-Spanish, many, including Samuel Toledano, see them as beautiful but impractical endeavors:

> I do not think that Judezmo should be made a vernacular language. I think that the Jews who want to do that or who are of Spanish tradition, ancestry or culture need to speak modern Spanish. . . . Judezmo is a jewel, and I read it with great personal interest, but it should not be perpetuated as a vehicle of communication. What is necessary is that Spanish-speaking Jews—and there are many of them—learn modern Spanish. It would be appropriate to teach Spanish in Israel and in Sephardic communities. Judezmo as such cannot resist the pressure of the modern world. . . . One must live in the present, conscious of the past, but it is impossible to live in the past. If we do not live in the present, the Hispanic character of hundreds of thousands of Sephardic Jews will be lost because they will not be able to find in Judezmo what they look for in a language. . . . What bothers me is not that Judezmo is being lost in

22. [AN] Personal interview with the author, 21 July 1983; the following quotations are also from the interview.

the younger generations. If they substitute Spanish for it, I am in total agreement. What is not acceptable is its substitution by English, French or any other language.

Toledano even has a proposal for the deliberate and definitive re-Hispanization of the Sephardim:

> I would like the study of Spanish to be taken seriously, with concrete syllabi, with the necessary facilities available, with the creation—in Israel at first and wherever else there are Sephardic communities—of Spanish Houses, Spanish Culture Houses, which have teachers and modern teaching aids. . . . Why should we not promote Spanish? If not, the alternative is not Judezmo; it is English.

Not all Sephardim think alike. In any case, such a program is unlikely to imbue the Sephardim scattered throughout the world with Spanish culture. In this regard we must bear in mind Toledano's words: "The dissemination of Spanish culture is something that Spain has *always* abandoned, and not only among Jews."

SEPHARDIC STUDIES

In contrast to those who propose the integration of the Sephardim into modern Spanish culture are those whose interest is the preservation, study, and even the revival of Sephardic culture. It usually happens that when something is in decline and on the way to extinction that interest in studying it arises. That is what has happened in the case of the Sephardim. The West "discovered" the Sephardic world when that world was decaying. As the decline becomes more pronounced, and only traces remain of the venerable flowering Sephardic culture, efforts to preserve and study it are increasing.

Consequently, hardly any traces remain of the old communities in what used to be the geographic environment of Levantine Sephardim, but institutions have been established to preserve their memory and study their past glory. What used to be a part of daily reality is now found in museums, libraries, or more or less erudite publications. It is to be seen in the Jewish Museum of Greece in Athens or the Jewish Historical Museum in Belgrade. It is found in the activities of the Jewish cultural society of Bulgaria or in the pages of the journals *Jevrejski Almanah* and *Zbornik* (from Yugoslavia) or *Godisnik* (from Bulgaria).

The Sephardim themselves have organized groups to learn, study, and disseminate their culture and history. This is the aim of several institutions in countries of the Second Diaspora, such as the Centre de Recherches sur le Judaïsme de Salonique [Center for research on Salonikan Judaism], founded in Tel Aviv by Jews from Salonika; the Foundation for the Advancement of

Sephardic Studies and Culture, established in New York in 1962; the Parisian Centre d'Études Don Isaac Abravanel [Isaac Abravanel studies center]; the Centro de Estudios Sefardíes [Sephardic studies center] in Caracas, under the auspices of the Asociación Israelita de Venezuela [Venezuelan Israelite association]; and the Centro de Investigación y Difusión de la Cultura Sefardí [Center for research and dissemination of Sephardic culture] in Buenos Aires. These institutions and others like them serve both as links among the Sephardim of a given country (encouraging community life with cultural and social activities) and promoters of cultural knowledge by means of libraries, speakers, study groups, and publications.

Some of these Sephardic associations in search of their own past have adopted an assertive or even combative attitude. Their aim is not only knowledge of the past but revival of the Judeo-Spanish language and culture, for they feel that traditional literature must not be lost. *Romanzas* and *canticas* must be disseminated (even if by recordings or radio broadcasts). Judezmophones must continue to produce literature in that language. The youth must learn Judeo-Spanish (through course work, for those who can no longer learn it from their elders). Typically Sephardic customs and traditional foods must be retained.

Reviving Sephardic culture—if even for just one more generation—and trying to transmit it to the younger generation are the objectives of associations such as Vidas Largas [Long lives], founded by Haim Vidal Séphiha in Paris in 1979. Vidas Largas calls itself an "Association for the Retention and Dissemination of the Judeo-Spanish Language and Culture." It publishes a bulletin and nonperiodical literature; distributes books on Sephardic themes published by other organizations; and offers or supports Judeo-Spanish classes in Paris and other French-speaking cities, such as Lyon, Marseilles, and Geneva.

A similar organization is Adelantre! [Forward!], founded in New York in 1975 by David Bunis (who is Ashkenazi) and Stephen Levy. Its aim was "to stimulate popular and academic interest in all aspects of Sephardic language, literature, history, music and folklore." It published the journal *Ké Xaver?* [Judeo-Spanish, What's up?] and a series called *Working Papers in Sephardic and Oriental Jewish Studies,* and also offered classes in Judeo-Spanish.

None of these efforts, however, has borne as much fruit as that of Moshé Shaul in Israel, because he has a powerful ally—the radio. Since the 1950s, Israel's national radio has broadcast a short daily program in Judeo-Spanish. In the 1970s, Shaul took control of the program, and he conceived of the plan of using this communication medium in order, in his words, *empesar en una verdadera "Operasion Renasensia" ke mos permetera, si se realizan muestras esperansas, de meter en marcha un proseso kultural a la fin del kual es posible ke se termine la "agonia" del Djudeo-Espanyol i ke muestra lengua torne a ser avlada i eskrita por un numero mas i mas grande de personas . . . pensamos . . . espandir muestras aktividades a otros kampos tambien, empesando de la organizasion de kursos de Djudeo-Espanyol para todos los ke keren embezarlo, pasando por konferensias, seminarios i tadradas folklorikas i asta la produksion de filmos i video-kasetas sovre temas atados a muesra istoria i kultura. (Aki Yerushalayim 9, 3—4)*

[to start a true "Operation Renaissance" that would allow us, if our hopes are realized, to initiate a cultural process whose aim is possibly ending the "agony" of Judeo-Spanish and having our language again spoken and written by an increasing number of people . . . we hope . . . to expand our activities to other areas as well, beginning with the organization of classes in Judeo-Spanish for all those who want to learn it, going then to conferences, seminars and folkloric evenings and even the production of movies and video-cassettes dealing with themes related to our history and culture.]

His activities have resulted in the publication of the Judeo-Spanish journal *Aki Yerushalayim* [Here is Jerusalem] and the implementation of a folklore project among his listeners, to collect and classify Sephardic folkloric materials. The project has yielded some very interesting samples of oral literature, folkways, customs, and Sephardic gastronomy.

There are also Jewish institutions that call themselves "Sephardic," using the term in its broadest sense of "non-Ashkenazi" and consequently including the so-called "Sephardim" from Arabic, Eastern Mediterranean, and African countries. These organizations promote or in one way or another support the study and understanding of Sephardim. Such is the case of the World Sephardi Federation, originally headquartered in London, which now has branches in every country that has any sizable non-Ashkenazi Jewish communities. It fosters Sephardic and Oriental Jews' knowledge of their own background through publications such as *Le Judaïsme Sephardi* and *Sephardi World,* symposia, speakers, and other activities.

Misgav Yerushalayim is also in this group of organizations, founded in Jerusalem in 1977 by an agreement among the Council of Sephardic and Oriental Communities in Israel, the World Sephardi Federation, and Hebrew University of Jerusalem. The list of sponsoring agencies makes clear that only part of its activities are dedicated to Sephardim in the strict sense of the word; more of its work is focused on Oriental Jewry. This became apparent during its first conference in Jerusalem in 1978, whose proceedings were published under the title of *The Sephardi and Oriental Jewish Heritage.* Two subsequent conferences were held in 1984 and 1988; another is planned for 1992.

Another important institution that gives a considerable part of its attention to the so-called Sephardim is Yeshiva University, the religious Jewish university headquartered in New York City. It has had a Sephardic studies program since 1974, and it sponsors the American Society of Sephardic Studies (ASOSS). Its publications are the journals *The American Sephardi* (for the Sephardic studies program) and *The Sephardic Scholar* (for the ASOSS).

Yeshiva University also has one of the great Hebraic libraries, with a large collection of Sephardica. The United States has other Judaica libraries with Sephardic collections as well. Among them are the libraries of the Jewish Theological Seminary of America and the YIVO Institute (dedicated to the study of Yiddish), both in New York, and Hebrew Union College in Cincinnati. In Israel, libraries that should be mentioned are the Jewish National and University Library in Jerusalem (and its collection of recordings), and the one at the Ben Zvi Institute, also in Jerusalem. In Europe there is the Etz Haim Seminary in Amsterdam.

Sephardica collections are found not only in Jewish institutions but also in some of the world's largest libraries and in miscellaneous archives. Three collections are in the British Museum in London, the Library of Congress in Washington, and at Harvard University. The Archivo Menéndez Pidal in Madrid also merits special mention: it has preserved the melodies and lyrics of Hispanic ballads and traditional songs collected by Menéndez Pidal, his collaborators, and their successors. More than twenty-five hundred of the texts collected there are Sephardic ballads and songs, most still unedited.

Sephardic studies have also been a part of the academic world whenever a professor or researcher capable of offering courses in the discipline has been at an institution under conditions that permitted developing the field. Wherever there have been departments of Hebraic studies or Hispanic studies, and a scholar interested in the interdisciplinary area of Sephardic studies, it has been possible for interested individuals to write theses and dissertations and to organize conferences in the field. Such activities have been in progress for quite a while at the universities in Granada, Madrid, and Paris, and now also at the Universidad del País Vasco in Spain. The English-speaking world has been especially active. Sephardic studies are or have been carried out at the University of Pennsylvania, Columbia University, and the University of California at Davis. In Israel, these activities are going on at universities in Jerusalem, Haifa, Beersheba and Tel Aviv.

Occasionally these almost individualized initiatives have resulted in the creation of a chair of Sephardic Language and Literature, as at the Universidad Autónoma in Madrid from the 1972–73 to the 1974–75 academic years, and also at the Sorbonne in Paris and the Hebrew University of Jerusalem.

On other occasions these efforts have resulted in the organization of con-ferences more or less specifically geared to Sephardic studies. One of the earliest conferences was the First Symposium of Sephardic Studies, held in Madrid in 1965. In 1975 the University of California at San Diego held a conference entitled "The Re-Discovery of the Hispano-Judaic Past," which included papers on converts and Spanish Jews in the Middle Ages as well as others on strictly Sephardic topics, such as the ballad, folklore, and music. In 1980 a series of Jornadas de Estudios Sefardíes [Happenings in Sephardic studies] were presented at the University of Extremadura (in Cáceres, Spain), during which presentations about Sephardim alternated with others on the history of Jews in Extremadura and the Hebrew presence in Hispanic litera-ture. In 1981, the Ramos de Castro Foundation organized a conference called "Forgotten Spain: The Jews" in Zamora (Spain). Leeds (United King-dom) was the seat of another conference on Sephardic Judaism in 1982. In 1982, 1983, and 1984, Encuentros de las Tres Culturas [Meetings of the three cultures] (Christian, Jewish, and Muslim) took place in Toledo (Spain), where presentations about Sephardim were given in the sections dedicated to Spanish Judaism. The municipality and the University of Cordova (Spain) cosponsored a commemoration of the 850th anniversary of Maimonides's birth in 1985 with presentations and cultural activities dealing with the Se-phardim. Binghamton, New York, was the 1987 site of the International and Interdisciplinary Conference on Sephardic Studies; a second conference was held there in 1991. 1989 was the year of the Jornadas Sefardíes [Sephardic happenings] in Castile-Leon and Medina del Campo (Spain).

Usually conferences focusing on Jewish culture in general include sections dealing with Sephardim, among them the World Congress of Jewish Studies, which has held eight conferences in Jerusalem, and the Jewish Folklore Con-ferences of the Association for Jewish Studies in the United States. Confer-ences on linguistics, Romance philology, Spanish literature, and the ballad also may include some Sephardic content. Examples are the Reuniones de Teatro y Poesía [Meetings on theater and poetry] held in Malaga (Spain) in 1973 and 1974 respectively, the Conference on Nordic and Anglo-American Ballad Research in Seattle in 1977, the Second International Symposium on the Hispanic Ballad in Davis, California the same year, the Third and Fourth International Colloquia on the Ballad (Madrid, 1982, and Puerto de Santa María, 1987), and the First International Congress on Troubador Literature (Madrid, 1984).[23] These meetings are international and academic in charac-

23. The American Association of Teachers of Spanish and Portuguese has included at least one session on Sephardic studies in each of its annual meetings since 1986.

ter; they promote fellowship among scholars in their respective fields. Proceedings subsequently published are refereed and often contain essential articles in the area of Sephardic studies.

Part of all the above characteristics (center dedicated to Judaic studies with special attention to Sephardica, library and collection of sources, group of active researchers, classes, academic conferences and publications) are to be found in the Instituto Arias Montano—now part of the Instituto de Filología—within the Consejo Superior de Investigaciones Científicas. Founded in 1940 in Madrid, it is subtitled the institute "for Hebraic, Sephardic and Near Eastern studies." Along with people who work in biblical studies and pre-expulsion Spanish Judaism are a group of specialists on Sephardic language and literature. The Institute's library has a large collection of Sephardic bibliography and sources (books in *aljamiado,* manuscripts, newspapers, and so on); its journal, *Sefarad,* always includes relevant articles. In 1966 the journal began to include a section called "Sephardica," which later became a separate volume, *Estudios Sefardíes.* It has now been reabsorbed as the third issue in each volume of *Sefarad.*

The Instituto Arias Montano organized the First Symposium on Sephardic Studies in 1964, and its members taught courses on Sephardic language and literature at the Universidad Autónoma in Madrid. Several important books have been published under the Institute's sponsorship and a good deal of academic work on the Sephardim has been carried out there.

Another Spanish institution dedicated to the same field is the Sephardic Museum in Toledo, located in the famous Samuel Levi Synagogue (also known as "sinagoga del Tránsito"). The museum was established in 1965 "with the mission of exhibiting all items of Hebreo-Spanish culture that could be collected and for the purpose of becoming a center for studies and dissemination of the same" (founding decree, in *Actas,* 614). The museum, which is really more Judeo-Hispanic than Sephardic, has a small collection of exhibits and a Judaica library that includes copies of Sephardic *aljamiado* booklets. In 1989, the Association of Friends of the Sephardic Museum was created to foster cultural activities.

Thanks, then, to the efforts of a small group of scholars, there have been some significant developments in the field of Sephardic studies in Spain, developments that have extended well beyond the borders of that country. Despite these successes, the same scholars have repeatedly deplored the lack of Sephardic studies in university curricula, even as purely elective courses. Iacob M. Hassán made some significant remarks about the situation in an article in *El País:*

While Sephardic Spanish (literature and language) is not included in our university curriculum—no more or less than Catalan, Galician or Basque—, Spain's debt to the Sephardim will not be repaid. It is a debt that Spain has to herself, because without knowledge of Sephardic literature, the knowledge of Hispanic letters will be incomplete.[24]

RECOMMENDED READING

For the current situation of the Sephardim in various world areas, see Haim Vidal Séphiha, *L'agonie des judéo-espagnols* (Paris: Entente, 1977), esp. 49–126. On Turkish Jewry in particular, see Shaul Tuval, "Las komunidades djudías de Turkia en muestros días," *Aki Yerushalayim* 4, no. 15 (Oct. 1982): 6–10. The same journal has published other articles with current data on contemporary Sephardic communities: see Adolfo Arditi, "Los djudios de Mexico," *Aki Yerushalayim* 5, no. 19–20 (Oct. 1983–Jan. 1984): 5–7; Gabriel E. Benatar, "Los djudios sefaradis en la Afrika sentral," *Aki Yerushalayim* 9, no. 32–33 (Jan.–June 1987): 5–8; and Avraam Haim, "La komunidad sefaradi de Miami Beach en Estados Unidos," *Aki Yerushalayim* 6, no. 22–23 (July–Oct. 1984): 21–22. On Sephardim in the United States, see Marc D. Angel, *The Sephardim of the United States: An Exploratory Study* (New York: Union of Sephardic Congregations, 1974), esp. 114–36. A good summary of the situation in Israel is offered in Tracy K. Harris, "The Prognosis for Judeo-Spanish: Its Description, Present Status, Survival and Decline, with Implications for the Study of Language Death in General" (Ph.D. diss., Georgetown University, 1979), 349–50. See also Ignacio Cembrero, "Los judíos sefardíes," *El País,* 3 July 1983, Sunday supp., 14–19 and 22, and Moshé Shaul and José Ramón Magdalena Nom de Déu, "El Mundo Sefardí. Los Sefardíes," in *Nuestro Mundo '85–'86* (Madrid: Agencia Efe–Espasa Calpe, 1985), 1521–27. The collection of Sephardic traditions in Jewish communities in Canada is described by Oro Anahory-Librowicz in "Folklore y tradiciones sefardíes en *Yahasrá,*" in *Los sefardíes: Cultura y literatura,* ed. Paloma Díaz-Mas (San Sebastián: Universidad del País Vasco, 1987), 233–44.

On the establishment and evolution of the new Jewish communities in Spain, see Haim Avni, *Spain, the Jews, and Franco,* trans. Emanuel Shimoni (Philadelphia: Jewish Publication Society of America, 1982), esp. 40–50 and 204–8.

24. [AN] Iacob M. Hassan "Tópicos y duedas" ["Topics and debts"], *El País,* 3 July 1983, Sunday supp., 3, col. *c*.

BIBLIOGRAPHY

This is not an exhaustive bibliography on the Sephardim, nor does it necessarily include all of the works consulted in preparing this book. It is a collection of the works cited in notes and the "Recommended Reading" sections at the end of each chapter, and includes full bibliographic citations for the abbreviations used within the text. It does not list the Sephardic publications mentioned in chapter 4; they appear in the index of titles and first lines.

Translator's note: It is not uncommon in Hispanic societies for people to use two last names: the father's family name comes first, followed by the mother's maiden name. Consequently, entries may be alphabetized by the next-to-last name. For example, sources by Ramón Menéndez Pidal will be listed under Menéndez Pidal, Ramón.

Actas = *Actas del Primer Simposio de Estudios Sefardíes,* ed. I. M. Hassán with M. T. Rubiato and E. Romero. Madrid: CSIC, 1970.
Agonie, see Séphiha, *L'agonie des judéo-espagnols.*
Altabé, David F. "The Romanso, 1900–1933: A Bibliographical Survey," *Sephardic Scholar* 3 (1977–78): 96–106.
Alvar, *Boda* = Alvar, Manuel. *Cantos de boda judeo-españoles.* Madrid: CSIC, 1971.
Alvar, Manuel. "Un *descubrimiento* del judeo-español." In *Studies in Honor of M. J. Benardete,* ed. Izaak A. Langnas and Barton Sholod, 363–66. New York: Las Americas, 1965.
Alvar, *Endechas* = Alvar, Manuel. *Endechas judeo-españolas.* Rev. and enl. ed. Madrid: CSIC, 1969.
Amistad, (1982) [Bulletin of Amistad España-Israel, Madrid].
Anahory-Librowicz, Oro. "Folklore y tradiciones sefardíes en *Yahasrá.*" In *Los sefardíes: Cultura y literatura,* ed. Paloma Díaz-Mas, 233–44. San Sebastián: Universidad del País Vasco, 1987.
Anahory-Librowicz, Oro, and Judith R. Cohen. "Modalidades expresivas de los cantos de boda judeo-españoles," *Revista de Dialectología y Tradiciones Populares* 41 (1986): 189–209.
Angel, Marc D. *The Sephardim of the United States: An Exploratory Study.* New York: Union of Sephardic Congregations, 1974. (Rept., with changes, from *The American Jewish Yearbook 1973,* 75–138.)
Arditi, Adolfo. "Los djudios de Mexico," *Aki Yerushalayim* 5, no. 19–20 (Oct. 1983–Jan. 1984): 5–7.

Armistead, see *Cat.-Ind.*
Armistead–Silverman, *En torno* = Armistead, Samuel G., and Joseph H. Silverman. *En torno al Romancero sefardí (Hispanismo y balcanismo de la tradición judeo-española)*. Madrid: Seminario Menéndez Pidal, 1982.
Armistead–Silverman, see also Nahón, *Romances.*
Armistead–Silverman, *Tres calas* = Armistead, Samuel G., and Joseph H. Silverman. *Tres calas en el Romancero sefardí (Rodas, Jerusalén, Estados Unidos)*. Madrid: Castalia, 1979.
Armistead–Silverman, *Yoná* = Armistead, Samuel G., and Joseph H. Silverman. *The Judeo-Spanish Ballad Chapbooks of Yacob Abraham Yoná*. Berkeley and Los Angeles: University of California Press, 1971.
Atienza, Juan G. *Guía judía de España*. Madrid: Altalena, 1981.
Atlas, see Gilbert.
Attias, *Cancionero* = Attias, Moshé. *Cancionero judeo-español*. Jerusalem: Centro de Estudios sobre el judaísmo de Salónica, Tel-Aviv, 1972.
Attias, *Romancero* = Attias, Moshé. *Romancero sefardí: Romanzas y cantes populares en judeo-español*. Jerusalem: Ben Zvi Institute, [1956] 1961.
Avishay, "Supervivientes" = Avishay, Mordehay. "Los últimos supervivientes de la Salónica judía," *El Olivo* 5–6 (Jan.–June 1978): 78–84.
Avni = Avni, Haim. *Spain, the Jews, and Franco*. Trans. Emanuel Shimoni. Philadelphia: Jewish Publication Society of America, 1982.
Baer, Yitzhak. *A History of the Jews in Christian Spain*. Trans. Louis Schoffman et al. 2 vols. Philadelphia: Jewish Publication Society of America, 1961 and 1966. A later translation into Spanish by José Luis Lacave is valuable for its more current bibliography: *Historia de los judíos en la España cristiana*. 2 vols. Madrid: Altalena, 1981.
Ben-Ami, Issachar, ed. *The Sephardi and Oriental Jewish Heritage*. Jerusalem: Magnes Press—Hebrew University, 1982.
Benardete, *Hispanic Culture* = Benardete, Mair José. *Hispanic Culture and Character of the Sephardic Jews*. 2d ed. Ed. Marc D. Angel. New York: Sepher-Hermon Press, 1982.
Benardete, Mair José. *Hispanismo de los sefardíes levantinos*. Madrid: Aguilar, 1963.
Benatar, Gabriel E. "Los djudios sefaradis en la Afrika sentral," *Aki Yerushalayim* 9, no. 32–33 (Jan.–June 1987): 5–8.
Benbassa = Benbassa-Dudonney, Esther. "El Kazamyento de los djudyos-espanyoles en Turkiya a la fin del dizimueven siglo." In *Actas de las Jornadas de Estudios Sefardíes de 1980,* ed. Antonio Viudas Camarasa, 31–37. Cáceres: Universidad de Extremadura, 1981.
Bénichou, Paul. "Notas sobre el judeo-español de Marruecos en 1950," *Nueva Revista de Filología Hispánica* 14 (1960): 307–12.
Bénichou, "Observaciones" = Bénichou, Paul. "Observaciones sobre el judeoespañol de Marruecos," *Revista de Filología Hispánica* 7 (1945): 209–58.
Bénichou, Paul. *Romancero judeo-español de Marruecos*. Madrid: Castalia, 1968.
Benoliel, José. *Dialecto judeo-hispano-marroquí o hakitía*. Reprint. Madrid: n.p., 1977.
Benoliel, "Hakitía" = Benoliel, José. "Dialecto judeo-hispano-marroquí o hakitía," *Boletín de la Real Academia Española* 13 (1926): 209–33, 342–63, 507–38; 14 (1927): 137–68, 196–234, 357–73, 566–80; 15 (1928): 47–61, 188–223; 32 (1952): 255–89.
Ben-Rubi, "Don Quijote" = Ben-Rubi, Itzhak. "Don Quijote y los judíos sefarditas," *Anales Cervantinos* 2 (1952): 374–75.
Ben-Sasson, H. H., ed. *Historia del pueblo judío*. 3 vols. Madrid: Alianza, 1988.

Ben-Sasson, H. H., ed. *A History of the Jewish People.* London: Weidenfeld & Nicholson, 1976.

Bensasson = Bensasson, M. *Los Israelitas Ispañoles: España y Sus Hijos de Oriente.* Alicante, 1905.

Borrás = Borrás, Tomás. *La pared de tela de araña.* 5th ed. Madrid: Bullón, 1963.

Bunis, David M. *The Historical Development of Judezmo Orthography.* Working Papers in Yiddish and East European Studies no. 2. New York: YIVO Institute, 1974.

Bunis, David M. *Problems in Judezmo Linguistics.* Working Papers in Sephardic and Oriental Jewish Studies, no. 1. New York: American Sephardi Federation, 1975. Rept. in "Some Problems in Judezmo Linguistics," *Mediterranean Language Review* 1 (1983): 103–38.

Bunis, *Sephardic Studies* = Bunis, David M. *Sephardic Studies: A Research Bibliography.* New York and London: Garland Publishing, 1981.

Bunis, "Types" = Bunis, David M. "Types of Nonregional Variation in Early Modern Eastern Spoken Judezmo," *International Journal of the Sociology of Language* 37 (1982): 41–70.

Camhy, "Purim" = Camhy, Gina. "Purim," *Vidas Largas* 2 (Apr. 1983): 38–43.

Cancionero = Hassán, I. M., Elena Romero, and Paloma Díaz-Mas. *Del Cancionero sefardí.* Madrid: Ministerio de Cultura, 1981. (Accompanies recordings by Joaquín Díaz.)

Carracedo, see also Romero, Elena, and Leonor Carracedo.

Carracedo, Leonor. "Coplas sefardíes del tiempo de Juan Chabás," *Dianium* (1987): 213–57.

Carracedo, Leonor. "Misoginia en textos proverbiales sefardíes," *Revista de Dialectología y Tradiciones Populares* 43 (1988): 87–93.

Carracedo, Leonor. "Refranero sefardí: Colecciones aljamiadas," *Estudios Sefardíes* 4 (forthcoming).

Carracedo, Leonor, and Elena Romero. "Refranes publicados por Ya'acob A. Yoná (edición concordada) y bibliografía del refranero sefardí," *Sefarad* 41, no. 3 (1981): 389–560.

Castro, "Entre los hebreos" = Castro, Américo. "Entre los hebreos marroquíes: La lengua española de Marruecos," *Revista Hispano-Africana* 1, no. 5 (May 1922): 145–46.

Cat.-Ind. = Armistead, Samuel G., et al. *El Romancero judeo-español en el Archivo Menéndez Pidal (Catálogo-índice de romances y canciones).* 3 vols. Madrid: Cátedra–Seminario Menéndez Pidal, 1978.

Cembrero, Ignacio. "Los judíos sefardíes," *El País,* 3 July 1983, Sunday supp., 14–19, 22.

Cohen, Judith R. See Anahory-Librowicz.

Crews, Cynthia M. "Extracts from the *Meam Loez* (Genesis) with a Translation and Glossary," *Proceedings of the Leeds Philosophical and Literary Society: Literary and Historical Section,* vol. 9, 13–106. Leeds: Leeds Philosophical and Literary Society, 1960.

Crews, Cynthia M. "Some Linguistic Comments on Oriental and Moroccan Judeo-Spanish." *Estudios sefardíes* 2 (1979): 3–20.

Díaz, see *Cancionero.*

Díaz-Mas, see also *Cancionero.*

Díaz-Mas, Paloma. "El cancionero popular sefardí." In *Los sefardíes: Cultura y literatura,* ed. Díaz-Mas, 191–222. San Sebastián: Universidad del País Vasco, 1987.

Díaz-Mas, Paloma. "Los españoles ante lo judío: Sobre un prejuicio de simpatía," *Raíces: Revista judía de cultura* 5 (Mar. 1989): 13–16.

Díaz-Mas, Paloma. "El Judaísmo: Religión y cultura." In *Los sefardíes: Cultura y literatura*, ed. Díaz-Mas, 23–34. San Sebastián: Universidad del País Vasco, 1987.

Díaz-Mas, Paloma, ed. *Los sefardíes: Cultura y literatura*. San Sebastián: Universidad del País Vasco, 1987.

Díaz-Mas, *Tópicos* = Díaz-Mas, Paloma. *Temas y tópicos en la poesía luctuosa sefardí*. Madrid: Universidad Complutense, 1982.

Elbaz, André E. "Moslem Influences in the Folktales of Canadian Sephardim," *Sephardic Scholar* 4 (1979–82): 54–64.

Elnecave, Nissim. *Los hijos de Ibero-franconia: Breviario del Mundo sefaradí desde los Orígenes hasta nuestros días*. Buenos Aires: La Luz, 1981.

Enciclopedia Judaica Castellana, 10 vols. Mexico: Enciclopedia Judaica Castellana, 1948–51.

Encyclopaedia Judaica, 17 vols. Jerusalem: Keter Publishing House, 1971–72.

En torno, see Armistead–Silverman.

España–Israel: Horizonte de un reencuentro. Toledo: Junta de Comunidades de Castilla-La Mancha, 1988.

Estrugo, *Retorno* = Estrugo, José M. *El retorno a Sefarad: Un siglo después de la inquisición*. Madrid: Imprenta "Europa," 1933.

Fernández, Africano. *España en Africa y el peligro judío: Apuntes de un testigo desde 1915 a 1918*. Santiago de Compostela: El Eco Franciscano, 1918.

Franco, M. *Essai sur l'Histoire des Israélites de l'Empire Ottoman depuis les Origines jusqu'a nos jours*. Reprint. Paris: Centre d'Études Don Isaac Abravanel, 1981.

Galanté, Abraham. *Histoire des Juifs d'Istanbul depuis la prise de cette ville, en 1435, par Fatih Mehmed II, jusqu'à nos jours*. Istanbul: Hüsnütabaiat, 1942.

Galanté, Abraham. *Histoire des Juifs de Rhodes, Chio, Cos, etc.* Istanbul: Société Anonyme de Papeterie et d'Imprimerie (Fratelli Haim), 1935.

Gaon, M. D. *A Bibliography of the Judeo-Spanish (Ladino) Press*. Jerusalem: Ben Zvi Institute, 1965.

Gilbert, Martin. *Jewish History Atlas*. London: Weidenfeld & Nicholson, 1969.

Gold, David L. "Dzhudezmo," *Language Sciences* 47 (Oct. 1977): 14–16.

Gold, David L. "An Introduction to Judezmo." In *Los sefardíes: Cultura y literatura*, ed. Paloma Díaz-Mas, 61–86. San Sebastián: Universidad del País Vasco, 1987.

Gold, David L. "Jewish Intralinguistics as a Field of Study," *International Journal of the Sociology of Language* 30 (1981): 31–46.

Gold, David L. "Where Have All the Sephardic Jews Gones?" In *Los sefardíes: Cultura y literatura*, ed. Paloma Díaz-Mas, 143–70. San Sebastián: Universidad del País Vasco, 1987.

Gonzalo Maeso, David, and Pascual Pascual Recuero. "Prolegómenos," *Me'am Lo'ez: El gran comentario bíblico sefardí*. Madrid: Gredos, 1964.

Haim, Avraam. "La komunidad sefaradi de Miami Beach en Estados Unidos," *Aki Yerushalayim* 6, no. 22–23 (July–Oct. 1984): 21–22.

Harris, Tracy K. "The Prognosis for Judeo-Spanish: Its Description, Present Status, Survival and Decline, with Implications for the Study of Language Death in General." Ph.D. diss., Georgetown University, 1979.

Hassán, see also *Cancionero*.

Hassán, Iacob M. "Las *Coplas de Yosef haṣaḍic*," *Módulo Tres* 2 (Mar.–Apr. 1973): 8–10.

Hassán, Iacob M. "Coplas sefardíes de *Las hazañas de José*: Ediciones ciertas e inciertas," *Sefarad* 46 (1986): 235–52.

Hassán, "De los restos" = Hassán, Iacob M. "De los restos dejados por el judeo-español en el espanõl de los judíos del Norte de Africa." In *Actas del XI Congreso Internacional de Lingüística y Filología Románicas,* 2127–40. Madrid: n.p., 1968.

Hassán, Iacob M. "La Diáspora sefardí." In *España-Israel: Horizonte de un reencuentro,* 25–34. Toledo: Junta de Comunidades de Castilla-La Mancha, 1988.

Hassán, Iacob M. "El estudio del periodismo sefardí," *Sefarad* 26 (1966): 229–35.

Hassán, Iacob M. "Un género castizo sefardí: Las coplas." In *Los sefardíes: Cultura y literatura,* ed. Paloma Díaz-Mas, 103–24. San Sebastián: Universidad del País Vasco, 1987.

Hassán, Iacob M. "Hacia una visión panorámica de la literatura sefardí." In *Actas de las Jornadas de Estudios Sefardíes de 1980,* ed. Antonio Viudas Camarasa, 51–68. Cáceres: Universidad de Extremadura, 1981.

Hassán, Iacob M. "Los sefardíes como tópico," *Raíces* 1 (Apr. 1986): 32–38.

Hassán, Iacob M. "Los sefardíes: Concepto y esbozo histórico." In *Los sefardíes: Cultura y literatura,* ed. Paloma Díaz-Mas, 11–22. San Sebastián: Universidad del País Vasco, 1987.

Hassán, Iacob M. "Tópicos y deudas," *El País,* 3 July 1983, Sunday supp., 3.

Hassán, Iacob M. "Transcripción normalizada de textos judeoespañoles," *Estudios Sefardíes* 1 (1978): 147–50.

Hassán, Iacob M. "Una versión ¿completa? de las *Coplas de Yoçef* publicadas fragmentariamente por González Llubera." In *Actas del I Encuentro de las Tres Culturas,* 283–88. Toledo: Ayuntamiento, 1983.

Hassán, Iacob M. "Visión panorámica de la literatura sefardí," *Hispania Judaica,* vol. 2, 25–44. Barcelona: Puvill Libros, 1982.

Hassán, Iacob M., and Elena Romero. "Poesía luctuosa judeoespañola: Quinot paralitúrgicas." In *Proceedings of the VI World Congress of Judaic Studies,* 7–16. Jerusalem: n.p., 1980.

Hassán, Iacob M., and Elena Romero. "Quinot paralitúrgicas: Edición y variantes," *Estudios Sefardíes* 1 (1978): 3–57.

Hassán Benasayag, Simón. "El desconocido, ese judío," *Raíces: Revista judía de cultura* 5 (Mar. 1989): 18.

Hirschberg, H. Z. (J. W.) *From the Ottoman Conquest to the Present Time.* Vol. 2 of *A History of the Jews in North Africa.* Leiden: Brill, 1981.

Lacave, José Luis. "Los judíos en la época de la Expulsión." In *Los sefardíes: Cultura y literatura,* ed. Paloma Díaz-Mas, 35–48. San Sebastián: Universidad del País Vasco, 1987.

Landau, Luis. "La Antología del *Me'am Lo'ez* y sus fuentes," *Estudios Sefardíes* 5 (forthcoming).

Larrea, *Cuentos* = Larrea Palacín, Arcadio de. *Cuentos populares de los judíos del norte de Marruecos.* 2 vols. Tetuan: Editora Marroquí, 1952–53.

Larrea, *Rituales* = Larrea Palacín, Arcadio de. *Cancionero judío del norte de Marruecos: Canciones rituales hispano-judías.* Madrid: CSIC, 1954.

Leibovici, Sarah. *Chronique des juifs de Tétouan (1860–1896).* Paris: Maisonneuve et Larose, 1984.

Leibovici, Sarah. "Nuestras bodas sefarditas. Algunos ritos y costumbres," *Revista de Dialectología y Tradiciones Populares* 41 (1986): 163–88.

Levy, *Chants* = Levy, Isaac. *Chants judéo-espagnols.* 3 vols. London: World Sephardi Federation, 1959–61.

Lévy, Isaac Jack. *Prolegomena to the Study of the Refranero Sefardí.* New York: Las Americas, 1969.

Librowicz = Anahory-Librowicz, Oro. *Florilegio de romances sefardíes de la diáspora (Una colección malagueña)*. Madrid: Cátedra–Seminario Menéndez Pidal, 1980.

Link, Pablo. *Bases del judaísmo*. Buenos Aires: n.p., 1948.

Maeso–Pascual, *Me'am Lo'ez*, see Gonzalo Maeso, David.

Magdalena Nom de Déu, see Shaul, Moshé.

Malinowski, Arlene C. "Aspects of Contemporary Judeo-Spanish in Israel Based on Oral and Written Sources." Ph.D. diss., University of Michigan, 1979.

Malinowski, Arlene C. "A Report on the Status of Judeo-Spanish in Turkey," *International Journal of the Sociology of Language* 37 (1982): 7–23.

Maranos = "Los Maranos, Drama Judeoespañol de T. Yaliz," ed. Julio F. Neira, *Módulo Tres* 6 (June 1974): 13–32.

Marquina, Antonio, and Gloria Inés Ospina. *España y el judíos en el siglo XX*. Madrid: Espasa-Calpe, 1987.

Marquina Barrio, Antonio. "La acción exterior de España y los judíos sefarditas en los Balcanes. In *Encuentros en Sefarad, Actas del Congreso Internacional "Los judíos en la historia de España,"* 417–40. Ciudad Real: Instituto de Estudios Manchegos, 1987.

Martínez Ruiz, Juan. "Poesía sefardí de carácter tradicional (Alcazarquivir)," *Archivum* 13 (1963): 79–215.

Martín Heredia, María. "Las Coplas de Hanuká." In *Actas de las Jornadas de Estudios Sefardíes de 1980,* ed. Antonio Viudas Camarasa, 115–22. Cáceres: Universidad de Extremadura, 1981.

Martín Heredia, María. "Hanuká: luminarias y coplas (A propósito de Cansinos y una festividad judía)," *Dianium* (1987): 259–70.

Menaché, "Suvenires" = Menaché, David. "Suvenires de chiquez: Sabatot y Selijot," *Revista de Dialectología y Tradiciones Populares* 15 (1959): 118–21.

Mendes Chumaceiro, Rita. "Language Maintenance and Shift among Jerusalem Sephardim," *International Journal of the Sociology of Language* 37 (1982): 28–39.

Menédez Pidal, "Catálogo" = Menéndez Pidal, Ramón. "Catálogo del romancero judío-español," *Cultura Española* 4 (1906): 1045–77; 5 (1907): 161–99.

Menéndez Pidal, Ramón. *Los Romances de América y otros estudios*. Madrid: Espasa-Calpe, 1958.

Molho, *Lit.* = Molho, Michael. *Literatura sefardita de Oriente*. Madrid and Barcelona: CSIC, 1960.

Molho, *Usos* = Molho, Michael. *Usos y costumbres de los sefardíes de Salónica*. Madrid and Barcelona: CSIC, 1950.

Muchnik, Mario. *Mundo judío: Crónica personal*. Barcelona: Lumen, 1983.

Nahón, *Romances = Romances judeo-españoles de Tánger*. Coll. Zarita Nahón. Ann. and ed. S. G. Armistead and J. H. Silverman. Madrid: Cátedra–Seminario Menéndez Pidal, 1977.

Nehama, Joseph. *Histoire des Israélites de Salonique*. Vols. 1–4. Paris: Durlacher, 1935–36; Vol. 5. London: World Sephardi Federation, 1959; Vols. 6–7. Salonika: Communauté Israélite de Thessalonique, 1978.

Ortega 1919 = Ortega, Manuel L. *Los hebreos en Marruecos*. Madrid: Editorial Hispano-Africana, 1919.

Ortega 1929 = Ortega, Manuel L. *Los hebreos en Marruecos,* rev. ed. Madrid: Cia. Ibero-Americana de Publicaciones, 1929, rpt. 1934.

Ospina, Gloria Inés, see Marquina.

Pulido = Pulido Fernández, Angel. *Españoles sin Patria y La Raza Sefardí*. Madrid: Estab. Tip. de E. Teodoro, 1905.

Pulido Fernández, Angel. *Los Israelitas Españoles y el Idioma Castellano.* Madrid: Librería de Fernando Fé, 1904.

Révah, I. S. "Formation et évolution des parlers judéo-espagnols des Balkans," *Iberida* 6 (Dec. 1961): 173–96. Rept. in *Hispania Judaica,* vol. 3, 61–82. Barcelona: Puvill Libros, 1982.

Révah, I. S. "Hispanisme et judaïsme des langues parlées et écrites par les Sefardim." In *Actas del Primer Simposio de Estudios Sefardíes,* ed. Iacob M. Hassán, María Teresa Rubiato and Elena Romero, 233–42. Madrid: CSIC, 1970. Rept. in *Hispania Judaica,* vol. 3, 61–82. Barcelona: Puvill Libros, 1984.

Rodríguez Marín = Rodríguez Marín, Francisco. *Cantos populares españoles.* 5 vols. Madrid: Ibiza, n.d.

Romero, see also *Cancionero,* Carracedo, and Hassán.

Romero, Elena. "Aspectos literarios y sociológicos del teatro de los sefardíes de los Balcanes." In *Los sefardíes: Cultura y literatura,* ed. Paloma Díaz-Mas, 171–90. San Sebastián: Universidad del País Vasco, 1987.

Romero, Elena. "*L'avare* de Molière en el teatro de los sefarditas del Oriente." In *The Sephardi and Oriental Jewish Heritage,* ed. Issachar Ben-Ami, 269–76. Jerusalem: Magnes Press–Hebrew University, 1982.

Romero, Elena. "La canción sefardí *El merecimiento de los patriarcas* y su vida tradicional," *Sefarad* 48 (1988): 357–71.

Romero, "Coplas" = Romero, Elena. "Las coplas sefardíes: Categorías y estado de la cuestión." In *Actas de las Jornadas de Estudios Sefardíes de 1980,* ed. Antonio Viudas Camarasa, 69–98. Cáceres: Universidad de Extremadura, 1981.

Romero, Elena. "Generalidades acerca de la literatura judeoespañola." In *Los sefardíes: Cultura y literatura,* ed. Paloma Díaz-Mas, 87–102. San Sebastián: Universidad del País Vasco, 1987.

Romero, Elena. "*Maimónides el mago:* Versión sefardí de un cuento tradicional judío," *Revista de Dialectología y Tradiciones Populares* 43 (1988): 507–12.

Romero, Elena. *Repertorio de noticias sobre el mundo teatral de los sefardíes orientales.* Madrid: CSIC, 1983.

Romero, *Teatro* = Romero, Elena. *El teatro de los sefardíes orientales.* 3 vols. Madrid: CSIC, 1979.

Romero, "Tu-bišbat" = Romero, Elena. "Complas de Tu-bišbat," *Poesía* [I Reunión de Málaga de 1974], 277–311. Málaga: Diputación, 1976.

Romero, Elena. "La última jornada del hombre en una copla sefardí de moral," *Estudios Sefardíes* 3/*Sefarad* 41 (1981): 403–13.

Romero, Elena. "Una versión judeoespañola del midraš hebreo *Yesirat havalad*," *Sefarad* 47 (1987): 383–406.

Romero, Elena, and Leonor Carracedo. "Poesía judeoespañola admonitiva," *Sefarad* 37 (1977): 429–51.

Ruiz Gómez, Francisco, and Manuel Espadas Burgos, eds. *Encuentros en Sefarad. Actas del Congreso Internacional "Los judíos en la historia de España."* Ciudad Real: Instituto de Estudios Manchegos, 1987.

Sala, Marius. *Estudios sobre el judeoespañol de Bucarest.* Mexico: Universidad Autónoma, 1970. Also available in French as *Phonetique et phonologie du judéo-espagnol de Bucarest.* Trans. Ioana Vintila-Radulescu. The Hague and Paris: Mouton, 1971.

Sala, *Judéo-Espagnol* = Sala, Marius. *Le Judéo-Espagnol.* Paris: Mouton, 1976.

Sánchez García-Arcicollar, María Dolores. "El género narrativo en la literatura judeoespañola." In *Actas de las Jornadas de Estudios Sefardíes de 1980,* ed. Antonio Viudas Camarasa, 107–13. Cáceres: Universidad de Extremadura, 1981.

Saporta, see *Torre.*

Schlesinger, Erna C. *Manual de religión judía: Principios, ritos y costumbres,* 3d ed. Buenos Aires: Instituto Judío Argentino de Cultura e Información, 1955.

Scholem, Gershom. *Sabbataï Sevi. The Mystical Messiah.* Trans. R. J. Zwi Werblowski. Princeton, N.J.: Princeton University Press, 1973.

Scholem, Gershom. *Sabbataï Tsevi: Le messie mystique (1626–1676).* Paris: Verdier, 1983.

Séphiha, Haïm Vidal. *L'agonie des judéo-espagnols.* Paris: Entente, 1977.

Séphiha, Haïm Vidal. *Le judéo-espagnol.* Paris: Entente, 1986.

Séphiha, Haïm Vidal. *Le Ladino (judéo-espagnol calque): Deuteronome, versions de Constantinople (1547) et de Ferrare (1553). Edition, étude linguistique et lexique.* Paris: Institut d'Études Hispaniques, 1973.

Séphiha, Haïm Vidal. *Le Ladino (judéo-espagnol calque): Structure et évolution d'une langue liturgique.* 2 vols. Paris: Association Vidas Largas, 1979.

Séphiha, Haïm Vidal. "El ladino verdadero o judeoespañol calco, lengua litúrgica." In *Actas de las Jornadas de Estudios Sefardíes de 1980,* ed. Antonio Viudas Camarasa, 15–29. Cáceres: Universidad de Extremadura, 1981.

Séphiha, Haïm Vidal. "Problématique du judeoespañol," *Bulletin de la Société de Linguistique de Paris* 69 (1974): 158–89.

Shaul, Moshé. "La poezia djudeo-espanyola kontemporanea," *Aki Yerushalayim* 10, no. 36–37 (Jan.–June 1988): 28–30.

Shaul, Moshé, and José Ramón Magdalena Nom de Déu. "El Mundo Sefardí. Los Sefardíes." In *Nuestro Mundo '85–'86,* 1521–27. Madrid: Agencia Efe–Espasa Calpe, 1985.

Suárez Fernández, Luis. *Judíos españoles en la Edad Media.* Madrid: Rialp, 1980.

Toledano, Samuel. Speech given on May 30, 1981 in Miranda de Ebro, under auspices of the Fundación Cantera Burgos, typed copy. Printed in *Estudios Mirandeses* 1 (1982): 153–65.

Tópicos, see Díaz-Mas.

Torre = Saporta y Beja, Enrique. *En torno de la Torre Blanca.* Paris: Vidas Largas, 1982.

Tuval, Shaul. "Las Komunidades djudías de Turkia en muestros días," *Aki Yerushalayim* 4, no. 15 (Oct. 1982): 6–10.

Vázquez, Angel. *La vida perra de Juanita Narboni.* Barcelona: Planeta, 1976.

Viaje = Villalón, Cristóbal de. *Viaje de Turquía (La odisea de Pedro de Urdemalas).* Ed. Fernando G. Salinero. Madrid: Cátedra, 1980.

Vilar, "Emigrantes" = Vilar, Juan Bautista. "Emigrantes Judeo-Marroquíes en América durante el siglo XIX," *Maguén/Escudo,* 2d ser., 48 (July–Sept. 1983): 21–24.

Vilar, *Tetuán* = Vilar Ramírez, Juan Bautista. *La judería de Tetuán (1489–1806) y otros ensayos.* Murcia: Universidad de Murcia, 1969.

Wagner, *Caracteres* = Wagner, Max L. *Caracteres generales del judeo-español de Oriente.* Madrid: Centro de Estudios Históricos, 1930.

Waxman, Meyer. *Introduction à la vie juive.* Paris: Albin Michel, 1958.

Yoná, see Armistead–Silverman.

TRANSLATOR'S
ADDITIONAL
BIBLIOGRAPHY

In the interests of American readers, some sources, most of them in English, have been added by the translator. These works were not available to Dr. Díaz-Mas when she wrote *Los sefardíes* nor when she did the subsequent revisions for this translation. Consequently, it was felt that adding them as a separate bibliography would be best, since the reader would realize that those works were not among the ones consulted by the author.

Aguilar, Manuel, and Ian Robertson. *Jewish Spain: A Guide*. Madrid: Altalena, 1984.

Angel, Marc. *La America: The Sephardic Experience in the United States*. Philadelphia: Jewish Publication Society of America, 1982.

Angel, Marc. *The Jews of Rhodes: The History of a Sephardic Community*. New York: Sepher-Hermon Press, 1978.

Cohen, Hayim J. *The Jews of the Middle East, 1860–1972*. Trans. Z. and L. Alizi. New York: Wiley, [1973].

Hertz, J. H., ed. *The Pentateuch and Haftorahs*. 2d ed. London: Soncino Press, 1966.

Israel, Jonathan Irvine. *Empires and Entrepots: The Dutch, the Spanish Monarch, and the Jews, 1585–1713*. London and Roncevert, W. Va.: Hambledon Press, 1990.

Laskier, Michael M. *The Alliance Israélite Universelle and the Jewish Communities of Morocco, 1862–1962*. Albany: State University of New York Press, 1983.

Lazar, Moshe. *The Sephardic Tradition: Ladino and Spanish-Jewish Literature*. Texts trans. David Herman. New York: Norton, [1972].

Lévy, Isaac Jack. *And the World Stood Silent: Sephardic Poetry of the Holocaust*. Urbana: University of Illinois Press, 1989.

Lévy, Isaac Jack. "En torno a la interpretación del término gabba." *Romance Notes* 9, no. 1 (1967): 170–79.

Lévy, Isaac Jack. *Jewish Rhodes: A Lost Culture*. Berkeley, Calif.: Judah L. Magnes Museum, 1989.

Lipschitz, C. U. *Franco, Spain, the Jews, and the Holocaust*. New York: Ktav Publishing House, 1984.

Raphael, Chaim, ed. *A Feast of History*. New York: Simon and Schuster, 1972.

Rodrigue, Aron. *French Jews, Turkish Jews: The Alliance Israélite Universelle and the Politics of Jewish Schooling in Turkey (1860–1925)*. Bloomington and Indianapolis: Indiana University Press, 1990.

INDEX

217

theater, 145; Institute for Sephardic
Studies, 165; interest in Sephardim, 166;
Jewish communities, 195–96; Jewish im-
migration from Latin America, 193–94;
Judeo-Spanish, 197; law of religious free-
dom, 166; saving Jews during World
War II, 162–64, 193; Second Republic
(1931–36), 161; Sephardic immigration,
50; World Sephardic Bibliographic Exposi-
tion, 165
Spain-Israel Friendship Association, 196
"Spaniards without a homeland," xi, 151,
155, 169
Spinoza, Baruch, 37
St. Jean de Luz, 36
story, 115–17
strangers, 52
Sublime Porte, 38
šuadit, 72
Sudan, 54
Sue, Eugène, 137
sugar refining, 54
sukkah, 18, 19
Sukkot, 18
Suleiman the Magnificent, 40, 41
Surinam, 66
Sueño de la hija, 122
synagogue, 14; Samuel Levi synagogue, 204

tálamo, 30
tallith, 14
Talmud, 11; Babli, 11; Yerushalmi, 11
Tamuz, 15
Tanach, 10
tanid, 90
Tangier, 53, 54, 57, 58, 61, 159, 161, 184
taqqanah, 52
taqqanot, 52
Taqqanot, 6
Tarragona, 2
tavan, 84
tax collecting, 5
teba, 14
tebilah, 30
tefelimes, 90
tefelines, 90, 91
tefillin, 28
tefilot, 14
Tehilim, 11
Tekirdag, 180

Tel Aviv, 188
Telégrafo, El, 132, 133, 134, 136
tenay, 83
Ten Commandments, 25
tengoy, 89
tenŷere, 84
Tere'asar, 11
Tereśa Raquén, 144
Tesabeá, 26
teshpeshti, 22
testamento del rey Felipe, El, 120, 121, 124
Tetuan, 52, 53, 55, 57, 160, 161, 183–84;
Castilian Cemetery, 68; Spanish taking of,
60–61, 152
Tevet, 15
theater, 49, 139–45
Thousand and One Nights, 105
Three Kings, Battle of, 58
Tiberias, 16, 41, 48
Tiempo, El, 132, 133, 134, 136
Tiempos pasados, 142
Tisha b'av, 26, 109, 124, 128, 129
Tishrei, 15
Tobias, Book of, 10
Toledano, Rahma, 154
Toledano, Samuel, 198–99
Toledano family, 56
Toledo, Abraham, 110, 146
Toledo, Spain, 203; Councils of, 2
Tolstoy, 136, 145
tomar sar, 83
tomimos, 89
Topaź, 144
tophane, 47
topí, 81
topimos, 81
Torá, la Torá, La, 126
Torah, 9, 10
Toral, Captain Domingo de, 151
Toronto, 186
Tortosa, 2
Toshavim, 52
Toulouse, 36
Translators' School, 4
Trastamara, 5
Travels, 105
tref, 12, 13
trefah, 12
tres consejos de Salomón, Los, 117
"*treśladados,*" 136